A Research Agenda for the Entrepreneurial University

T0327341

Elgar Research Agendas outline the future of research in a given area. Leading scholars are given the space to explore their subject in provocative ways, and map out the potential directions of travel. They are relevant but also visionary.

Forward-looking and innovative, Elgar Research Agendas are an essential resource for PhD students, scholars and anybody who wants to be at the forefront of research.

Titles in the series include:

A Research Agenda for the Entrepreneurial University

Edited by

ULLA HYTTI

Department of Management and Entrepreneurship, University of Turku, Finland

Elgar Research Agendas

Cheltenham, UK • Northampton, MA, USA

Published by
Edward Elgar Publishing Limited
The Lypiatts
15 Lansdown Road
Cheltenham
Glos GL50 2JA
UK

Edward Elgar Publishing, Inc.
William Pratt House
9 Dewey Court
Northampton
Massachusetts 01060
USA

Paperback edition 2022

A catalogue record for this book
is available from the British Library

Library of Congress Control Number: 2020952252

This book is available electronically in the **Elgar**online
Business subject collection
http://dx.doi.org/10.4337/9781788975049

ISBN 978 1 78897 503 2 (cased)
ISBN 978 1 78897 504 9 (eBook)
ISBN 978 1 0353 0024 2 (paperback)

Printed and bound by CPI Group (UK) Ltd, Croydon, CR0 4YY

Contents

Figures

Tables

Contributors

Lise Aaboen, Professor of technology-based entrepreneurship, Department of Industrial Economics and Technology Management, Norwegian University of Science and Technology, Norway.

Leena Aarikka-Stenroos, Professor, Department of Industrial Engineering and Management, Tampere University, Finland.

Anna Alexandersson, Senior Lecturer, Department of Organisation and Entrepreneurship, Linnaeus University, Sweden.

Karin Berglund, Professor of Entrepreneurship, Stockholm Business School, Stockholm University, Sweden.

Andrew Creed, Author, Researcher and Educator in the Department of Management, Faculty of Business and Law, Deakin University, Australia.

James A. Cunningham, Professor of Strategic Management, Department of Entrepreneurship, Innovation and Strategy, Newcastle Business School, Northumbria University, United Kingdom.

Anna Dubois, Professor of Industrial Marketing and Purchasing, Department of Technology Management and Economics, Chalmers University of Technology, Sweden.

Mari Elken, Senior Researcher, The Nordic Institute for Studies in Innovation, Research and Education (NIFU), Norway.

Maribel Guerrero, Professor of Entrepreneurship, Faculty of Business and Economics, Universidad del Desarrollo, Chile and Northumbria Centre for Innovation, Regional Transformation and Entrepreneurship (iNCITE), Newcastle Business School, Northumbria University, United Kingdom and Centre for Innovation Research (CIRCLE), Lund University, Sweden.

Jarna Heinonen, Professor of Entrepreneurship, Department of Management and Entrepreneurship, University of Turku, Finland.

Lenita Hietanen, Adjunct Professor in Entrepreneurship Education, Department of Music, Art and Culture Studies, University of Jyväskylä, and University Lecturer in Music Education, Faculty of Education, University of Lapland, Finland.

Ulla Hytti, Professor of Entrepreneurship, Department of Management and Entrepreneurship, University of Turku, Finland.

Marina Jogmark, Senior Lecturer, Department of Organisation and Entrepreneurship, Linnaeus University, Sweden.

Rita Kaša, Assistant Professor, Nazarbayev University Graduate School of Education, Kazakhstan.

Saija Katila, Senior University Lecturer, Department of Management Studies, Aalto University, School of Business, Helsinki, Finland.

Ari Kuismin, Postdoctoral Researcher, Department of Management Studies, Aalto University, School of Business, Finland.

Katja Lahikainen, Junior Researcher, Industrial Engineering and Management, LUT University, Finland.

Pikka-Maaria Laine, Senior University Lecturer (Management), Faculty of Social Sciences, University of Lapland, Finland.

Valentina Lazzarotti, School of Industrial Engineering, LIUC Università Cattaneo, Italy.

Raffaella Manzini, School of Industrial Engineering, LIUC Università Cattaneo, Italy.

Kristel Miller, Senior Lecturer in Strategy, Department of Management Leadership and Marketing, University of Ulster, United Kingdom.

Miira Niska, Postdoctoral Researcher, Faculty of Social Sciences, University of Helsinki, Finland.

Elena Oikkonen, Associate Professor, Industrial Engineering and Management, LUT University, Finland.

Anders Paalzow, President and Rector, Professor, Stockholm School of Economics in Riga, Stockholm School of Economics in Russia, and the Baltic International Centre for Economic Policy Research (BICEPS).

Kati Peltonen, Research, Development and Innovation Director, LAB University of Applied Sciences, Finland.

Gloria Puliga, School of Industrial Engineering, LIUC Università Cattaneo, Italy.

Ida Sabelis, Associate Professor of Organization Sciences, Faculty of Social Sciences, Vrije Universiteit Amsterdam, the Netherlands and Extraordinary Professor at Education and Human Rights in Diversity (Edu-HRight) Research Unit, Faculty of Education, North-West University, Potchefstroom, South Africa.

Elisa Salvador, Professor of Managing Innovation and Creativity, ESSCA School of Management, Paris, France.

Malin Tillmar, Professor of Entrepreneurship, Department of Organisation and Entrepreneurship, Linnaeus University, Sweden.

David Urbano, Professor of Entrepreneurship, Department of Business and Centre for Entrepreneurship and Social Innovation Research (CREIS), Universitat Autònoma de Barcelona, Spain.

Andrea Urbinati, School of Industrial Engineering, LIUC Università Cattaneo, Italy.

Anu Valtonen, Professor of Cultural Economy, Faculty of Social Sciences, University of Lapland, Finland.

Karen Verduijn, Senior Lecturer, School of Business and Economics, Vrije Universiteit Amsterdam, the Netherlands.

Kari Mikko Vesala, Docent, Lecturer in Social Psychology, Faculty of Social Sciences, University of Helsinki, Finland.

Jarrett B. Warshaw, Assistant Professor of Higher Education, Department of Educational Leadership and Research Methodology, Florida Atlantic University, USA.

Ambika Zutshi, Associate Professor in the Department of Management, Faculty of Business and Law, Deakin University, Australia.

Acknowledgements

I would like to thank Edward Elgar Publishing for their encouragement and support in the development of this book. I am also grateful for the reviewers listed below who helped in the selection and development of the chapters.

List of reviewers:

Lise Aaboen, Norwegian University of Science and Technology, Norway.

Anna Alexandersson, Linnaeus University, Sweden.

Karin Berglund, Stockholm University, Sweden.

Alexander Chepurenko, National Research University, Russia.

Andrew Creed, Deakin University, Australia.

James Cunningham, Northumbria University, UK.

Päivi Eriksson, University of Eastern Finland, Finland.

Ferran Giones, University of Southern Denmark, Denmark.

Maribel Guerrero, Universidad del Desarrollo, Chile and Northumbria University, UK.

Karin Gunnarsson, Stockholm University, Sweden.

Jarna Heinonen, University of Turku, Finland.

Norbert Kailer, Johannes Kepler University Linz, Austria.

Saija Katila, Aalto University, Finland.

Inna Kozlinska, University of Gröningen, the Netherlands.

Katja Lahikainen, LUT University, Finland.

Mona Mannevuo, University of Turku, Finland.

Iselin Mauseth Steira, Nord University, Norway.

Tönis Mets, Tarto University, Estonia.

Kirsi Peura, University of Turku, Finland.

Daniil Pokidko, Hanken University, Finland.

Seppo Poutanen, University of Turku, Finland.

Tommi Pukkinen, University of Turku, Finland.

Elisa Salvador, ESSCA School of Management, France.

Kelly Smith, Coventry University, UK.

Karen Verduijn, Free University Amsterdam, the Netherlands.

Jarrett B. Warshaw, Florida Atlantic University, USA.

Karen Williams Middleton, Chalmers University of Technology, Sweden.

1 Introduction: navigating the frontiers of entrepreneurial university research

Ulla Hytti

The entrepreneurial university as a concept and phenomenon was introduced more than two decades ago (Etzkowitz, 1998; Clark, 1998) in a context where universities aimed at strengthening their impact in society (Jarvis, 2013; Siegel and Wright, 2015). Since then, research into this area has been burgeoning (Fayolle and Redford, 2014; Foss and Gibson, 2015), as has been the practical interest when many universities are establishing themselves as entrepreneurial universities (Liu, 2018). In his pioneering work, Clark (1998) came up with five different pathways for universities when transforming into entrepreneurial universities. As the first two pathways, he suggested that universities should both strengthen their steering core and diversify their funding base so that they would have the ability and autonomy to make decisions about their strategy and future directions independently. Third, he recommended extending their developmental periphery by establishing non-academic units, such as technology transfer offices or other centres, to make it easier for university stakeholders to get in contact and build relations with the university. Fourth, he emphasised the importance of the academic heartland – research and teaching – at the core of the entrepreneurial university. Finally, Clark suggested developing a university-wide entrepreneurial culture as a means for universities to operate in a flexible and entrepreneurial way. In essence, Clark understood an entrepreneurial university as not only contributing to entrepreneurship around it but as an institutional entrepreneur itself. Institutional entrepreneurship refers to the 'activities of actors who have an interest in particular institutional arrangements and who leverage resources to create new institutions or to transform existing ones' (Maguire, Hardy and Lawrence, 2004, p. 657), such as the university.

Thereafter, research on the entrepreneurial university has depicted the (ideal) models for the entrepreneurial university and its evolution – what the entrepreneurial university is and what it does when contrasted against other (historic) types of universities (Etzkowitz, 2013; 2014). The goal has been to understand the different types of entrepreneurial universities in terms of their entrepreneurial architecture (Foss and Gibson, 2015): their structures, systems, leadership, strategies and culture (see also Bronstein and Reihlen, 2014). Often, authors make sense of the changes in universities by investigating the environmental or institutional forces (or determinants) that explain or help to understand the transition towards the entrepreneurial university (Foss and Gibson, 2015) and the changes this proposes to the value proposition and value creation (Cunningham and Miller, Ch 7, this volume).

However, technological advancements in digitalisation, robotisation, artificial intelligence and machine learning are transforming and disrupting societies, industries, businesses, governments, jobs, education and, to put it shortly, the way we live and experience our lives (e.g. Kile, 2013). Consequently, digitalisation may also contribute to transformations in the entrepreneurial university and its landscape, calling for new research in this area (Guerrero and Urbano, Ch 9, this volume; Salvador, Manzini, Urbinati, Puliga and Lazzarotti, Ch 13, this volume). University strategies on open data and open science (Hong and Walsh, 2009), as well as the more open and collaborative research processes, e.g. via citizen science (Follett and Strezov, 2015), create new layers to the entrepreneurial university and thus open up new research pathways. The deepening and diversifying collaboration with various stakeholders is giving birth to new roles and units within the university (thus similarly opening up the need to understand the dynamics within the university and in the relations with stakeholders (Warshaw, Ch 10, this volume; Creed, Heinonen and Zutshi, Ch 11, this volume)). As the processes of academic entrepreneurship and university–industry collaboration become more complex and many sided, generating knowledge of these processes is important (Aaboen, Dubois and Aarikka-Stenroos, Ch 12, this volume; Guerrero and Urbano, 2012).

The majority of prior research has focused on the societal and organisational levels as the units of analysis, and too little attention has been paid to what happens at the level of individuals and groups that actually work at universities. The organisational perspective could be enriched with individual-level analyses and benefit from an understanding of the activities and agency of university members, such as managers (Hytti, Eriksson, Montonen and Peura, 2020), faculty and students (Lahikainen, Peltonen, Hietanen and Oikkonen, Ch 8, this volume), in contributing to and shaping the entrepreneurial university.

However, researchers adopting a less optimistic view on entrepreneurial university warn us that there is also a risk that the entrepreneurial university becomes a taken-for-granted kind of pervasive ideology (du Gay, 2000) that cannot be challenged or questioned. Rather than being understood as concrete activities implemented to support entrepreneurship at the university, the entrepreneurial university becomes a rhetorical move in the neoliberal discourse (Niska and Vesala, Ch 6, this volume). The entrepreneurial university 'establishes neoliberal ideals, redefines the values of European university education, and generates [an] instrumental and one-dimensional understanding of the purpose of university education' (Laalo, Kinnari and Silvennoinen, 2019, p. 93). The entrepreneurial university could be seen as a vehicle to emphasise the new public management doctrine, meaning that universities should be more business-like and should focus on performance management and accountability, often accompanied by quantitatively measured financial and other targets (Jones et al., 2020). Thus, critical voices call for questioning the ideological underpinnings and pervasiveness of new managerialism or academic capitalism, as well as the notion of impact (for whom and how) (Deem, 2001; Mautner, 2005; Taylor, 2014).

Furthermore, research demonstrates how neoliberalism works by subjectifying the entrepreneurial self as something that we have voluntarily selected. It takes the shape of an ideal subject (Berglund, Hytti and Verduijn, 2020; Bröckling, 2015), i.e. to be a good academic is to be an entrepreneurial one. Despite the precariousness of their position, the entrepreneurial academic has internalised the goals to target and publish as much as possible in top journals and to seek and compete for research funding, for example. Hence, as we have believed that the effort to be entrepreneurial follows from our own desires (Fenwick, 2002), challenging and resisting it become difficult. Furthermore, the entrepreneurial university and related start-up events include a multisensory environment that intensifies the affectual sensation, contributing to our willingness to be a part of and identify with the entrepreneurial university by creating a sense of fun and excitement (Katila, Laine, and Parkkari, 2019; Katila, Kuismin, Laine and Valtonen, Ch 5, this volume).

In their editorial, Jones et al. (2020) wish to bring forth the opportunity for resistance for academics by opening up our own role and contribution to the performative university. By becoming aware and acknowledging our role, it opens up the possibility for agency. 'They (we?) keep on playing a role in audits, visitations, excellence exercises, funding schemes, and so on, activities which would grind to a halt, were academics to collectively refuse to play a role in them anymore' (Jones et al., 2020, p. 372). Obviously, the responsibility for resistance cannot be assigned to individuals; collective action is needed. Consequently, if we return to Clark (1998) and his ideas about the entrepreneurial university as an institutional entrepreneur with the aim of creating new institutions or transforming existing ones, it should be possible to envision a future of collective action in academia in order to engage in different acts, spaces, processes and mechanisms of resistance of the performative university and in coming up with alternatives (Jones et al., 2020) for the entrepreneurial university.

There is increasing awareness of global challenges, the so-called wicked problems, which the world and societies face today. Thus, the question is not only how universities are impactful in the areas they select but also how they enable global agendas to shape their own agenda. Solving societal challenges, climate change and sustainability and helping the world survive the global pandemic are giving rise to debates about 'societally responsible entrepreneurial universities' (Verduijn and Sabelis, Ch 3, this volume). Hence, the changes in and around universities transform how we think about entrepreneurial universities. The entrepreneurial university as an institutional entrepreneur gives prominence and a mandate, opportunity or even a responsibility to reflect on the challenges and changes society needs today – changes in which the entrepreneurial university can make a difference. Broadening the scope and understanding related to the entrepreneurial university opens up new opportunities for an 'alternative entrepreneurial university' (Berglund, Alexandersson, Jogmark and Tillmar, Ch 2, this volume), and the ability to envision different versions of the entrepreneurial university leaves more room for local and contextualised versions (Kaša, Elken and Paalzow, Ch 4, this volume). This also opens up the opportunity to break away from the narrow research commercialisation perspective. At the same time, we must be wary of promoting the entrepreneurial university (be it one directing research commercialisation, social change or other forms of alternative aims) as the only possible university form. Thus, when moving forward, we need to leave many doors open for 'academics and managers alike, to craft their institutions around a real social purpose' (Jones et al., 2020, p. 374).

The chapters in this book explore these subjects in forward-looking ways. Developing a closer link between the mainstream and critical perspectives allows us to bring in the axiological debate (Do we want to? Should we? How should we do it?) (Kyrö, 2015) to research on the entrepreneurial university and to be reflexive of how entrepreneurial universities are developed, by whom and for whom. When it comes to the individual chapters in this volume, I follow Czarniawska (2016) and abstain from summarising them. 'Readers need to familiarize themselves with the orginals, rather than relying on second-hand renditions. [...] All I can promise is that there is much to choose from' (Czarniawska, 2016, p. xiii).

Acknowledgement

The author would like to acknowledge the financial support provided by the Academy of Finland (grant number 295960).

References

Berglund, K., Hytti, U. and Verduijn, K. (2020). 'Navigating the terrain of entrepreneurship education in neoliberal societies'. *Entrepreneurship Education and Pedagogy*, 2515127420935444.

Bröckling, U. (2015). *The entrepreneurial self: Fabricating a new type of subject.* Sage, London, Thousand Oaks CA, New Delhi and Singapore.

Bronstein, J. and Reihlen, M. (2014). 'Entrepreneurial university archetypes: A meta-synthesis of case study literature'. *Industry and Higher Education*, **28**(4), 245–262.

Clark, B. R. (1998). *Creating entrepreneurial universities: Organizational pathways of transformation. Issues in higher education.* Elsevier Science Regional Sales, New York, NY.

Czarniawska, B. (Ed.). (2016). *A research agenda for management and organization studies.* Edward Elgar Publishing, Cheltenham, UK and Northampton, MA, USA.

Deem, R. (2001). 'Globalisation, new managerialism, academic capitalism and entrepreneurialism in universities: Is the local dimension still important?' *Comparative Education*, **37**(1), 7–20.

Du Gay, P. (2000). 'Enterprise and its futures: A response to Fournier and Grey'. *Organization*, **7**(1), 165–183.

Etzkowitz, H. (1998). 'The norms of entrepreneurial science: Cognitive effects of the new university–industry linkages'. *Research Policy*, **27**(8), 823–833.

Etzkowitz, H. (2013). 'Anatomy of the entrepreneurial university'. *Social Science Information*, **52**(3), 486–511.

Etzkowitz, H. (2014). 'The entrepreneurial university wave: From ivory tower to global economic engine'. *Industry and Higher Education*, **28**(4), 223–232.

Fayolle, A. and Redford, D. T. (2014). *Handbook on the entrepreneurial university.* Edward Elgar Publishing, Cheltenham, UK and Northampton, MA, USA.

Fenwick, T. J. (2002). 'Transgressive desires: New enterprising selves in the new capitalism'. *Work, Employment and Society*, **16**(4), 703–723.

Follett, R. and Strezov, V. (2015). 'An analysis of citizen science based research: Usage and publication patterns'. *PloS one*, **10**(11), e0143687.

Foss, L. and Gibson, D. V. (Eds.). (2015). *The entrepreneurial university: Context and institutional change.* Routledge, London.

Guerrero, M. and Urbano, D. (2012). 'The development of an entrepreneurial university'. *The Journal of Technology Transfer*, **37**(1), 43–74.

Hong, W. and Walsh, J. P. (2009). 'For money or glory? Commercialization, competition, and secrecy in the entrepreneurial university'. *The Sociological Quarterly*, **50**(1), 145–171.

Hytti, U., Eriksson, P., Montonen, T. and Peura, K. (2020). 'Navigating enterprise at universities: A discursive analysis of academic managers' identity work', paper presented at the British Academy of Management, Conference in the Cloud (virtual conference), 2–4 September 2020.

Jarvis, P. (2013). *Universities and corporate universities: The higher learning industry in global society.* Routledge, London.

Jones, D. R., Visser, M., Stokes, P., Örtenblad, A., Deem, R., Rodgers, P. and Tarba, S. Y. (2020). 'The performative university: "Targets", "terror" and "taking back control" in academia'. *Management Learning*, **51**(4), 363–377.

Katila, S., Laine, P. M. and Parkkari, P. (2019). 'Sociomateriality and affect in institutional work: Constructing the identity of start-up entrepreneurs'. *Journal of Management Inquiry*, **28**(3), 381–394.

Kile, F. (2013). 'Artificial intelligence and society: A furtive transformation'. *AI & Society*, **28**(1), 107–115.

Kyrö, P. (2015). 'The conceptual contribution of education to research on entrepreneurship education'. *Entrepreneurship & Regional Development*, **27**(9–10), 599–618.

Laalo, H., Kinnari, H. and Silvennoinen, H. (2019). 'Setting new standards for homo academicus: Entrepreneurial university graduates on the EU agenda'. *European Education*, **51**(2), 93–110.

Liu, W. (2018). Book Review. Lene Foss and David V. Gibson (eds.): *The entrepreneurial university: context and institutional change*, Routledge, London, 2015, 285pp, *Higher Education*, **75**, 743–745.

Maguire, S., Hardy, C. and Lawrence, T. B. (2004). 'Institutional entrepreneurship in emerging fields: HIV/AIDS treatment advocacy in Canada'. *Academy of Management Journal*, **47**(5), 657–679.

Mautner, G. (2005). 'The entrepreneurial university: A discursive profile of a higher education buzzword'. *Critical Discourse Studies*, **2**(2), 95–120.

Siegel, D. S. and Wright, M. (2015). 'Academic entrepreneurship: Time for a rethink?'. *British Journal of Management*, **26**(4), 582–595.

Taylor, Y. (Ed.). (2014). *The entrepreneurial university: Engaging publics, intersecting impacts.* Springer.

2 An alternative entrepreneurial university?

Karin Berglund, Anna Alexandersson, Marina Jogmark and Malin Tillmar

Introduction

Entrepreneurship, as an ideology, embraces human activity to engage relentlessly in the betterment of society and the progress of modernity (Ogbor, 2000). However, the ways in which entrepreneurship is played out historically, geographically and culturally varies (Baumol, 1990; Steyaert and Katz, 2004). In contemporary Western societies, entrepreneurship and innovation have been translated into a logic of enterprise, which has become a blueprint for reaching all kinds of goals, from innovating new groundbreaking technologies to managing the public sector and engaging in the pursuit of social change. No wonder that entrepreneurship has also been embraced by the institution of the university. The entrepreneurial society, perpetuated through neoliberalism, gives prominence to individualism, competitiveness, market logics and an economic rationality (e.g. Berglund, Lindgren and Packendorff, 2017). In such a society, everyone and everything is to be made more entrepreneurial; consequently, entrepreneurship can be described as a prescriptive force that is sweeping into present society as a strong current (Bröckling, 2015: 196, xiii).

The emergence of the entrepreneurial society has led some to advocate decreasing the role of the state and unleashing markets, in the hope of revitalising society by making it more (economically) efficient and reducing obstacles for innovation. This argument is met with opposition by Mazzucato (2015), who argues that the state, in the post-war US, was the main facilitator of innovation. Through long-term investments, the state enabled the public sector to instigate innovation, by providing citizens, NGOs, companies and the public sector (including universities) with a space and an arena where innovations could be developed.

Following the thesis of 'the entrepreneurial state', universities provided society with scientific knowledge and collaborated with other societal stakeholders to materialise this knowledge into concrete products, services, practices and technologies that would benefit society (Mazzucato, 2015). The construction of the first iPod is but one example of how a company (Apple) was able to build a product based on state-developed innovations and contribute to the development of the ICT market. One could say that universities then acted entrepreneurially, without having to present themselves as entrepreneurial. It is worth noting here that 'entrepreneurial' is linked to a system, rather than to a particular individual or organisation. Thus, the entrepreneurial and innovative state, with its visions, long-term investments, cross-sector collaborations and different logics, made it possible for citizens in various organisations to creatively enact ideas, co-create opportunities and bring about change: social, cultural and economic.

Following Mazzucato, the role of the entrepreneurial state is to be a visionary and a long-term investor that makes future realities possible. This implies that the state not only adjusts market conditions, which laissez-faire economics often warn against, but that it has been successful in creating and shaping markets. Mazzucato, however, admits that even in the US the entrepreneurial state has fallen by the wayside lately. Neoliberal logics have taken precedence, making it more difficult for the state to 'be entrepreneurial' in the same way as previously. Instead, the state is ensnared in a short-term enterprise logic of economic effectiveness, having to compete for resources and short-term results just like any other market actor.

In this chapter, the notion of the entrepreneurial state is the background to a discussion about the emergence of the entrepreneurial university (TEU) as well as alternative approaches to the entrepreneurial university (AEU). Although the entrepreneurial state had its heyday during the post-war era and the development of a welfare society from the 1950s to the 1970s, it can shed light on different approaches to making universities entrepreneurial in contemporary society. In this chapter, we conceptualise two of these approaches – TEU and AEU – to highlight the need to better contextualise how 'the entrepreneurial' is incorporated into the university, making us as researchers aware of the different research questions that can be posed in order to better understand the different attempts to make universities entrepreneurial.

The entrepreneurial university and its critics

The term entrepreneurial university denotes the potential connection between knowledge production, entrepreneurial activity and technological development through new venture creation in academic milieux (e.g. Foss and Gibson, 2015; Shane, 2004; Wright, Lockett, Clarysse and Binks, 2006; Wright, Clarysse, Mustar and Lockett, 2007). The academic is here transformed into an entrepreneur who can turn research knowledge into technologies that can become competitive products on the market (Shane, 2004). The imperative is to strengthen the role of higher education – and the institution of university – in a marketised society (Clark, 2001). By initiating Triple Helix collaborations, where universities work together with businesses and government agencies to focus their competencies, the foundation is laid for innovations to be developed and commercialised (Etzkowitz, 2006). However, critics claim that such a spread of entrepreneurial imperatives makes it more difficult for the university to function according to the Humboldtian Bildungsideal, emphasising the need to integrate the arts and sciences with research to achieve a more holistic view of learning, education and cultural knowledge.

The Humboldtian Bildungsideal gives prominence to the university's role to nurture critical reflection, since this makes it possible to understand human beings and their relations to themselves, others and society, which can be undermined if cause-effect explanations of innovative and effective solutions rule (Tunstall, 2018). The Bildungsideal also points to the formative potential of humans and societies by emphasising the ability to relate to a broad range of reflections, from historical to contemporary issues, making space for new understandings of the world we inhabit (Bornemark, 2018). The critics unanimously warn us that by following entrepreneurial imperatives we risk losing vital parts of learning reflected in concepts such as curiosity, the power of knowledge, critical reflection and democratic self-reflection. The entrepreneurial university, they claim, is incentivised to focus on research and development on market terms (e.g. Ball and Olmedo, 2013), to advance the connection between academic work and capitalist rationalities (e.g. Slaughter and Rhoades, 2004), and to foster the idea of entrepreneurial subjectivities as superior to other possible ways to live life (e.g. Dahlstedt and Fejes, 2019). This may undermine the reflective culture and space it takes for a Bildungsideal to flourish.

To advance our ambition to conceptualise TEU and AEU, we include the critique directed towards the entrepreneurial university by embracing the concept of Bildungsideal, which can shed light on the entrepreneurialisation of universities and whether there could be alternative interpretations of the university as entrepreneurial. A research question that can be formulated from this discussion is: Can a university claim to be entrepreneurial without submitting to the primacy of the market and losing contact with a Bildungsideal? To place the discussion in a context, we will use the case of Linnaeus University to describe efforts to 'go alternative', and thus to create a fruitful tension between TEU and AEU. During the past decade, Linnaeus University has presented itself as an entrepreneurial university blending different approaches in education and research.

Linnaeus University – an example of an (alternative) entrepreneurial university

The university website states that '[t]he overall purpose of the Entrepreneurial Linnaeus University will be to create the conditions for a broad entrepreneurship, which contributes to community building. This is done by equipping our students to consciously and critically contribute to providing space for socially, economically and ecologically sustainable entrepreneurship'. The priority is thus not primarily the researchers' ability to transform themselves into entrepreneurs, nor is it about the potential transformation of research results into commercial products and services. Rather, Linnaeus seeks to adopt a broad interpretation of entrepreneurship that paves the way for a multi-dimensional entrepreneurial impact on the university and its close surroundings. At Linnaeus, the entrepreneurial university is not simply a brand, used to describe a particular kind of activity, but a vision that has been supported by several projects that have been carried out with an aim to enact entrepreneurship-as-creativity (Larsson and Sjöstrand, 2014), and involve the regional context in the processes of socio-economic revitalisation (Final Report, 2016). We believe the alternative entrepreneurship-as-creativity approach (AEU) creates a fruitful tension to the technologically innovation driven university (TEU).

Linnaeus University consists of two campuses in the southern region of Småland: one in the city of Kalmar, close to the Baltic Sea, and the other, a merger of two previous independent universities, in the city of Växjö. The region is known for its entrepreneurial culture and relatively high proportion of small companies. The term 'Gnosjö spirit' has been used to describe its enterprising and networking culture (Wigren, 2003), as well as its propensity for reproducing entrepreneurship as male gendered (Pettersson, 2004). Småland is also the home of the Swedish entrepreneurial icon brand IKEA, founded by the late Ingvar Kamprad (1926–2018), that has spurred research on entrepreneurship (Karlsson, 2018), and leadership (Forslund, Lundgren, and Zambrell, 2016).

One of the forerunners of Linnaeus University, Växjö University, was also the home of Professor Emeritus Bengt Johannisson, who has contributed to the establishment and development of entrepreneurship as a research field (Steyaert, Hjorth and Gartner, 2011). His legacy is primarily the definition of entrepreneurship as creative organising and networking, working closely with the small business owners in the region through enactive research. His successors have continued this work by developing a critical understanding of entrepreneurship (Bill, Bjerke, and Johansson, 2010; Johansson, 1997) and highlighting the importance of context, gender and interactive research in understanding the role of entrepreneurship in the public sector and civil society (Tillmar, 2009). In teaching, artistic methods such as drama and photos have been used to broaden the view of what entrepreneurship can entail (Ellborg, 2018). What unites these researchers, and the research milieu of 'Entrepreneurship and Social Change', is an understanding of entrepreneuring as co-creation with surrounding society, and a curiosity to understand the mundanity of entrepreneuring in close relations with various empirical settings (Alexandersson, 2015; Fredin and Jogmark, 2017; Holmgren, 2018; Rosenlund and Rosell, 2017). Despite holding on to many conventional views of entrepreneurship – such as proactive men and women, a small company culture, the innovative IKEA – Linnaeus University simultaneously deviates from many of the characteristics ascribed to the entrepreneurial university, such as that of the high tech developer generating innovations commercialised through Triple Helix collaborations that generates numerous patents.

Through the entrepreneurship-as-creativity approach, Linnaeus exemplifies one possible approach to TEU, which raises questions about alternative understandings of the entrepreneurial university and its role in society. However, this does not mean that the technologically innovation-driven university (TEU) does not contribute and is out of play. On the contrary, both approaches to the entrepreneurial university may have their advantages and disadvantages. In the following sections, we want to explore this, and therefore view the tension between AEU and TEU as fruitful for furthering our understandings of how the entrepreneurial can be approached by universities. Against the backdrop of the entrepreneurial state and Bildungsideal we now move on to discuss the notions of democracy and truth and knowledge, and to develop research questions from the positions of AEU/TEU.

Democracy and the entrepreneurial university

In discussions about TEU, keywords such as technology, R&D and innovation often determine how universities are to integrate the 'entrepreneurial component' in their operations. Entrepreneurship becomes a specialised form of knowledge earmarked for particular explorative processes of the selected few: an entrepreneurial elite. This ideological reproduction tends to favour particular people, such as the Western, male subject with an interest in technology, whereby knowledge about entrepreneurship is made unavailable for students, teachers, researchers and university staff in general. Such a focus on the entrepreneur often leads to a business view of innovations as products and services that could and should reach the market.

Sceptical voices, however, warn that such a focus – with the individual and business as the operating nexus – may lead to a disruption of the Humboldtian ideal and to the loss of education for the sake of education. This undermines the ability for people both inside and outside the university to gain new understandings of societal phenomena, to re-think current dogmas, and to figure out innovative ways to navigate in contemporary societies (Berg and Seeber, 2016). Further, this direction fails to democratise universities, by operating in ways that specialise and favour particular functions, processes and areas. Innovation repeats itself in the sense that what we look for (or allocated resources and attention) is what we get. For that reason, we pose the following question: Does the entrepreneurial university that claims its direction need to specialise its innovative potential to reach the market, or could entrepreneurship education also serve as way forward to democratise higher education?

Considering that Linnaeus University seeks to inspire entrepreneurship not only among researchers, but also among students, and that it views not only global technological races but also the local setting as a resource, this suggests a more open and democratic view of the role that entrepreneurship can take in university settings. To gain an understanding of such a view of entrepreneurship, we move to the literature that has sought to detach entrepreneurship from its role as the engine of capitalism and instead expanded entrepreneurship by connecting it to concepts such as creativity, play, bricolage, aesthetics and collective action. The emergence of the broader view of entrepreneurship is shaped both from sceptical voices being raised, and efforts to find ways for how entrepreneurship can be re-directed. It has been suggested that entrepreneurship is limited by, and even locked into, an economic understanding (Steyaert and Katz, 2004) that it still highlights the white, Western man as a model (Ogbor, 2000) under which other cultures and social groups (based on gender, age, ethnicity, sexuality, etc.) are marginalised in our shared understanding of entrepreneurship. Further, entrepreneurship is expected to contribute not only to innovations, increased employment and continued growth, but also to ecological and social sustainability, cultural exploration and social change (Steyaert and Hjorth, 2006). Nowadays, entrepreneurial processes are also seen as contributing to social development and community building in general (Tillmar, 2009; Berglund, Johannisson and Schwartz, 2012).

These voices tell a different story from the usual one where entrepreneurship, underpinned by a market ideology, is seen as propelling business creation and economic growth. On the contrary, creativity is perceived as omnipresent, allowing entrepreneurship to become a social process where people – individually or collectively – perceive needs to be met, problems to be solved, and ideas that can be enacted and transformed in contexts where social, sustainable, cultural and economic logics interact. This broad definition of entrepreneurship is embraced at Linnaeus University. In particular, attention is directed towards the opportunities to develop synergies with the surrounding community and strengthen the area around the two campuses of Kalmar and Växjö. The democratisation of entrepreneurship is visible in the ambitions to create an entrepreneurial culture where students, teachers and researchers become active co-workers ready to create opportunities and participate in the local community as well as in global contexts.

Since 2001, one of the oldest bachelor programmes in entrepreneurship and business development in Sweden, namely Enterprising and Business Development (EBD), has been working primarily with business development in small businesses in this region (Johansson and Rosell, 2012) with the focus on small businesses as valuable agents in entrepreneurship and innovation. In spite of not representing the high-tech ideal, where specialised entrepreneurs in R&D are employed to innovate and apply for patents, the small business approach has long been the ambition of Linnaeus University (Johannisson, 1998). The interaction with the surrounding society has, however, not always been harmonious, and has at times been characterised by intense discussion as a result of research enacted by Bengt Johannisson (2005), who has provoked small business owners to re-think their own practices and teach the university how it can avoid a top-down transfer of entrepreneurship knowledge to 'unknowledgeable practitioners' in order to be effective. Instead, a scene where entrepreneurs are given a language to describe and understand what they actually do when they do entrepreneuring and networking has been created in close interaction between the university and its local business surroundings. These processes stress the permeable boundaries between the university and the local community, where there is no predefined direction for how knowledge 'flows'. Instead, the emphasis is on dialogue, learning and inclusion.

Another example is the master's in entrepreneurship at Linnaeus University, which aims to teach the students about entrepreneurial processes in all sectors of society, thus broadening the scope of entrepreneurship. A mapping of master programmes in entrepreneurship in Sweden and other parts of the world showed the focus was generally on strategic entrepreneurship, innovation and entrepreneurial management. The master's at Linnaeus, however, is centred on entrepreneurship in all sectors, with an emphasis on sustainability and social change. The students learn and work with projects in business, governmental agencies and NGOs, and cases from all sectors are used to show entrepreneurship in less common places, rather than the usual subjects among entrepreneurs. The aim is to showcase a diversity of entrepreneurs and entrepreneurial contexts.

This alternative approach to being an entrepreneurial university is further expressed in the desire to be involved in co-creation and interactive research, taken with the research platform of entrepreneurship and social change (www.lnu.se/ent). Interaction and co-creation with the surrounding society is an important feature of most projects within the platform. Inspired by a Penta-Helix approach (Björk, Hanson and Lundborg, 2014; Elg, Ellström, Kock and Tillmar, 2016), a co-creation council with representatives from organisations from different sectors of working life in Småland is linked to the platform. The private sector is included, along with municipalities and civil society organisations. Unlike the Triple-Helix approach discussed by Etzkowitz (2006), it is not commercialisation which is on the agenda here, but rather the role of entrepreneurship in democratic development (Carayannis and Campbell, 2012). The purpose of this interactive approach and co-creation within the ENT platform at Linnaeus University is joint learning for mutual benefit on equal terms (Svensson, Ellström and Brulin, 2007).

In and around the entrepreneurial university at Linnaeus there are consistent attempts to reach out to all students and to include both students and staff. Via the broader understanding of entrepreneurship, they are offered discursive resources to shape a story of what 'entrepreneurial' means to them, both in education and for their future professional life. In this vein, the experimentation with interactive teaching methods is aligned with the efforts to include both students and local actors in educational efforts. The broad reconceptualisation of entrepreneurship provides us with an entrepreneurship discourse which is inclusive and also makes it possible to avoid fixating the concept of entrepreneurship. Instead, a space is provided to reflect upon the role of entrepreneurship for the individual, organisations, societies and also for universities. This facilitates democratic self-reflection, always ubiquitous, but particularly necessary in times of turmoil when democratic institutions are challenged and dismantled. The democratic self-reflection might also make it possible to problematise and resist the societal expectations to become entrepreneurial. See Table 2.1 for conceputalisation of TEU and AEU.

Table 2.1   The entrepreneurial university and alternative entrepreneurial university

	The Entrepreneurial University (TEU)	Alternative Entrepreneurial University (AEU)
Assumption of entrepreneurship and democracy	Innovations are a result of knowledge-intensive processes. TEU can result in novel products and services that can revolutionise a democratic welfare society and benefit all its citizens. Examples of innovation could be new medical treatments, climate aware technology, etc. Innovations from the university can contribute to employment, societal progress and economic growth.	A broadened view of entrepreneurship is claimed, where entrepreneurship is seen as an integral part of human activity. This implies that the 'many people' should be invited and involved. There is a democratic right to be(come) an entrepreneur/entrepreneurial. Entrepreneurship is seen as contributing not only to economic growth, but also to ecological and social sustainability, cultural exploration, social change, and individual empowerment.
Examples of research questions posed within the two 'examples'	What technologies and advancements are of importance for various sectors in society? Which disciplines can contribute to solve a particular societal problem and how can they co-operate? How can existing technology be used in a new context or combined into innovations? → **Which technology can solve the problem?**	How can university practices – educational practices – facilitate reflexivity with regards to the role of entrepreneurship in late capitalism? A space is provided to reflect upon the role of entrepreneurship, for the individual, organisations, societies and also for universities. This facilitates democratic self-reflection, always ubiquitous, but in particular necessary in times of turmoil when democratic institutions are challenged and dismantled. → **Which society can solve the problem?**

Knowledge and truth to foster innovation and entrepreneurial activity

The fact that the universities are seen in the role of defender of the truth and scientific knowledge creates a particular tension in relation to entrepreneurial practice, which is concerned with making up new stories (Johansson, 2004), getting people involved, and 'acting as if' the idea is already (or on its way to being) realised (Gartner, Bird, and Starr, 1992). Entrepreneurial practice thus requires individuals to balance between acting out new ideas, drawing people in and gaining legitimacy for their ideas. This may involve a careful stretching of reality (Gartner et al., 1992), or a more brutal stretching where the boundary between truth and lie is blurred, as in the case of Stein Bagger (Bill, Jansson and Olaison, 2010), Fyre Festival (Smith, 2019) or Theranos (Carreyrou, 2018). Entrepreneuring, we suggest, always involves a fine line between 'speaking the truth' and 'bending the truth' in the unfolding of potentiality and possible futures. However, in a neoliberal society, where competition, the market and short-sighted endeavours are favoured, this means that the story that 'wins' thus gains acceptance, and may more easily be detached from the reality it seeks to unfold when maintaining attractiveness. This has come to have an effect on the educational community around Stanford. In an article from Stanford eCorner, Tom Byers writes:

> In early March this year, I met an educator […] Professor Geoff Sayre-McCord, [who] introduced himself to a table of entrepreneurship educators and administrators by saying, 'Entrepreneurs face a moral liability: that they will become liars.' It was a bold remark to make in a business school setting, and I was intrigued.

In this section we will engage with the following question: Do entrepreneurial practices in neoliberal late capitalism increasingly support post-truth regimes and twist enlightenment ideals? If so, does this not collide with the very ethos of university? Our response would be that with a more informed view of knowledge and truth we can understand how different knowledge approaches draw on entrepreneurship practices, and an ethical awareness can be evoked to prevent nurturing a practice that supports a brutal bending of the truth.

To answer this question, we turn to Flyvbjerg (2001), who picked up Aristotle's three approaches to knowledge: episteme, techne and phronesis. Whilst episteme is what we often understand as scientific knowledge, underpinned by a natural science ambition to define, measure, calculate and order phenomena, techne and phronesis are helpful to differentiate between the knowledge claims involved in entrepreneuring. With an epistemic claim for knowledge we can thus count, measure and define something. We can agree upon these 'facts' objectively, finding a universal 'truth' that is context-independent and based on general analytical rationality. Episteme recurs today in the term 'episte-mology', which points to its role in the academic community. To make some-thing work, however, we need technical knowledge, or 'know how', to solve a practical problem. Techne, the pragmatic approach is based on instrumental rationality (the cable was not inserted) ruled by a conscious goal (we need the computer to work) and is today found in terms such as technique, technical and technology. Third, there is the notion of disputing a way of reasoning that has come to be perceived as 'truth'; a knowledge claim Flyvbjerg refers to as phronesis, or practical wisdom. Phronesis describes a pragmatic knowledge, which is context dependent and based on value-rationality. We relate phrone-sis to the reflexive ethical practitioner that exercises her/his reflective judgment when enacting processes of emergence, as entrepreneurial processes have been described (Johannisson, 2011). The four questions that guide a phronetic research approach are: (1) Where are we going? (2) Who gains and who loses, and by which mechanisms of power? (3) Is this development desirable? and (4) What, if anything, should we do about it? (Flyvbjerg, 2001). These questions allow us to direct the focus towards if, and how, considered reason is involved in entrepreneurial processes.

What we can learn from the three approaches to knowledge – episteme, techne and phronesis – is to acknowledge how they take part in entrepreneurship edu-cation. Students entering both EBD and the master programme in entrepre-neurship at Linnaeus University have high expectations that they will learn the techne of entrepreneurship. They want to learn techniques that will turn them into successful entrepreneurs and to learn recipes to develop high growth busi-nesses. They also learn and use many different techniques in association with entrepreneurship and management during their studies, but are less inclined to associate entrepreneurship with episteme or phronesis. Entrepreneurship is associated neither with analysis nor with critical reflection-in-action. The stu-dents on programmes and stand-alone courses create new ideas and business models together with, or closely with, stakeholders. In the entrepreneurship master's programme, the students also create and implement entrepreneurial projects, sometimes in close cooperation with stakeholders. They are asked to create new ideas and business models by understanding the stakeholders and what works for them. These educational practices resemble techne, the prag-matic approach, which is based on instrumental rationality, ruled by a con-scious goal. Thus, students want 'tools' they can use to make something work.

The students from the EBD programme work continuously with partner organ-isations during their three-year studies. This approach provides them with space not only to develop their technical skills (e.g. how to present an idea, how to talk to a customer), but also to walk the walk of an entrepreneur (or, at least next to her/him) and exercise phronesis by developing an ability to reflect in action. Students at master level are also continuously asked, through a number of assignments, to reflect on the research and how it relates to their context and their future work life. The idea of entrepreneurship is reflected upon in relation to their own experiences, expectations and aspirations through a critical assessment method, by discussing the idea of entrepreneurship in relation to the personal level (What do I think?), the scientific level (What does the research say?) and the ethical level (What values/ethics should apply here?). By being exposed to a variety of theories and perspectives (e.g. effectuation, opportunity discovery and business model generation), students are not only taught to classify, categorise and analyse entrepreneurial processes according to epistemic ideals, but are also helped to reflect critically on entrepreneurship as practice and to position themselves in relation to that practice and incorporate elements of different theories and practices in their approach. This resembles phronesis, the pragmatic approach which is context-dependent, based on value-rationality. These practices help students gain experiences through which they can develop their ability to be the reflexive ethical practitioner that exercises her/his reflective judgment (cf. Schön, 2017).

In the emerging societal terrain where 'alternative facts' cause concern, universities are being challenged to hold on even more firmly to the concepts of knowledge and truth. Recent documentaries describing the dark side of entrepreneurship (e.g. Theranos and Fyre Festival) show how truth can be bent in entrepreneurial processes, which reminds us of the need for an academically developed entrepreneurship education (Berglund and Verduijn, 2018). Such an approach can be described as a balancing act (Tillmar, 2018), where ambitions to create conditions for entrepreneurship should not be aligned with the uncritical fostering of neoliberal subjects that perpetuate the status quo. Instead, students should be equipped with practical wisdom, through practising phronesis, so they can contribute to the betterment of society: ecologically, culturally, socially, and with the hope of a more sustainable future.

By being aware of the different claims to the truth that can be made, we can learn what is at stake, and how truth can be bent, as well as become better informed about how we can enact entrepreneurship in the post-truth society. The aim is not to diminish scientific knowledge, but to understand that what we perceive to be scientific knowledge is historically, socially and culturally rooted. Furthermore, truth always involves degrees of power and, apart from making epistemic knowledge claims, we should also learn to navigate the landscape of techne (how to do) and phronesis (wisdom and ethics) in entrepreneurship education as well as in the entrepreneurial university. We interpret 'acting as if' as the human ability to act upon the unknown by relating to one's experiences, ideas, visions, and hopes. The ability to sense this is essential if society wishes to nurture entrepreneurship practices. But if there is no institutional support to distinguish episteme from techne and phronesis, our students need to be grounded ethically, and well-informed about the various knowledge claims involved in entrepreneuring, so they will not be accused of telling lies, or bending the truth.

Whilst it can be easy to designate episteme as an important basis for the TEU to produce knowledge, and phronesis as the propelling mechanism in AEU, techne still has a role to play 'between' these two approaches. In furthering our understanding of how to make the university more entrepreneurial, the three approaches to knowledge help to remind us about the interplay of different knowledges in the making of change. We therefore suggest retaining the following research questions in order to discern what knowledge is left out/let in: (1) Are all three approaches to knowledge – episteme, techne and phronesis – emphasised in TEU versus AEU activities? (2) If not, what is suppressed/marginalised? (3) How can connections be made to facilitate a process where techne, episteme and phronesis are present?

University and the state: creating fruitful tensions and questions through TEU and AEU

In this chapter, we have sought to problematise the shift from the post-war welfare society, where universities acted entrepreneurially in alignment with overall visions of the entrepreneurial state, to contemporary neoliberal global society where universities have become market actors who compete with others by offering their entrepreneurial engagement in a desire to contribute to innovations and the betterment of society. This shift can also be described as a move from liberal democracy to neoliberal global capitalism. In the context of Sweden, which has served as a point of departure to discuss the case of Linnaeus University, the previously strong welfare state has undergone pervasive deregulation of the public sector along with increasing marketisation and privatisation, with far-reaching consequences for the educational system (Dahlstedt and Fejes, 2019). Arguments for making the shift – from state organised welfare to including market rules in the organisation of welfare – echo the critique of the US state, which Mazzucato argues was misaligned if a society wishes to be innovative, because viewing the state as lame, inefficient and an obstacle to innovation leads to the advocacy of another unidimensional solution, namely the market.

To complicate this picture, the public sector is typically pictured as less entrepreneurial than the market. There are some indicators that the market may benefit the many in some contexts (Rosling, 2018). However, research has shown severe limitations for entrepreneurship to develop in the Swedish private sector (Tillmar, 2005) and great opportunities for entrepreneurial renewal in the public sector (Sundin and Tillmar, 2008). Furthermore, the market is often accused of only benefiting the rich, at the expense of the poor, leading to a democratic decline. Even so, in neoliberal global capitalism, the emphasis is on competition rather than cooperation. Thus, public sector organisations exposed to market rules may be forced to help those who might benefit most, rather than those most in need (Eikenberry and Kluver, 2004). An ideological elevation of entrepreneurship also follows in the wake of the neoliberal tide. In short, it becomes attractive to present oneself as entrepreneurial – which applies as much to individuals as to organisations and societies. Being entrepreneurial is perceived as something desirable. Those are the people to follow. In this chapter we have pointed to how 'the entrepreneurial' in the world of higher education can be claimed in different ways. The concept is thus far from stable and unambiguous.

Consequently, neoliberal logics have taken precedence, making it more difficult for the state – and, we would argue, universities – to 'be entrepreneurial' in the way they have previously acted. Instead, universities are increasingly ensnared in the enterprise logic, having to compete for resources just as any other actor on the market. It is in this terrain we have placed the two conceptualisations of TEU and AEU with an ambition to point to collaborative advantages and, perhaps, opportunities to act more entrepreneurially together. We have described the technologically innovation-driven university (TEU) as being underpinned by an epistemic knowledge approach, propelled by the question: What kind of technologies can solve a situation or problem? In contrast, the alternative 'entrepreneurship-as-creativity' approach to the university (AEU), underpinned by a phronetic knowledge approach, focuses on the question: Which society can solve a situation or problem?

Following Mazzucato's (2015) description of the state in the post-war US context, the state acted entrepreneurially in the sense of its bold and visionary ideas (i.e. conquering space and the moon), but also in taking risks aligned with these visions by investing in long-term promising, yet risky, projects to make future realities possible. The state, and its members, was richly rewarded by new innovations, welfare development and a sense of societal progress (ibid.). The institution of education, and thus universities, played a key role in facilitating this entrepreneurial role of the state. However, while we cannot travel back in time and change the situation, we need to understand what we can learn from former societal structures. The elaboration of TEU/AEU in this chapter may help us to think anew about the role of universities in a society that needs innovation to thrive.

In particular, discussing the entrepreneurial university in terms of TEU and AEU teaches us that if the entrepreneurial university is coupled only with specialisation, efficiency, technology and innovations, we may have a situation where a single entrepreneurial logic is given precedence in education and knowledge production. The alternative of making entrepreneurship more inclusive, creative and a facilitator for all of us to enact co-creation with various stakeholders may also fall short unless there are improvements, such as technological innovations, that might bring about new markets that make it possible to establish structures to facilitate the emergence of a more sustainable and human society. Hence, TEU and AEU complement each other and could – if they joined forces – play the role of their predecessor, the university without the preface entrepreneurial. The interplay of TEU and AUE can set the stage for processes that aim to develop new innovations and, at the same time, processes seeking new ways of organising society. If – or when – these two approaches to the entrepreneurial university develop ways in which to cooperate, they may resist the temptation to compete with each other to be recognised as the entrepreneurial university, and instead find ways to create the stability and long-terms investments that are needed to turn new knowledge into both new technologies and novel ways of organising society for the betterment of society.

From our discussion and conceptualisations of AEU and TEU, we can now ask the following question: How can – and should – we study the entrepreneurial university? Below, we set out some guiding ideas for how we could – empirically, theoretically and methodologically – undertake a study of the university as entrepreneurial.

How to study entrepreneurial universities

In this chapter, we have used the example of Linnaeus University to highlight the fact that alternative interpretations co-exist with more conventional understandings of the entrepreneurial university. Further research should explore and identify more empirical cases of alternative practices in teaching, research and collaboration. By discussing firstly democracy, and then knowledge and truth, a number of questions and perspectives have been suggested to shed light on the variation the entrepreneurial university may take. From a more strategic viewpoint, we have also indicated how to 'build' an entrepreneurial university that is consistent with the values of a particular educational institution. Whilst we refrain from giving normative advice, we nonetheless imagine that the different aspects of TEU/AEU shed light on how the current orientation, context and ambition of a university can provide different routes for how it can be(come) 'entrepreneurial'. Discussing universities in terms of TEU and AEU also makes it possible to pose a number of new research questions about entrepreneurship education and research and its relation to the society.

Viewing the university through the lens of Bildungsideal allows us to recognise that knowledge about entrepreneurship is valuable not only for prospective entrepreneurs, but for all citizens in the era of late capitalism. From this perspective, we suggest that research on the entrepreneurial university can be guided by the following questions: (1) Does the entrepreneurial university educate its stakeholders to better understand the various practices and logics of entrepreneurship (i.e. spanning from creativity to marketing and selling), and in that case how? (2) In what way does the entrepreneurial university facilitate reflexivity and an ethical awareness to prevent 'acting-as-if' from turning into 'truth-bending' in entrepreneurial processes? And (3) How does the concept of Bildung – with its ambition to educate citizens at large – underpin practices in the entrepreneurial university to help society and its members to see through the smokescreens of both threat-mongers and preachers of promise?

With regards to our elaboration of TEU and AEU, the limitation of the former is the view of entrepreneurship as a neutral practice (based on neutral knowledge of techne and episteme), unpolitical and unproblematic, to be taught to entrepreneurial individuals. Although AEU seeks to democratise the idea of entrepreneurship, it is also limited to considering the implied (and perhaps naive) notion that, through practices of co-creation, entrepreneurship can circumvent the neoliberal ideology of markets and its short-term focus and provide space for collective action. To better understand these limitations, we suggest adopting a broader conceptualisation of entrepreneurship, theoretically supported by social science literature on power dynamics, change, and democratic self-reflection. Such a conceptualisation allows the following questions to be addressed: (1) Can employees and students resist becoming entrepreneurial in the entrepreneurial university? (2) If not, what kind of freedom can then be associated with knowledge?

Returning to the concepts of democracy as well as of truth and knowledge highlights the fact that entrepreneurial practices involve different forms of knowledge, which makes it possible to discuss two underlying questions: (1) Who should be educated? (2) Given the different approaches to knowledge, what should they learn? These two questions should not only be borne in mind by those researching the entrepreneurial university, but also spur ethical self-reflection among academics to reconsider how we want to live academic life. Ethnography, including auto-ethnography, as a methodological approach might help us, as researchers and teachers, to explore these questions and to study what happens when, for example, we strive to broaden the view of what entrepreneurship can entail and/or to create awareness of 'the dark sides' of entrepreneurialism. Addressing the entrepreneurial university from the perspective of TEU and AEU unfolds the political, ideological and ethical terrain of higher education. In short, conducting research in this area is political. We suggest that we always need to remember the bigger picture involving notions of democracy and knowledge while studying entrepreneurial universities. As researchers, it may be tricky to navigate this terrain, faced with both high expectations and deep distrust from a varied group of stakeholders. Nonetheless, we should take responsibility for the knowledge we produce, and must reflect upon how it can be used and who benefits from it (cf. Flyvbjerg). This does not mean that we should not study the entrepreneurial university from different angles, but it requires an awareness of why this is done and what it can lead to (Lindgren and Packendorff, 2007).

If we want to understand how the entrepreneurial university can emulate the entrepreneurial state, we should also study whether the university makes long-term investments that no other actor is interested in, and if so what kind, as well as how such long-term investments may facilitate a re-evaluation of entrepreneurial practice and knowledge processes. While wrapping up this chapter in mid-March 2020, most of us are, on a global scale, in some kind of quarantine because of Covid-19 and the coronavirus outbreak. Keeping long-term investments and the role of knowledge production in mind, one of the authors of this chapter came across a live interview with a vaccine researcher on a US media news channel, which spurred our interest. Searching for this institute we found a published interview with Dr Peter Hotez, Co-director of the Center for Vaccine Development at Texas Children's Hospital and Dean of the National School of Tropical Medicine at the Baylor College of Medicine in Houston. Dr Hotez described how the vaccine research group has for a long time dedicated its efforts to developing and testing vaccines that are not of interest for the biotech market (because vaccine is a risky product for the commercial market – it may not generate profit, or the profit required for the stock market).

Dr Peter Hotez says he made the pitch to anyone who would listen. After years of research, his team of scientists in Texas had helped develop a vaccine to protect against a deadly strain of coronavirus. Now they needed money to begin testing it in humans. But this was 2016. More than a decade had passed since the viral disease known as severe acute respiratory syndrome, or SARS, had spread through China, killing more than 770 people. That disease, an earlier coronavirus similar to the one now sweeping the globe, was a distant memory by the time Hotez and his team sought funding to test whether their vaccine would work in humans. 'We tried like heck to see if we could get investors or grants to move this into the clinic,' said Hotez.[1] However, in the interview it was emphasised how, against all odds, they continuously worked to prepare vaccines for all known viruses. Just in case. Because in a crisis, that would save us time and we would be better prepared to avoid extraordinary actions that might jeopardise both lives and societies.

Bearing this story in mind we would also ask how TEU as well as AEU can participate in creating a more stable, forethoughtful and sustainable – ecologically, socially, economically – future through preparing for the extraordinary. This implies dedicating research not only to those areas that are described as 'useful' when society works according to 'business as usual', but also putting energies and efforts into unfashionable areas; those that may not be profitable in the short term, but which may in the end benefit us all in a crisis. It is worth repeating the old and well-known motto to keep research free; allowing science to be curious and to explore unknown frontiers, irrespective of discipline and research area, may help societies to cope and heal through unexpected crisis. This requires an entrepreneurial university with integrity, one that can assess opportunities in the near future, but that can also prepare for the unexpected, by taking a long-term perspective on innovation and expecting new ideas to emerge by experimenting in a multitude of research directions.

Finally, in this chapter we have problematised the university's relationship/s with entrepreneurship. We imagine that the reader of the chapter might well think: 'Let's skip addressing university as entrepreneurial.' Addressing the university as something else would indeed be an opportunity. However, that does not mean that we can escape entrepreneurship. Neither can we avoid the progress of neoliberalism and its impact on individuals, organisations and societies. Nor can we hinder totalitarian ideological attempts to restrict liberalism. Instead, populism could play a part in setting unexpected boundaries, which might put even more restraints on research. So we need both strength and nerve to stay on course and learn more about the effects generated when we are swept away by the cheers of entrepreneurship, without neglecting the relation between university and entrepreneurship. We therefore need more research into how these relationships (because we believe this needs to be described in the plural) have emerged. Writing this chapter has raised questions not only about how we want to inhabit research life, but about how we can study the very context we inhabit.

Notes

1. See   https://www.nbcnews.com/health/health-care/scientists-were-close-corona virus-vaccine-years-ago-then-money-dried-n1150091 (accessed 16 March 2020).

References

Alexandersson, A. (2015), *Incubating Businesses*. (Doctoral dissertation). Växjö, Sweden: Linnaeus University Press.
Ball, S. J. and A. Olmedo (2013), 'Care of the self, resistance and subjectivity under neoliberal governmentalities', *Critical Studies in Education*, 54(1), 85–96.
Baumol, W. J. (1990), 'Entrepreneurship: Productive, unproductive and destructive', *Journal of Political Economy*, 98(5), 893–921.
Berg, M. and B. K. Seeber (2016), *The Slow Professor: Challenging the Culture of Speed in the Academy*. Toronto: University of Toronto Press.
Berglund, K. and K. Verduijn (Eds.) (2018), *Revitalizing Entrepreneurship Education*. New York: Routledge.
Berglund, K., B. Johannisson and B. Schwartz (Eds.) (2012), *Societal Entrepreneurship: Positioning, Penetrating, Promoting*. Cheltenham, UK and Northampton, MA, USA: Edward Elgar Publishing.
Berglund, K., M. Lindgren and J. Packendorff (2017), 'Responsibilising the next generation: Fostering the enterprising self through de-mobilising gender', *Organization*, 24(6), 892–915.
Bill, F., B. Bjerke and A. W. Johansson (Eds.) (2010), *(De)mobilizing the Entrepreneurship Discourse: Exploring Entrepreneurial Thinking and Action*. Cheltenham, UK and Northampton, MA, USA: Edward Elgar Publishing.
Bill, F., A. Jansson and L. Olaison (2010), 'The spectacle of entrepreneurship: A duality of flamboyance and activity' in F. Bill and A. W. Johansson (Eds.), *(De)mobilizing the Entrepreneurship Discourse: Exploring Entrepreneurial Thinking and Action* (pp. 158–175). Cheltenham, UK and Northampton, MA, USA: Edward Elgar Publishing.
Björk, F., J. Hansson and D. Lundborg (2014), *An Ecosystem for Social Innovation in Sweden: A Strategic Research and Innovation Agenda*. Lund: Lund University.
Bornemark, J. (2018), *The Renaissance of the Immeasurable: A Settlement with the Pedants' World Domination*. [English translation], Stockholm: Volante.
Bröckling, U. (2015), *The Entrepreneurial Self: Fabricating a New Type of Subject*. Newcastle Upon Tyne: Sage.
Carayannis, E. G. and D. F. J. Campbell (2012), *Mode 3 Knowledge Production in Quadruple Helix Innovation Systems: 21st-Century Democracy, Innovation, and Entrepreneurship for Development*. Berlin: SpringerBriefs in Business.

Carreyrou, J. (2018), *Bad Blood – Secrets and Lies in a Silicon Valley Startup*. New York: Penguin Random House.
Clark, B. (2001), 'The entrepreneurial university: New foundations for collegiality, autonomy, and achievement', *Higher Education Management*, 13(2), 9–24.
Dahlstedt, M. and A. Fejes (Eds.) (2019), *Neoliberalism and Market Forces in Education: Lessons from Sweden*. Oxford: Routledge.
Eikenberry, A. M. and J. D. Kluver (2004), 'The marketization of the nonprofit sector: Civil society at risk?', *Public Administration Review*, 64(2), 132–140.
Elg, M., P. E. Ellström, H. Kock and M. Tillmar (2016), Impact evaluation report: Helix Vinn Excellence Centre 2006–2015.
Ellborg, K. (2018), 'Visualizing entrepreneurship – Using pictures as ways to see and talk about entrepreneurship in educational settings' in C. H. Matthews and E. Liguori (Eds.), *Annals of Entrepreneurship Education and Pedagogy – Vol III* (pp. 79–98). Cheltenham, UK and Northampton, MA: Edward Elgar Publishing.
Etzkowitz, H. (2006), 'The new visible hand: An assisted linear model of science and innovation policy', *Science and Public Policy*, 33(5), 310–320.
Final Report (2016), *The Entrepreneurial University – Open*. Report published by Linnaeus University.
Flyvbjerg, B. (2001), *Making Social Science Matter: Why Social Inquiry Fails and How it can Succeed Again*. Cambridge: Cambridge University Press.
Forslund, M., M. Lundgren and K. Zambrell (2016), *Småländskt ledarskap: inledande betraktelser*. [English translation], Växjö: Linnaeus University Press.
Foss, L. and D. V. Gibson (2015), 'The entrepreneurial university: Context and institutional change' in L. Foss and D. Gibson (Eds.), *The Entrepreneurial University: Context and Institutional Change* (pp. 27–43). New York: Routledge.
Fredin, S. and M. Jogmark (2017), 'Local culture as a context for entrepreneurial activities', *European Planning Studies*, 25(9), 1556–1574.
Gartner, W. B., B. J. Bird and J. A. Starr (1992), 'Acting as if: Differentiating entrepreneurial from organizational behavior', *Entrepreneurship Theory and Practice*, 16(3), 13–32.
Holmgren, C. A. (2018), *The Shaping of the Entrepreneurial Teacher. Entrepreneurial Learning as Governmentality*. [English translation] (Doctoral dissertation), Växjö: Linnaeus University Press.
Johannisson, B. (1998), 'Personal networks in emerging knowledge-based firms: Spatial and functional patterns', *Entrepreneurship & Regional Development*, 10(4), 297–313.
Johannisson, B. (2005), *The Essence of Entrepreneurship*. [English translation], Lund: Studentlitteratur.
Johannisson, B. (2011), 'Towards a practice theory of entrepreneuring', *Small Business Economics*, 36(2), 135–150.
Johansson, A. W. (1997), *Understanding Counselling to Small Business Owners*. [English translation] (Doctoral dissertation), Lund: Lund University Press.
Johansson, A. W. (2004), 'Narrating the entrepreneur', *International Small Business Journal*, 22(3), 273–293.
Johansson, A. W. and E. Rosell (2012), 'Academic and non-academic education for societal entrepreneurship' in K. Berglund, B. Johannisson and B. Schwartz (Eds.), *Societal Entrepreneurship: Positioning, Penetrating, Promoting*. Cheltenham, UK and Northampton, MA, USA: Edward Elgar Publishing.
Karlsson, M. (2018), *Infinitely Demanding Entrepreneurship*. (Doctoral dissertation), Växjö: Linnaeus University Press.

Larsson, D. and G. Sjöstrand (2014), 'The entrepreneurial university – Linnaeus university! Evaluation'. [English translation], December 2014. Report published by Linnaeus University, Faculty of Social Sciences.
Lindgren, M. and J. Packendorff (2007), *Construction of Entrepreneurship. Theory, Practice and Interaction.* [English translation], Örebro: Forum för Småföretagsforskning.
Mazzucato, M. (2015), *The Entrepreneurial State: Debunking Public vs. Private Sector Myths, Vol. 1.* London: Anthem Press.
Ogbor, J. O. (2000), 'Mythicizing and reification in entrepreneurial discourse: Ideology-critique of entrepreneurial studies', *Journal of Management Studies*, 37(5), 605–635.
Pettersson, K. (2004), *Enterprising Men and Invisible Women; The Discourse of Gnosjö from a Gender Perspective.* [English translation] (Doctoral dissertation), Uppsala: Uppsala University.
Rosenlund, J. and E. Rosell (2017), 'Using dialogue arenas to manage boundaries between sectors and disciplines in environmental research projects', *International Journal of Action Research*, 13(1), 24–38.
Rosling, Hans (2018), *Factfulness – Ten Tips to Help you Understand the World.* [English translation], Johanneshov: MTM.
Schön, D. A. (2017), *The Reflective Practitioner: How Professionals Think in Action.* Oxford: Routledge.
Shane, S. (2004), *Academic Entrepreneurship: University Spinoffs and Wealth Creation.* Cheltenham, UK and Northampton, MA: Edward Elgar Publishing.
Slaughter, S. and G. Rhoades (2004), *Academic Capitalism and the New Economy, Markets, State, and Higher Education.* Baltimore: The Johns Hopkins University Press.
Smith, C. (2019), 'Fyre: The Greatest Party That Never Happened', Documentary available at Netflix. Imdb: https://www.imdb.com/title/tt9412098/.
Steyaert, C. and D. Hjorth (Eds.) (2006), *Entrepreneurship as Social Change: A Third Movements in Entrepreneurship Book.* Cheltenham, UK and Northampton, MA, USA: Edward Elgar Publishing.
Steyaert, C. and J. Katz (2004), 'Reclaiming the space of entrepreneurship in society: Geographical, discursive and social dimensions', *Entrepreneurship & Regional Development*, 16(3), 179–196.
Steyaert, C., D. Hjorth and W. B. Gartner (2011), 'Six memos for a curious and imaginative future scholarship in entrepreneurship studies', *Entrepreneurship & Regional Development*, 23(1–2), 1–7.
Sundin, E. and M. Tillmar (2008), 'A nurse and a civil servant changing institutions: Entrepreneurial processes in different public sector organizations', *Scandinavian Journal of Management*, 24(2), 113–124.
Svensson, L., P.-E. Ellström and G. Brulin (2007), 'Introduction – On interactive research', *International Journal of Action Research*, 3(3), 233–249.
Tillmar, M. (2005), 'Våffer gör di på detta viset? Villkor för småföretagande inom omsorgen ur ett institutionellt perspektiv' [English translation], *Kommunal Politik och Ekonomi*, 9, 3–9.
Tillmar, M. (2009), 'Societal entrepreneurs in the health sector: Crossing the frontiers', *Social Enterprise Journal*, 5(3), 282–298.
Tillmar, M. (2018), 'Foreword: Critique, entrepreneurship, practice: A prolegomenon' in K. Berglund and K. Verduijn (Eds.), *Revitalizing Entrepreneurship Education: Adopting a Critical Approach in the Classroom* (pp. xv–xvi). Oxford: Routledge.

Tunstall, R. (2018), 'Education or exploitation? Reflecting on the entrepreneurial university and the role of the entrepreneurship educator' in K. Berglund and K. Verduijn (Eds.), *Revitalizing Entrepreneurship Education: Adopting a Critical Approach in the Classroom* (pp. 25–40). Oxford: Routledge.

Wigren, C. (2003), *The Spirit of Gnosjö: The Grand Narrative and Beyond* (Doctoral dissertation), Jönköping: Jönköping International Business School.

Wright, M., B. Clarysse, P. Mustar and A. Lockett (2007), *Academic Entrepreneurship in Europe*. Cheltenham, UK and Northampton, MA, USA: Edward Elgar Publishing.

Wright, M., A. Lockett, B. Clarysse and M. Binks (2006), 'University spin-out companies and venture capital', *Research Policy*, 35(4), 481–501.

3 The societally entrepreneurial university

Karen Verduijn and Ida Sabelis

Introduction

This ambition to be societally entrepreneurial can be traced across the globe, and appears in many guises, sharing a commitment to improving universities' societal engagement. The aim of this chapter is to address this development in the context of the struggle of universities to cope with neoliberal tendencies such as the performativity that has found its way into our higher educational institutions, with the emphasis on striving for 'excellence', and the need to strike a (new) balance. In other words, we wonder how to avoid this ambition becoming either merely another marketing tool, or just the next way to acquire the money that especially European universities are lacking.

In doing so, we bring to the fore the phenomenon of community engagement initiatives in higher education (cf. Barinaga, 2016; Fenwick, 2016; Berglund and Verduijn, 2018), and look in particular at the concept of 'community service learning' (CSL) (Jacoby, 2015), or simply 'service learning'. We wonder if such an endeavour can do enough to help universities find that new balance and if that is sufficient, given the precarious situation in which many European universities find themselves (De Vita and Case, 2016; Gianiodis et al., 2016; Tunstall, 2018; Donskis et al., 2019). Ultimately, we ponder – taking up on the notion of affirmative critique (cf. Braidotti, 2011; Andersen, 2017; Gunnarsson and Hohti, 2018) – on what could be done differently in order to commensurate universities' striving for survival with their societal responsibilities and role as academic education institutes.

Precarious universities

The momentum of writing about a 'societally entrepreneurial university' is contextualized by a 'reorientation of university strategies and policies to promoting entrepreneurship and societal impact' (Hytti, 2018, p. 228). This relates to the delicate situation of many (European) universities, which for their survival used to be largely dependent on tax money from governments, but now find themselves in a situation of competition and internal accountability (Ball, 2003), and a lack of money through heavy cutbacks in funding and simultaneously increasing numbers of students (van Loon, 2019). In a context in which ever more students enter universities and governments increasingly seem to downplay the importance of academic 'Bildung' (reflective education) by downscaling the funding, universities see themselves forced to find new sources of income, while at the same time having to better 'market' themselves (thus, to (better) perform) in the sense that their 'products' (students and research, and relevant knowledge) grow. Already in 1996 authors like Parker and Jary, and Georg Ritzer described the dawning of a 'McUniversity', likening the workings of universities to that of 'fast food', for the mind that is, and arguing how this is based on a concomitant organizational system of industrial performance, which stresses the importance of (growing) numbers and increases in funding.

In comparison, universities based in the North Americas have a different tradition in terms of raising money than their European counterparts – their neoliberal traditions helped establish the normality of, e.g., private funding whereas the Rhineland traditions as informing European universities' fundaments (e.g. Karsten, 1999; Martin and Collinson, 2002) are based on communal funding and the levelling of class-based differences with regards to entering (higher) educational programmes. With the rise of student numbers following the emancipatory movements since the 1950s, and the increasing realization of how more students require more funding, European higher education seems to have turned to market thinking and its concomitant habits of commercialization and commodification. And this obviously brings along different policies in relation to the organization of higher education as it is aimed at (structural) growth rather than at, for instance, cooperation, and the deepening of knowledge to benefit society (Nelson 2011; Bauman and Donskis, 2013). An amalgam of market-inspired policies and an overall switch towards more individualization, in tandem with a decrease of attention for reproductivity, or 'care' (Biesecker and Hofmeister, 2013;[1] Bauman, 2000) then paved (and paves) the way for what Ball (2012) termed the centrality of performativity. As Tammy Shefer argues in the foreword to *Academia in Crisis* (2019): 'the helpful and well-argued critique of the marketisation [...] and corporatisation (with digitalisation as a key component) of the university, [is] shaped by larger global capitalist imperatives' (Shefer in Donskis et al., 2019, p. 10). The capitalist imperative rather exploits the realm of reproduction and care (home, volunteering, etc.) than taking into account what has largely become private: the support of all that is 'productive'. Many colleagues have by now criticized this newly adopted 'cookie factory' style (Sabelis, 2019a, p. 195) and its deteriorating effects due to the predominantly money-based management and governance of universities (e.g. Lorenz, 2012; Ball, 2012; Radice, 2013; De Vita and Case, 2016; Collini, 2012; Flikkema and ten Have, 2016; Donskis et al., 2019). The first signs of how this development feeds into more superficial and output-oriented scholarship (Collini, 2012) become visible. The lack of 'Bildung' (Sabelis, 2019b, pp. 132 ff) for which the European universities traditionally were known, can only cause frustration and, paradoxically, undermine the same performativity it is striving for, as it ultimately pushes fast and repetitive knowledge instead of gradually developing and broadening reflected insights aimed to provide more understanding of societal problems and contexts for all.

So, the expansion of universities as almost-industrial institutes, embracing market-driven models, in fact turns around the same goals promoted in the slogans and mission statements universities have adopted from global business. Universities striving for excellence all-at-the-same-time, and promoting a 'broader mind' while organizing bigger programs are only symptoms of a university that eats (from) its own children instead of feeding them. As Martha Nussbaum puts it:

> If [corporatization of higher education] continues, nations all over the world will soon be producing generations of useful machines, rather than complete citizens who can think for themselves, criticize tradition, and understand the significance of another person's sufferings and achievements (Nussbaum, 2010, p. 2).

This has an effect on how society is involved and implied, and how the academy's audience regards its relevance. With Shefer (2019) we share the felt need for 'a critical hope to open up spaces for resistance and change, even if only in small pockets and through slow movements, and to allow a different "imaginary" of what the university can be and do' (p. 16). Indeed, one of the issues is how academia can evolve, especially when departing from a critical perspective in which the education of 'complete citizens' (Nussbaum, 2010) is argued for. Not all critique brings with it the 'seed of change'; a lot of critiques on the neo-liberalization of universities (e.g. Lorenz, 2012) bear a high level of TINA (there is no alternative, cf. Bauman and Donskis, 2013). But universities could and probably also will still contribute to, if not in terms of solutions, then at least by offering guidance and inspiration to deal with society's problems, be it only because students also increasingly speak up about their desire to 'learn'. And then, after all, rather than having the focus on 'production', a fruitful way to develop and promote academic attitudes, knowledge and research can be to invent different links to the societies of which universities are a part, and to co-develop research while explicitly involving neighbourhoods, alternative projects, and social institutions. Some clouds of change in that sense can be seen in, for instance, the struggle for decolonialization of knowledge in South Africa, and at some European universities,[2] e.g. in the initiative of Ghent University, Belgium,[3] to leave the uniformity of the rat-race and find their own mode in reinventing ways for what they themselves consider quality no matter what others decide.

Universities dealing with society's problems

In this chapter we interrogate the recent trend towards developing 'entrepreneurial universities', especially where this trend is likened to the 'societally entrepreneurial'. We do this against the backdrop of how understandings of entrepreneurship in general have moved from a 'narrow' understanding (entrepreneurship as (new) business creation, and the dominant adoption of psychological and economic lenses and models) to broader ones, in which entrepreneurship is seen as 'fundamentally a process of social change' (Calás et al., 2009, p. 553), and thus to 'not only bring about new firms, products and services but also new openings for more liberating forms of individual and collective existence' (Verduijn et al., 2014, p. 98). A similar shift applies specifically to the concept of the entrepreneurial university, which witnesses not only the more 'regular' approaches (stimulating spin-offs, etc.), but also the perceived need to 'give back' to society, and the emergence of a variety of community engagement initiatives. We introduce and discuss a particular example of such an initiative: (community) service learning, as one example of how universities deal with societal problems.

Community service learning

Community service learning (CSL) has a long tradition, originating in the US and now gradually gaining ground in Europe. CSL generally appears as a (1) course-based, (2) credit bearing educational experience, in which students (3) participate in mutually identified and organized service activities that benefit the community, and (4) reflect on the service activity in such a way as to (5) gain further understanding of course content, a broader appreciation of the discipline, and an enhanced sense of personal values and civic responsibility (Bringle and Clayton, 2012, p. 105). Examples include students becoming 'buddies' for refugees, helping them find their way in a local community, initiating activities to liven up particular neighbourhoods, and the creating of community gardens to help foster a more sustainable local environment. Students' involvement in such initiatives is – via CSL – part of the coursework, and thus students also gain credits for their involvement. An example from our home university is a course in which students are asked to design a logistical solution to help a particular food bank initiative work more efficiently. The students literally need to join the people collecting and distributing the food in order to understand the situation, and come up with a suitable solution.

Thus, a community engagement pedagogy such as CSL fits well with the growing awareness that universities need to prepare students to deal with today's (and tomorrow's) complex, pluralistic and dynamic societal challenges (Bringle and Clayton, 2012) and not just 'produce' knowledge for growth and profit. It fits the realization that there is a pressing need to address how we understand contemporary society as part of all (higher) education. Or, after Nussbaum (2010), it fits the need to foster 'complete citizens' who can think for themselves, criticize tradition, and understand the significance of other persons' presences. Obviously, not only (abstract) knowledge is needed to do that, but also an actual (reciprocal) connection with the communities from which knowledge is developed, as with the food bank example. Having students engage in community initiatives should stimulate students' 'sense of social responsibility' (Fenwick, 2016, p. 257), with social responsibility not being a 'concept to be taught', but rather a 'living force to be engaged with' (ibid.). This results in a deep(er) engagement between university and communities, for the greater benefit of both. There is a strong element of care in such community servicing (Flikkema and ten Have, 2016). And there is an overarching (utopian) sense of hope, a hope that a better, more egalitarian, just world is possible. However, inspired by so-called 'critical' traditions in science (ibid.), we would not suggest proceeding on the path of the utopian. Rightfully, a comment on CSL is thus that it is too 'uncritical' – as it leans too much on the utopian, and as it actually comes forward from within the framing of univer-sities striving for growth and profit; and therefore one should not assume, for instance, that reflexivity is automatically entailed. Furthermore, community service is associated with voluntary or 'social work', and risks providing unpaid work where formerly jobs have been cut, or outsourced. In other words, CSL combined with universities' need for money means that the entrepreneurial elements in community service can be regarded as an extra source of cheap labour, while students – under the header of gaining work experience – first and foremost provide labour (Edwards et al., 2001).

All in all, community service as such does not directly or straightforwardly contribute to the university's problems; it might distract from its entrepreneurial ventures by co-opting students and staff into 'attractive' (and time-consuming) projects, while business-as-usual continues the neoliberal trend, and CS(L) actually forms just another reputation-enhancing asset ('our students help solve societal issues'). At the same time, there is a need for the work experience students gain, for the skills to be acquired, and we contend that there is a need for change, preferably via well-skilled and reflexive citizens we hope to educate via our teaching. And for staff, the research provides new insights, and the possibility for academia and its social surroundings to benefit from having better insight into each other's problems, values, and (potential) contributions.

Given that CSL has actually acquired a prominent role at our home university, we use some quotes to illustrate:

> For the students CSL has added value on an academic, professional and personal level. The most prominent example of improved academic skills is a deeper understanding of the scientific theory. When the CSL activities are properly related to the scientific knowledge on that theme, students will be encouraged to move between the real world and scientific theory. The professional added value for students is related to the improvement of communication skills and the development of their professional network. The personal added value of CSL revolves around diversity, openness to change and discovering new interests.[4]

We indeed see the general corporate language surface here: 'the development of their professional network' and 'personal added value'. But, given the overall aim to (re)connect academia with society and society's needs and challenges, we would actually expect more emphasis on developing a sense of collectivity, and a deepened (critical) understanding of the roots of named challenges, rather than just 'move between the real world, and scientific theory'.

And, as per above (polishing a university's reputation):

> CSL offers the opportunity to be better informed on and more involved in societal issues. Offering a CSL-activity can play a role in attracting motivated students. The knowledge that students gain can offer new perspectives and input for discussions during lectures. Also, CSL-activities can easily be coupled to research and publications.[5]

Indeed, 'attracting motivated students', and 'offering opportunities' is another example of how performativity, and market logics, seem to have found their way in, even in this particular reorientation to societal concerns. Lacking here is how, according to Fenwick (2016), involving students in community engagement initiatives means that we 'attune students and educations critically' (p. 250) to concerns of 'the global political economy' (ibid.). And, as argued above, this is precisely what we deem lacking in CSL.

Worth mentioning here as an alternative is Barinaga (2016) who writes about activism in business education in particular, with activism being offered 'as a pedagogic approach to raise awareness, develop humility and mobilize students' (p. 299). She describes how 'two concerns [...] translate into [the] pedagogical design: (1) to promote reflection on the extent to which market rationalities and business tools are appropriate to work with a range of social issues; and (2) to help students deepen their understanding of the social mechanisms at the root of the problems they may be working with inside and outside the classroom' (p. 300). This actually resonates more with the kind of societal engagement we would like to see emerge against the backdrop of the precariousness in which contemporary (European) universities find themselves. We want to stipulate that community engagement initiatives in higher education need to depart from a critical awareness (thus, address those concerns of the global political economy, and go to the root of the problems) if they are to help universities deal with society's problems without falling into the trap of re-establishing and re-producing the same principles that have caused the same to find themselves in a precarious situation – or, for that matter, to educate students as clones of that system, thus actually preventing raising them as aware and critical citizens. That 'critical awareness' is the basis, so to speak, from which possibilities for social change and empowerment can be enacted.

This is theoretically connected to the notion of affirmative critique (Braidotti, 2011; Andersen, 2017). Affirmative critique raises the vital question whether 'critique [will] be able to change the things we critique' (Gunnarsson and Hohti, 2018, p. 3) – and preferably from the inside, the experience of being closely involved. Affirmative critique is about raising the 'difficult (critical) questions', of which there is no 'innocent escape' (ibid.), and at the same time realizing 'the result of such critique' (ibid.). Whereas critique itself is needed for investigating and uncovering what is 'underneath', and 'behind' certain problems in terms of power structures, disciplining, oppression and discrimination (Gunnarsson and Hohti, 2018), it does not necessarily bring about change (ibid.). Indeed, it might even immobilize people, and situations; for students may come out of the experience with a feeling of 'now I see all that is "underneath", and now what…?' – which points at a critical awareness, but with a lack of (visible/palpable) possibilities for action, be that patience, humility, or hands-on attitudes. That is why the affirmative emphasizes the need to foster the opportunity for making a difference, and to wonder if the critique will be able to genuinely change the very things we set out to critique instead of 'just' learning skills and gaining a feeling of the problems at hand. According to Andersen (2017), this entails 'a shift to the affirmative where you can take on the misery in the world, but also a larger sense of the possible' (p. 438), where it is more viable to resist, re-articulate, and affirm alternatives (ibid., p. 439). To us, the notion of affirmative critique underscores not only what we have argued with regards to developing a (critical) awareness, but also to the need to intervene, and thus fight the TINA notion. The one cannot go without the other, and critical awareness implies realizing that the critique, coupled with intervention, will always change a status quo. That requires different tactics, and a return to 'Bildung', rather than a continuation on the road to becoming almost-industrial institutes. It requires asking such questions as what productive possibilities can be opened up, and thus also what (dominant) practices need altering/resisting: what happens if we intervene? How can we cater for long-term effects? How can we include more community members and 'empower' a neighbourhood? It means, in the example of the food bank case, not only coming up with a suitable solution, but (and) with sustainable solutions that serve the interest of all social actors involved, rather than have the account right at the end of the month; while at the same time opening up for change in positions – perhaps longer term involvement of volunteers, gradually producing jobs for young people, and providing training and education on the job. This is all about thinking through, in the development of solutions, longer-term desired and undesired effects instead of going for 'quick fixes'. In short, it calls for an openness to new life possibilities, by allowing (and guiding) people to go beyond current limits (Hjorth and Holt, 2016), both within our institutions, and when stimulating students to 'go out there'.

Wrapping up – our research agenda for the entrepreneurial university

In sum, we commend stimulating students' civic engagement, and fostering 'citizenship' as a token of universities' societal engagement. We however consider that such a pedagogy as 'community service learning' does not suffice, and that with it, we run the risk of reproducing the kind of pitfalls and risks universities are facing nowadays, in relation to the newly acquired core paradigm of earning money and fostering growth. The profit motive, or at least the accountability motive, is never far away. Rather, we see pedagogies based on citizenship and care – 'wild pedagogies' perhaps (Jickling et al., 2018), that do not 'just' care for the social, but for nature and, more widely, a combination of social and global sustainability.

This chapter contributes to a research agenda for the entrepreneurial university by offering our specific thoughts on how our understanding of the notion of the entrepreneurial university needs to shift (back) from a focus on economic development and market logics, to one of societal responsibility and engagement. 'From science to society via start-up' is a phrase we literally stumbled upon the other day, illustrating the seed of commercialization in the valorization of science for society. It was used as an invitation to a meeting hosted by our university. What might seem to be a well-intended 'giving back' to society (reasoned from within academia), however, is just another example of the current-day pitfalls of the entrepreneurial university.

We propose to develop a critical agenda for the understanding of the entrepreneurial university, with an eye to how this can be enacted as affirmative critique, for there lies the potential to bridge 'academia' and 'society', to connect 'practice' and 'reflexivity' – the very notions that are now being kept (too) far apart.

That agenda should entail:

- A thorough discussion, to start with, about motives and methods for such pedagogies as CSL. It will not be enough to promote service learning as part of a next mission statement, enhancing the marketing program of universities. A first step should entail agreement about content, possibilities and limits of universities to contribute to society via sharing knowledge and skills.
- Following from this, an inventory of good practices might be required. It is not the case that universities and 'society' are completely apart, or that society 'desperately' needs academic interference. Cooperation between faculties and their societal counterparts (research partners and funding bodies, community based groups involved in participatory methods, and other levels of shared knowledge development projects) has always been there, usually based on interdependence and collective interests. CSL is not about reinventing a wheel, but can perhaps be about reinforcing existing partnerships.
- In line, we should address the capitalization of academic work, e.g. by refraining from just publishing in international (i.e. English-based) jour-

nals, as genuinely society-driven CSL might not be so interesting to the 'global debate', not in first instance in any case. Indeed, CSL should not be added to the list of requirements to which all academics are subject. Rather, CSL could, and should, be used as a chance to revise the burdens neoliberal practices have caused over the last couple of decades. The lens of affirmative critique allows for not merely introducing 'new ways', but especially to revise 'old habits': genuine change in understanding what 'useful' knowledge is might shed light on how some knowledge currently evaporates from 'users' via publication (and related research project) practices that build new ivory towers, inaccessible to those who have no access to open access journals and books.

• Finally, on to the dream of 'affirmative citizenship': students usually demonstrate engagement in many ways. Be it via university bodies (student councils for one), or via jobbing and thus partaking in social life almost in a random manner, students enter the university with one foot in the institution, but the other in social worlds that sometimes make up exactly the realms CSL might be aimed at. It is our contention, talking affirmative change, that this should not be so much about inviting students to engage in community service projects, but rather that universities themselves could use CSL to rethink the taken-for-granted nature of 'publish or perish', of tenure tracks that mould students into complying, competing colleagues, and of an addiction to big-grant projects that ultimately do not serve to rethink university's uses (Ahmed, 2018) in society.

We agree with Braidotti (2019), when she claims that universities have such a brilliant, noble pedigree, and in wondering why universities would take 'corporation' as model, whilst they have – already for many centuries – been able to educate decent, discerning, creative citizens. So, in a nutshell, we propose an interventionist agenda, with an emphasis on reflexivity, and on performing (creative) 'counter actualizations' (Andersen, 2017), so as to alter these hard-to-alter practices. There is a need to rethink, and intervene, in such practices, not so much in terms of a new road ahead, more in terms of returning to the important functions universities have always had, and renewing those towards a better future.

Notes

1. Biesecker and Hofmeister have, mainly in German, made it their lives' work to stress the importance of RE/-productivity from a politically feminist perspective. This brings in the more current concept of 'care' (*Sorge, Vorsorge* in German)

      to highlight not only productivity as a one-sided concept, but also the lack of attention for what it takes to be productive, and how implicitly a hierarchy (classification) of work, e.g. between genders, classes, and socio-ecological action, is maintained. See also Biesecker and Hofmeister (2015; and Das Argument (2011)).

2.   This is yet another debate, decolonization and 'transformation' of higher education. It seems as though this movement shows some similarity with the critique on neoliberalization of universities as yet another form, a contemporary variant of control over knowledge development and its role in education and valorization.

3.   https://www.insidehighered.com/news/2019/01/23/ghent-university-belgium-embraces-new-approach-faculty-evaluation-less-focused.

4.   https://www.vu.nl/en/about-vu-amsterdam/mission-and-profile/csl/index.aspx (accessed on 8 April 2019).

5.   https://www.vu.nl/en/about-vu-amsterdam/mission-and-profile/csl/index.aspx (accessed on 8 April 2019).

References

Ahmed, S. (2018), 'Uses of use: Diversity, utility and the university', http://www.crassh.cam.ac.uk/gallery/video/sara-ahmed-uses-of-use-diversity-utility-and-the-university.

Andersen, C. E. (2017), 'Affirmative critique as minor qualitative critical inquiry: A storying of a becoming critical engagement with what happens', *International Review of Qualitative Research*, **10** (4), 430–449.

Ball, S. J. (2003), 'The teacher's soul and the terrors of performativity', *Journal of Education Policy*, **18** (2), 215–228.

Ball, S. J. (2012), 'Performativity, commodification and commitment: An I-Spy Guide to the neoliberal university', *British Journal of Educational Studies*, **60** (1), 17–28.

Barinaga, E. (2016), 'Activism in business education: Making sociology practical for social entrepreneurs', in T. Beyes, M. Parker and C. Steyaert (eds), *The Routledge Companion to Reinventing Management Education*. London: Routledge.

Bauman, Z. (2000), *Liquid Modernity*. Cambridge: Polity Press.

Bauman, Z. and L. Donskis (2013), *Moral Blindness: The Loss of Sensitivity in Liquid Modernity*. Cambridge: Polity Press.

Berglund, K. and K. Verduijn (eds) (2018), *Revitalizing Entrepreneurship Education. Adopting a Critical Approach in the Classroom*. New York: Routledge.

Biesecker, A. and S. Hofmeister (2013), 'Zur Produktivität des "Reproduktiven". Fürsorgliche Praxis als Element einer Ökonomie der Vorsorge', *Feministische Studien: Zeitschrift für Interdisziplinäre Frauen-und Geschlechterforschung*, **31** (2), 240–252.

Braidotti, R. (2011), *Nomadic Theory: The Portable Rosi Braidotti*. New York: Columbia University Press.

Braidotti, R. (2019), 'The critical posthumanities'. Talk at Harvard University's Graduate School of Design, https://www.youtube.com/watch?v=0CewnVzOg5w.

Bringle, R. G. and P. H. Clayton (2012), 'Civic education through service learning: What, how, and why?', in *Higher Education and Civic Engagement* (pp. 101–124). New York: Palgrave Macmillan.

Calás, M., L. Smircich and K. Bourne (2009), 'Extending the boundaries: Reframing "entrepreneurship as social change" through feminist perspectives', *Academy of Management Review*, **34** (3), 552–569.

Collini, S. (2012), *What are Universities for?* London: Penguin.

Das Argument (2011), 'Care – eine feministische Kritik der politischen Ökonomie', *Das Argument*, **292** (53).

De Vita, G. and P. Case (2016), 'The smell of the place: Managerialist culture in contemporary UK business schools', *Culture and Organization*, **22** (4), 348–364.

Donskis, L., I. Sabelis, F. Kamsteeg and H. Wels (eds) (2019), *Academia in Crisis. The Rise and Risk of Neoliberal Education in Europe*. Leiden, New York: Brill Publishers, VIBS 335.

Edwards, B., L. Mooney and C. Heald (2001), 'Who is being served? The impact of student volunteering on local community organizations', *Nonprofit and Voluntary Sector Quarterly*, **30** (3), 444–461.

Fenwick, T. (2016), 'What matters in sociomateriality: Towards a critical posthuman pedagogy in management education', in T. Beyes, M. Parker and C. Steyaert (eds), *The Routledge Companion to Reinventing Management Education*. London: Routledge.

Flikkema, M. and S. ten Have (2016), *Sense of Serving. Reconsidering the Role of Universities Now*. Amsterdam: VU University Press.

Gianiodis, P. T., G. D. Markman and A. Panagopoulos (2016), 'Entrepreneurial universities and overt opportunism', *Small Business Economics*, **47** (3), 609–631.

Gunnarsson, K. and R. Hohti (2018), 'Why affirmative critique?', *Reconceptualizing Educational Research Methodology*, **9** (1), 1–5.

Hjorth, D. and R. Holt (2016), 'It's entrepreneurship, not enterprise: Ai Weiwei as entrepreneur', *Journal of Business Venturing Insights*, **5**, 50–54.

Hytti, U. (2018), 'Critical entrepreneurship education: A form of resistance to McEducation?', in K. Berglund and K. Verduijn (eds), *Revitalizing Entrepreneurship Education. Adopting a Critical Approach in the Classroom* (pp. 228–234). New York: Routledge.

Jacoby, B. (2015), *Service-Learning Essentials. Questions, Answers and Lessons Learned*. San Francisco: Jossey-Bass.

Jickling, B., S. Blenkinsop, N. Timmerman and M. D. D. Sitka-Sage (eds) (2018), *Wild Pedagogies: Touchstones for Re-negotiating Education and the Environment in the Anthropocene*. New York: Springer.

Karsten, S. (1999), 'Neoliberal education reform in The Netherlands', *Comparative Education*, **35** (3), 303–317.

Lorenz, C. (2012), 'If you're so smart, why are you under surveillance? Universities, neoliberalism, and new public management', *Critical Inquiry*, **38** (3), 599–629.

Martin, P. Y. and D. Collinson (2002), 'Over the pond and across the water: Developing the field of "gendered organizations"', *Gender, Work & Organization*, **9** (3), 244–265.

Nelson, C. (2011), *No University is an Island: Saving Academic Freedom*. New York: NYU Press.

Nussbaum, M. C. (2010), *Not for profit: Why Democracy Needs the Humanities* (Vol. 2). Princeton, NJ: Princeton University Press.

Parker, M. and D. Jary (1995), 'The McUniversity: Organization, management and academic subjectivity', *Organization*, **2** (2), 319–338.

Radice, H. (2013), 'How we got here: UK higher education under neoliberalism', *ACME: An International E-Journal for Critical Geographies*, **12** (3), 407–418.

Ritzer, G. (1996), 'McUniversity in the postmodern consumer society', *Quality in Higher Education*, **2** (3), 185–199.

Sabelis, I. (2019a), 'Epilogue', in L. Donskis, I. Sabelis, F. Kamsteeg and H. Wels (eds) (2019), *Academia in Crisis. The Rise and Risk of Neoliberal Education in Europe* (pp. 195–198). Leiden, New York: Brill Publishers.

Sabelis, I. (2019b), 'Timescapes in academic life; Cubicles of time control', in L. Donskis, I. Sabelis, F. Kamsteeg and H. Wels (eds) (2019), *Academia in Crisis. The Rise and Risk of Neoliberal Education in Europe* (pp. 129–149). Leiden, New York: Brill Publishers.

Shefer, T. (2019), 'Introductory thoughts', in L. Donskis, I. Sabelis, F. Kamsteeg and H. Wels (eds) (2019), *Academia in Crisis. The Rise and Risk of Neoliberal Education in Europe* (pp. 1–10). Leiden, New York: Brill Publishers.

Tedmanson, D., C. Essers, P. Dey and K. Verduyn (2015), 'An uncommon wealth ... transforming the commons with purpose, for people and not for profit!', *Journal of Management Inquiry*, **24** (4), 439–444.

Tunstall, R. (2018), 'Education or exploitation? Reflecting on the entrepreneurial university and the role of the entrepreneurship educator', in K. Berglund and K. Verduijn (eds), *Revitalizing Entrepreneurship Education. Adopting a Critical Approach in the Classroom* (pp. 25–40). New York: Routledge.

van Loon, J. (2019), 'A nomad of academia. A thematic autobiography of privilege', in L. Donskis, I. Sabelis, F. Kamsteeg and H. Wels (eds), *Academia in Crisis. The Rise and Risk of Neoliberal Education in Europe* (pp. 150–168). Leiden, New York: Brill Publishers.

Verduijn, K., P. Dey, D. Tedmanson and C. Essers (2014), 'Emancipation and/or oppression? Conceptualizing dimensions of criticality in entrepreneurship studies', *International Journal of Entrepreneurial Behavior & Research*, **20** (2), 98–107.

4 Entrepreneurial universities in post-Soviet countries

Rita Kaša, Mari Elken and Anders Paalzow

Introduction

The question of university transformation is relevant in any context as universities are social systems that evolve or deteriorate depending on their external and internal environments (Pervin, 1967). The concept of entrepreneurial university as an analytical construct is one way for understanding why some universities develop as self-reliant confident organizations and some find it harder to do. The concept of entrepreneurial university as introduced by Clark (1998) outlines five pathways for university transformation into a self-reliant entrepreneurial organization (Clark, 2004). This chapter reviews existing scholarly knowledge about entrepreneurial higher education institutions in the former Soviet Union, focusing also on the extent to which institutions in these regions seem to develop in this direction. By doing this, the chapter identifies gaps in existing knowledge and provides suggestions for future research.

The question about knowledge of university transformation into entrepreneurial organizations in the 15 post-Soviet countries – Armenia, Azerbaijan, Belarus, Estonia, Georgia, Kazakhstan, Kyrgyzstan, Latvia, Lithuania, Moldova, Russia, Tajikistan, Turkmenistan, Ukraine and Uzbekistan – is relevant for several reasons. One reason is that new knowledge is generated when we account for what is already known. There is limited research that examines the whole post-Soviet region (Smolentseva et al., 2018). Existing research on entrepreneurial university concept is heavily driven by information that exists on universities in the context of developed liberal democracies. References to evidence generated on universities in the context of political, economic and social transition are much less numerous. This forms a gap in our understanding of the notion of entrepreneurial universities. In Western Europe, one can argue that universities are embedded in a relatively stable institutional context.

As institutions, universities are enduring and recognizable (Olsen, 2007, p. 27). Even when their governance and steering systems may change substantially and sometimes lead to dramatic changes in higher education systems, the basic state structure has remained intact. The context for higher education institutions in post-Soviet region is fundamentally different. After the collapse of the Soviet Union in 1991, universities in all newly independent countries found themselves in circumstances of uncertainty. Their former highly centralized higher education system had collapsed. Not only was there in many instances a necessity to build up new higher education systems, but the countries also simultaneously needed to establish a basic state structure. As countries were determining their new development trajectories after (re)independence processes, so were the universities.

Another reason to look at research generated in the contexts of former Soviet Union countries is the diversity of these contexts, and the different trajectories in which these countries have evolved. In a sense, the set of countries represents a form of natural laboratory, where from a shared starting point, countries have taken different pathways. While often lumped together as the "post-Soviet" bloc of countries, the directions for the development of the former Soviet Union countries have been different, leading to diverse higher education systems in each individual country (Huisman et al., 2018). While some countries have embarked on widespread reform processes oriented towards Western models from the very early years of the collapse of the Soviet Union and have now joined the EU, societal change processes in other countries have taken a different direction. This diversity is furthered by different university characteristics in each context. Evidence shows that even in the same national context in a transition economy, universities can evolve by different pathways (e.g., Rezaev and Starikov, 2017). Thus, it is relevant to ask how research that exists on entrepreneurial universities in post-Soviet countries captures the diversity of university characteristics.

The aim of the chapter is not to take a normative position on the desirability of the entrepreneurial university model for this region, but instead examine the available research evidence on entrepreneurial university transformations in this region, and in this manner also critically discuss the concept and its relevance in the region and in the context of countries in transition. To provide an outlook on entrepreneurial university research in post-Soviet countries available for international readership in English, this chapter first presents a literature review focused on these countries. The review examines what we already know about the dimensions of entrepreneurial universities in 15 post-Soviet countries and uses this as a basis to discuss avenues for future research, given the contextual specifics of these nations.

Entrepreneurial university – dimensions, dilemmas and data

Starting point for the review

"Entrepreneurial university" (Clark, 1998) as a concept is a result of the context for higher education around the millennium. It is one of several concepts that were introduced in a short period of time to denote the necessity for universities to be more flexible and adaptable towards environmental demands. The triple helix model proposed by Etzkowitz and colleagues (Etzkowitz and Leydesdorff, 2000; Etzkowitz et al., 2000) represents another. Other concepts, such as e.g. academic capitalism (Slaughter and Leslie, 1997) suggest that universities in the US had been embarking on such entrepreneurial activities for some time, leading to fundamental effects on universities. The perceived success of the US higher education model was at the time also a prominent ideal in European policy debates about higher education (Olsen and Maassen, 2007). The wider context in which both "entrepreneurial university" and "triple helix" models were introduced was marked by a more pronounced policy emphasis on the needs of the knowledge society and the perceived inability of traditional universities to cater for these needs. In European policy discussions about higher education, universities were viewed as cumbersome and slow, limited in their ability to respond to the rapid changes in the environment and the new demands set upon them. Yet, the two concepts also represent a rather different view on the main unit of analysis. Where Clark's focus was on the university as a self-reliant institution, the perspective from Etzkowitz and colleagues was more instrumental, where university is perceived as an instrument for knowledge production in a wider ecosystem of actors.

In his seminal work, Clark (1998, 2004) outlined five pathways for universities to become more flexible entrepreneurial institutions. These pathways were diversification of funding base, strengthened steering core, extended developmental periphery, revitalized academic heartland and an entrepreneurial culture. In an entrepreneurial organization income is generated from diverse sources that include various public grants, tuition revenue, industry contracts, income from commercialization of research, etc. For a university to be able to develop self-reliance, it needs to establish a steering core that enables balancing across multiple levels and departments of a university. The steering capacity depends on collegial connections in daily operations between academics and administrators as well as an organizational structure that enables university to be administratively strong at the top, the middle and the bottom (Clark, 2004). Entrepreneurial university also needs structures that work in unconventional ways, cutting across disciplines and departments, engaging with populations typically outside university boundaries (Clark, 1998). This leads to the emergence of parallel administrative structures to the traditional academic departments, which Clark (1998) calls the "extended developmental periphery" (p. 6). An academic heartland concept recognizes that strong universities are built on strong departments that carry out the core university activities, which are teaching and research (Clark, 2004). Entrepreneurialism in academic departments means that the department is a dynamic place that is attractive to faculty, students and resource providers; entrepreneurial academic departments will seek to innovate in ways that bring additional resources for a university (p. 176). University-wide entrepreneurial culture as the fifth element in Clark's (1998, 2004) classification of entrepreneurial university characteristics means "repeated vigorous assertion" of university's identity. If a university reaches high cultural or organizational identity, it gains a strong reputation that enables the organization to advance.

In total, these five dimensions suggest that in order to become an entrepreneurial university, both structural and cultural changes are necessary. While this perspective explicitly emphasizes external linkages, it also acknowledges the role of the "academic heartland", where the core of academic endeavor is located. Yet, one can also argue that in order to engage with the pathways outlined by Clark, universities need to have the necessary capacity and autonomy to engage in such change processes.

The method and results of literature review on entrepreneurial university in the post-Soviet context

The ample literature generated on entrepreneurial characteristics of Western universities demonstrates that this concept is versatile and can be examined empirically in various ways. In order to allow for a broad overview of scholarly literature in English about the phenomenon of entrepreneurial university in 15 post-Soviet countries, we conducted a structured search of articles in Google Scholar, Scopus, and Web of Science. The timeline for the literature search was set from 1991 to February 2019, when the countries in focus here emerged on the map as independent nations, with a repeated search in Google Scholar, Academic Search Premiere, and Taylor & Francis applying a narrower timeline from 1998 to November 2019. The narrower timeline coincided with concepts of entrepreneurial university (Clark, 1998) and triple helix (Etzkowitz et al., 2000) gaining attention in higher education research. The repeated search with a narrower timeline verified the initial search results and identified additional relevant articles.

The search terms used in conjunction with the term "university" were "entrepreneurial" and "entrepreneurship", adding the name of a country. While this search strategy will not identify all contributions that concern systemic changes in these countries (e.g. studies that have discussed changes in funding models in these countries in more general terms), our emphasis is on the explicit discussion of the "entrepreneurial universities" concept in research about these countries. The literature search returned articles ranging from peer-reviewed publications in well-established scholarly journals to conference proceedings and journals that do not vet their publications in a rigorous peer-review process. The review followed predetermined steps of searching for literature, reviewing the quality of the contributions and systematically summarizing the results concerning various dimensions of entrepreneurial universities. An obvious limitation in this search is that it does not capture contributions in local languages. Thus, while the review of literature in this chapter does not pretend to be exhaustive, it provides a relevant snapshot for further discussion.

The search results for each country returned a higher number of results than those that were qualified by the applied criteria to be included in this literature review. The articles were thus first screened for their relevance, assessing whether the article was an original research paper, providing empirical evidence, and identifying the sources of information clearly. In the result of the first literature search, 31 full-text articles were retained as meeting the criteria for inclusion in this chapter. An additional 10 full-text articles were retained after the second round of literature search. In total, 41 articles were included for the review in this chapter (see Table 4.1).

The largest number of relevant articles retained for a review in this chapter were about universities in Estonia (14 sources) and Russia (11 sources). There were no research articles qualifying for this review on universities in Georgia, Moldova, Kyrgyzstan, Tajikistan, Turkmenistan, and Uzbekistan. One descriptive article speaking about the creation of innovation labs in five countries of Central Asia was retained. Armenia, Azerbaijan, Belarus, Kazakhstan, Latvia, Lithuania and Ukraine included a small number of studies, and a few articles compared two or more countries. This literature was systematically organized and assessed according to the source, unit of analysis, methodology and dimensions addressed and which of the two models (Clark or Etzkowitz) the study employed.

Table 4.1   Articles reviewed for analysis in this chapter

Country	Source	Unit of analysis	Dimensions of entrepreneurial university addressed	Reference to Bruton Clark	Reference to Henry Etzkowitz	Methodology
Azerbaijan, Belorussia, Kazakhstan	Belitski, Aginskaja and Marozau (2019)	Commercialization of knowledge	Diversified funding base; Expanded developmental periphery	No	Yes	Mixed methods
Armenia	Inzelt (2015)	Governmental policy context and factors conditioning university–industry links	University–industry–government framework	No	Yes	Qualitative
Belorussia	Marozau (2015)	University	Diversified funding base; Expanded developmental periphery; Integrated entrepreneurial culture	Yes	Yes	Quantitative
Estonia	Kelli, Mets and Jonsson (2014)	Intellectual property management system at a university	University–industry links	No	Yes	Case study research design
	Kelli, Mets, Jonsson, Pisuke and Adamsoo (2013)	Innovation support system at a university	Expanded developmental periphery; University–industry links	No	Yes	Qualitative

Country	Source	Unit of analysis	Dimensions of entrepreneurial university addressed	Reference to Bruton Clark	Reference to Henry Etzkowitz	Methodology
	Kirs, Karo and Lumi (2017)	Behavior of university research groups	Academic heartland	No	Yes	Case study research design
	Mets (2006)	University spin-offs in biotech sector	University-industry-government framework	No	Yes	Case study research design
	Mets (2010a)	Intellectual property management at a university	Expanded developmental periphery; University-industry links	Yes	No	Case study research design
	Mets (2010b)	Knowledge production at a university	University-industry-government framework	No	Yes	Case study research design
	Mets, Andrijevskaja and Varblane (2008)	University and its context	University-industry-government framework; Expanded developmental periphery	Yes	Yes	Qualitative
	Mets, Kozlinska and Raudsaar (2017)	Entrepreneurial competences among university students	Academic heartland	No	No	Quantitative
	Mets, Leego, Talpsep and Varblane (2007)	Intellectual property protection at university spin-offs	University-industry links	No	No	Case study research design

Country	Source	Unit of analysis	Dimensions of entrepreneurial university addressed	Reference to Bruton Clark	Reference to Henry Etzkowitz	Methodology
	Paes, Raudsaar, Roigas and Barkalaja (2014)	Entrepreneurship learning among students of arts	Academic heartland	No	No	Qualitative
	Poder, Kallaste, Raudsaar and Venesaar (2017)	Entrepreneurial capacities of universities	Integrated entrepreneurial culture	Yes	Yes	Quantitative
	Taks, Tynjala and Kukemelk (2016)	Entrepreneurship learning among engineering students	Academic heartland	No	No	Qualitative
	Varblane, Mets and Ukrainski (2008)	Links between university and industry	University-industry-government framework	No	Yes	Case study research design
	Voolaid and Ehrlich (2016)	University	Integrated entrepreneurial culture	No	Yes	Quantitative
Kazakhstan	Kirichok (2013)	Differences in perspectives on business education	University-industry-government framework	No	Yes	Case study research design
	Smirnova (2016)	Mutual perceptions between universities and telecommunication companies	University-industry links	No	No	Mixed methods

Country	Source	Unit of analysis	Dimensions of entrepreneurial university addressed	Reference to Bruton Clark	Reference to Henry Etzkowitz	Methodology
Kazakhstan, Kyrgyzstan, Tajikistan, Turkmenistan and Uzbekistan	Leal, Gobel and Morris (2017)	Developing university–industry–government linkages and entrepreneurial culture	Expanded developmental periphery; University–industry–government framework	No	Yes	Multiple sources of evidence, research for project development
Latvia	Adamsone-Fiskovica, Kristapsons, Tjunina and Ulnicane-Ozolina (2009)	Engagement of universities with industry and general public	University–industry–government framework	No	No	Qualitative
	Kaša, Elken, Paalzow and Pauna (2019)	University responses to pressures of entrepreneurialism	University steering core	Yes	Yes	Qualitative
Latvia, Lithuania	Melnikova, Grunwald, Ahrens and Zaščerinska (2017)	Entrepreneurship learning among students in education sciences	Academic heartland	No	No	Qualitative
	Melnikova and Zaščerinska (2016)	Entrepreneurship learning among students in education sciences	Academic heartland	No	No	Qualitative

Country	Source	Unit of analysis	Dimensions of entrepreneurial university addressed	Reference to Bruton Clark	Reference to Henry Etzkowitz	Methodology
Lithuania	Binkauskas (2014)	Governmental policy context and factors conditioning university–industry links	University–industry–government framework	Yes	Yes	Case study research design
	Kazakeviciute, Urbone and Petraite (2016)	Entrepreneurship learning among students of engineering, science, health, IT	Academic heartland	No	No	Pre-post research design
	Leisyte, Vilkas and Staniskiene (2017)	University	Steering core; Academic heartland	No	No	Case study research design
	Secundo, Perez, Martinaitis and Leitner (2017)	Measurement of university "third mission" performance	Integrated entrepreneurial culture	Yes	Yes	Qualitative
Moldova, Russia	Kwiek (2009)	Entrepreneurial traits of private universities	Diversified funding base; Strengthened steering core; Expanded developmental periphery; Academic heartland	Yes	No	Qualitative
Russia	Budyldina (2018)	Characteristics of entrepreneurial universities	Academic heartland; Diversified funding base	Yes	Yes	Case study research design

Country	Source	Unit of analysis	Dimensions of entrepreneurial university addressed	Reference to Bruton Clark	Reference to Henry Etzkowitz	Methodology
	Balzer and Askonas (2016)	Interaction of university–industry–government factors	University–industry–government framework	No	Yes	Qualitative
	Bychkova (2016)	University and industry approaches to structuring collaboration	University–industry–government framework	Yes	Yes	Case study research design
	Bychkova, Chernysh and Popova (2015)	Links between university and industry	University–industry–government framework	Yes	No	Qualitative
	Dezhina (2015)	University–industry mobility of researchers	University–industry–government framework	No	No	Qualitative
	Dezhina and Etzkowitz (2016)	Innovation system development	University–industry–government framework	No	Yes	Qualitative
	Grasmik (2015)	University spin-offs and impact on innovation	University–industry links; Expanded developmental periphery	No	Yes	Quantitative
	Ivaschenko, Kiryushin and Engovatova (2016)	Assessment of interdisciplinary education program	Academic heartland; Expanded developmental periphery	Yes	Yes	Case study research design

Country	Source	Unit of analysis	Dimensions of entrepreneurial university addressed	Reference to Bruton Clark	Reference to Henry Etzkowitz	Methodology
	Williams and Kluev (2014)	Development of entrepreneurial university	Diversified funding base; Expanded developmental periphery; Integrated entrepreneurial culture	Yes	Yes	Case study research design
	Williams, Bedny and Terlyga (2015)	Development of entrepreneurial university	Diversified funding base; Expanded developmental periphery; Integrated entrepreneurial culture	Yes	Yes	Case study research design
	Yashin, Klyuev and Bagirova (2018)	Entrepreneurship learning among students in diverse majors	Academic heartland	No	No	Quantitative
Ukraine	Yegorov and Ranga (2014)	Developing university-industry-government links	University-industry-government framework	No	No	Qualitative

Entrepreneurial universities in the post-Soviet bloc – status of knowledge

The review of this literature reveals that some of the identified change processes in the region can be associated with the dimensions in Clark's framework (1998, 2004) or with the triple helix concept of university–industry–government relations (Etzkowitz, 2008; Etzkowitz and Leydesdorff, 2000; Etzkowitz et al., 2000). While nearly all studies referenced Clark or Etzkowitz, or both, few would explicitly and systematically examine the existence of these models in detail in the post-Soviet countries. This implies that the review cannot confirm that there is substantive research on the "entrepreneurial model" in the post-Soviet bloc, or even a specific post-Soviet version of an entrepreneurial university. Nor does this review suggest a convergence of university models among the countries in focus. The number of studies in most countries is too small to establish broad conclusions of convergence. Even though some dimensions of entrepreneurial university such as university-industry relations have been identified and analyzed in some countries, idiosyncratic features in these countries are strongly present (see Figure 4.1).

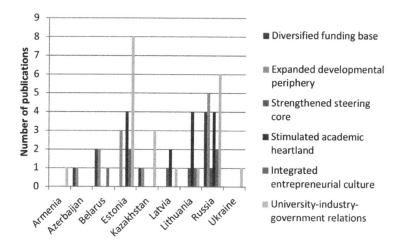

Figure 4.1 Dimensions of entrepreneurial university in reviewed studies by country

Compared to other countries and regions such as Central Asia and South-Caucasus, the number of studies for the Baltic region and Russia is broader. The next section provides a more detailed view on findings of entre-preneurial university study in the Baltic region and Russia for which a larger number of studies on entrepreneurial university were identified.

A detailed view on two contexts

Baltic countries

The Baltic region represents a set of countries and education systems that have re-integrated with Europe, being all early signers of the Bologna Declaration and members of the EU since 2004. As a region, this is among those most covered within the literature, yet also here the picture that emerges is some-what fragmented, with some aspects covered more and some less. Extended developmental periphery was captured most in Estonia due to many studies focusing on university–business–government collaboration through the prism of spinoffs and research groups. Even though diversification of university funding through entrepreneurial activities was not the primary focus in any of the articles, the theme of funding re-occurred in most articles as an impor-tant factor in conditioning organizational behavior and interactions between universities, industry and government. Funding was identified as a crucial element in supporting successful university–business collaboration in Estonia (Kelli et al., 2013). Research on university–industry knowledge transfer within the biotechnology sector in Estonia identified that public funding for basic science continued to be the main source for research-based business funding (Mets, 2006) and there were multiple context constraints for university spin-off companies to generate profit through patenting activities (Mets et al., 2007). Insufficiency of public funding for research was acknowledged as a significant driver for university collaboration with business in order to sup-plement university budgets in Latvia (Kaša et al., 2019).

A common theme that emerged in studies applying the triple helix model in Estonia (Kelli et al., 2013; Mets et al., 2008) and Lithuania (Binkauskas, 2014) was the lack of mutual understanding and divergence of company and university interests, hindering this cross-sectoral collaboration in research. Discussing the "reform of the statist Triple Helix model in the former Soviet bloc", Varblane et al. (2008, p. 376) emphasized the centrality of managerial and organizational competence in transitioning from a linear innovation model to an interactive and learning-based approach. Questions of developing a balance between university academic and market orientation dominated studies concerned with university steering in Baltics. Research groups in

Estonia (Kirs et al., 2017) and university leadership in Latvia (Kaša et al., 2019) showed conscious selective decisions about how and to what degree organizations and their units engage in market-oriented activities, even though access to resources was an important factor in these decisions. Findings from a longitudinal qualitative case study at a large public university in Lithuania added that attempts of the university's leadership to rebalance the university's academic and market orientation may lead to mutual distrust between the academic staff and the university's leadership (Leisyte et al., 2017).

Concerning the academic heartland, the review primarily uncovered studies on entrepreneurship education learning outcomes in Estonia (e.g. Mets et al., 2017), Latvia and Lithuania (e.g. Melnikova et al., 2017) showing that entrepreneurial education strengthens entrepreneurial potential of students. Findings in another study from Estonia revealed that universities differ in their entrepreneurial capacity (Poder et al., 2017) and, yet, it is possible to implement an entrepreneurial education model in a conservative academic environment even though it takes much effort (Paes et al., 2014). Examining cultural dimensions within the institutions and speaking to integrated entrepreneurial culture, a case study of Estonia (Voolaid and Ehrlich, 2016) suggested that a university with higher organizational learning rates higher on measures of entrepreneurship.

Russia

University–industry–government relations, diversified funding base, expanded developmental periphery, and academic heartland were the most addressed topics in current research about entrepreneurial universities in Russia. Fewer in focus were questions of university steering core and integrated entrepreneurial culture. Applying the triple helix framework, research established that national government policy conditions university entrepreneurship (Balzer and Askonas, 2016; Dezhina and Etzkowitz, 2016). Bychkova (2016) examined the results of national "innovation enforcement" (p. 518) policy for fostering university–industry interaction, finding that organizations engaged in various strategic responses, even suboptimal ones, in order to secure their future well-being. Dezhina (2015) identified limited intersectoral mobility of researchers as a factor constraining university–industry interaction success.

Studies addressing revenue diversification concurred that there is an association between a university's characteristics and its revenue diversity. Budyldina's (2018) research showed that diversified funding and higher licensing incomes were characteristic of regionally integrated universities that engaged in industry-specific research commercialization activities. The same study also found that a higher share of publication activity was related to a higher share of funding from non-public sources of funding (Budyldina, 2018). This was because the quality of academic research signaled to the industry the potential quality of a university as a partner. Capturing universities' approaches to creating parallel administrative structures and developing integrated entrepreneurial culture, Williams et al. (2015) argued that internal institutional factors are important in shaping universities' strategic orientation and outcomes as entrepreneurial university. Their study of entrepreneurial transformation of two leading Russian universities showed different pathways towards entrepreneurial university. While one focused on advancing internal systems supporting entrepreneurial behavior and embedding entrepreneurship in broader curricula, the other prioritized links with industry over entrepreneurship education. This university case study echoed observations that the initial understanding of entrepreneurship as a strategic objective of universities in Russia has been rather narrow, focused on new start-ups and not the development of broader entrepreneurial behaviors and attitudes in staff and students (Williams and Kluev, 2014). Yashin et al. (2018) corroborated this finding, concluding that curricula at Russia's universities focused less on developing soft skills of future entrepreneurs and prioritized hard skills. Yet, there was also contrasting case study evidence (Ivaschenko et al., 2016) on how implementation of a graduate studies program in biotechnology contributed to the developing innovation ecosystem of the university.

Research agenda on entrepreneurial university in post-Soviet countries

Clark (2004) argues that "the work of higher education is highly localized [...] The best way to find out how universities change the way they operate is to proceed in research from the bottom-up and the inside-out" (p. 2). This means that an in-depth qualitative study of university cases is the most beneficial approach for understanding the dynamics of entrepreneurial university transformations. Having said that, examples of studies on post-Soviet contexts (e.g. Belitski et al., 2019 in Table 4.1) show that empirical examination of entrepreneurial university operations sheds much light on how these goals are accomplished on a broader scale. Thus, a research agenda on entrepreneurial universities in post-Soviet countries should build on qualitative and quantitative research methodologies to advance knowledge on diversity and outcomes of entrepreneurial university transformations and outcomes.

While there are more studies on Estonia and Russia, it can be questioned whether this would suggest that higher education systems and institutions in Estonia and Russia have witnessed a systematic shift towards the entrepreneurial university model. After all, the two countries suggest significantly different political context and steering regimes for higher education. Here, one can perhaps turn a critical eye on the notion of entrepreneurial universities in Clark's conceptualization and the underlying assumption of this representing a strategic choice and the necessary organizational capacity that underpins this understanding. Stensaker and Benner (2013) discussed the entrepreneurial university and how, rather than only being a desirable normative model of a more adaptive and responsive university, it can also become a path-dependent model for new universities in developed countries. While these universities can be less prestigious and have shorter historical legacies, they are still embedded in a stable democratic context.

Here, the post-Soviet countries represent a principally different context as societies and also higher education institutions have been going through a more substantial and comprehensive transformation process. While Guy Neave referred to European higher education systems as being characterized by "shocking diversity" (Neave, 2003, p. 151), the post-Soviet bloc represents a double shock. Not only are the specific choices concerning higher education diverse, but the social and political context in which they are embedded also shows considerable diversity in terms of system stability. The Soviet legacies did not disappear after the collapse of the Soviet Union. For example, the relationship between teaching and research remains diverse across the region. Several of the studies in this review also point towards the importance of contextual factors and how emphasis on entrepreneurial aspects are narrow, limited and constrained by environmental factors. All these dimensions should be further explored in studying university transformations in the region.

Context matters in several ways. There is a pattern that emerges when comparing the entrepreneurial university research on countries with more publications and countries with fewer publications. In the former case, many publications acknowledge research grants supporting these publications. Post-Soviet countries that are less represented in entrepreneurial university research tend not to name grants supporting the respective research. This means that for a systematic research agenda on entrepreneurial university in post-Soviet contexts there needs to be common larger project framework with a formal expectation of reputable publications.

Etzkowitz et al. (2000) and Etzkowitz (2008) emerge as the most frequently addressed issue in the scope of research on entrepreneurial university in post-Soviet countries. In most instances, the articles are concerned with the role of universities in contributing to innovation that have potential for commercialization. A pessimistic interpretation of this is that it can be linked to simple resource dependency, as universities in the region are severely under-funded in most of the countries. Or it can also be a formal response to the dominant official discourse calling for innovations.

The way forward concerning entrepreneurial universities as a concept studied in post-Soviet contexts should consider three aspects. First, entrepreneurial university probably should not be seen as a normative model. It is necessary to adapt these ideas, developed in politically stable contexts, to more volatile and unstable environments that are still in transition, defining the boundaries and norms for university and state interactions as well as for the interaction between the university and the public and private sector at the local and regional levels. Second, it is important to acknowledge that entrepreneurialism in many cases is a necessity rather than choice in contexts of scarce resources. This does not have to be an issue in itself, but it can limit universities' capacity to broaden the scope of diversified funding sources. That, in turn, conditions university approaches in developing new institutional structures and practices. Third, the importance of organizational capacity means that it is not only academic capacity but also administrative capacity that has to be professional-ized. The focus on transformational dynamics within universities considering competencies not only of academic staff and high-level leadership but also of lower-level administrative staff would benefit advancing the understanding of entrepreneurial universities in the contexts of recent societal transitions. All three aspects or research directions are particularly well suited for case studies that will illuminate how the entrepreneurial university has emerged and evolved during the close to 30 years since the collapse of the Soviet Union.

While it may seem that this very diverse region of 15 countries has a number of shared challenges to strengthen the entrepreneurial capacity of its universities, the transition context also offers opportunities, in particular for comparative studies. Clark's (1998, 2004) core argument was about responsiveness and adaptability – where individual universities need to have sufficient agency to engage in a path of transformation. While a transition context can represent a situation where universities have, through multiple adaptation processes, already developed certain entrepreneurial knowledge, this would imply that the region could also generate a number of entrepreneurial universities in the long run. A core aspect in this argument is, however, that they need sufficient autonomy and capacity to engage in the processes of entrepreneurial behavior. At this point it is by no means a given that all of the various national institu-tional frameworks in the region provide this kind of context. Studying these aspects through comparative case studies should facilitate the development of typologies that will shed light on the development of the entrepreneurial university in an environment (within the university as well as in society at large) that to a large extent is still characterized by transition.

Conclusion

This literature review of entrepreneurial university in post-Soviet countries has revealed an uneven body of knowledge by country as well as by research questions in focus. Questions of entrepreneurial university have been most studied in Estonia and Russia while there was not a single English language original research article identified to address this topic about universities in Georgia, Moldova, Kyrgyzstan, Tajikistan, Turkmenistan and Uzbekistan. Armenia, Azerbaijan, Belarus, Kazakhstan, Latvia, Lithuania and Ukraine were represented by up to six articles. This literature, although not exhaustively and within the individual articles, speaks in some manner to the dimensions in Clark's (1998) model of entrepreneurial university, which are diversification of university funding, strengthened steering core, expanded developmental periphery, strengthened academic heartland and integrated academic culture. The most prevalent, however, has been the angle of university–industry–government relations applying the framework by Etzkowitz and colleagues (e.g. 2000, 2008). The uneven knowledge of the entrepreneurial university phenomenon in 15 countries that (re)emerged in 1991 suggests that a research agenda for entrepreneurial university in each country might be different. The value of cross-country comparison would be in fostering the understanding of how different trajectories of country development, redefining state to society relations, drive and condition university transformations into what Clark calls resilient institutions.

References

Adamsone-Fiskovica, A., Kristapsons, J., Tjunina, E. and Ulnicane-Ozolina, I. (2009). Moving beyond teaching and research: Economic and social tasks of universities in Latvia. *Science and Public Policy*, **36**(2), 133–137.

Balzer, H. and Askonas, J. (2016). The Triple Helix after communism: Russia and China compared. *Triple Helix*, **3**(1). https://doi.org/10.1186/s40604-015-0031-4.

Belitski, M., Aginskaja, A. and Marozau, R. (2019). Commercializing university research in transition economies: Technology transfer offices or direct industrial funding? *Research Policy*, **48**(3), 601–615. https://doi.org/10.1016/j.respol.2018.10.011.

Binkauskas, G. (2014). The formation of innovation system in the context of the participants and their relationships: The case of Lithuania. *International Journal of Technology Management and Sustainable Development*, 13(3), 251–264.

Budyldina, N. (2018). Entrepreneurial universities and regional contribution. *International Entrepreneurship and Management*, 14(2), 265–277.

Bychkova, O. (2016). Innovation by coercion: Emerging institutionalization of university–industry collaborations in Russia. *Social Studies of Science*, 46(4), 511–535.

Bychkova, O., Chernysh, A. and Popova, E. (2015). Dirty dances: Academic–industry relations in Russia. *Triple Helix*, 2(13). https://doi.org/10.1186/s40604-015-0019-0.

Clark, B. (1998). *Creating entrepreneurial universities: Organizational pathways of transformation*. Bingley: Emerald.

Clark, B. (2004). *Sustaining change in universities: Continuities in case studies and concepts*. New York, NY: Open University Press.

Dezhina, I. (2015). Intersectoral mobility of researchers in Russia: Trends and policy measures. *Triple Helix*, 2(6). https://doi.org/10.1186/s40604-015-0020-7.

Dezhina, I. and Etzkowitz, H. (2016). Path dependence and novelties in Russian innovation. *Triple Helix*, 3(11). https://doi.org/10.1186/s40604-016-0042-9.

Etzkowitz, H. (2008). *The Triple Helix: University–industry–government innovation in action*. New York, NY: Routledge.

Etzkowitz, H. and Leydesdorff, L. (2000). The dynamics of innovation: From national systems and "Mode 2" to a Triple Helix of university–industry–government relations. *Research Policy*, 29(2), 109–123.

Etzkowitz, H., Webster, A., Gebhardt, C. and Cantisano Terra, B. (2000). The future of the university and the university of the future: Evolution of ivory tower to entrepreneurial paradigm. *Research Policy*, 29(2), 313–330.

Grasmik, K. (2015). Spin-off as an indicator of regional innovation. *Triple Helix*, 2(10). https://doi.org/10.1186/s40604-015-0022-5.

Huisman, J., Smolentseva, A. and Froumin, I. (Eds.). (2018). *25 years of transformations of higher education systems in post-Soviet countries: Reform and continuity*. Cham: Palgrave Macmillan.

Inzelt, A. (2015). Re-aligning the Triple Helix in post-Soviet Armenia. *Triple Helix*, 2(15). https://doi.org/10.1186/s40604-015-0025-2.

Ivaschenko, N., Kiryushin, P. and Engovatova, A. (2016). Developing innovation ecosystem of the university through implementation of interfaculty Master's program: The case of LMSU. In I. Aaltio and M. Tunkkari Eskelinen (Eds.), *Proceedings of the 11th European Conference on Entrepreneurship and Innovation* (pp. 303–310). Jyvaskyla: Academic Conferences and Publishing International.

Kaša, R., Elken, M., Paalzow, A. and Pauna, D. (2019). Conditioned entrepreneurialism: Strategic responses of universities in Latvia and Norway. *European Education*, 51(4), 253–269. https://doi.org/10.1080/10564934.2019.1637266.

Kazakeviciute, A., Urbone, R. and Petraite, M. (2016). Curriculum development for technology-based entrepreneurship education: A cross-disciplinary and cross-cultural approach. *Industry and Higher Education*, 30(3), 202–214.

Kelli, A., Mets, T. and Jonsson L. (2014). Management of intellectual property rights in academia: The Estonian and Swedish perspectives. *International Journal of Technology Management & Sustainable Development*, 13(3), 219–236.

Kelli, A., Mets, T., Jonsson, L., Pisuke, H. and Adamsoo, R. (2013). The changing approach in academic–industry collaboration: From profit orientation to innovation support. *Trames*, 17(67/62), 215–241.

Kirichok, O. (2013). Business and academia in Kazakhstan: Living a cat and dog life? On reconstruction of education policy in Kazakhstan. *Life Science Journal*, **10**(12s), 732–737.

Kirs, M., Karo, E. and Lumi, P. (2017). Strategic behaviour of research groups within the entrepreneurial university policy rhetoric: the Estonian biotechnology sector. *Science and Public Policy*, **44**(6), 802–820.

Kwiek, M. (2009). Entrepreneurialism and private higher education in Europe. In M. Shattock (Ed.), *Entrepreneurialism in universities and the knowledge economy* (pp. 100–120). Maidenhead: Open University Press.

Leal, X., Gobel, H. and Morris, D. (2017). Designing user-centered and context appropriate strategies for university–industry strategies for university–industry interaction: Innovation labs in Central Asia. Conference International Conference for Entrepreneurship, Innovation and Regional Development, Thessaloniki, Greece, 31 August to 1 September 2017. http://www.diva-portal.org/smash/record.jsf?pid= diva2%3A1152560&dswid=-288.

Leisyte, L., Vilkas, M., Staniskiene, E. and Zostautiene, D. (2017). Balancing countervailing processes at a Lithuanian university. *The Learning Organization*, **24**(5), 327–339. https://doi.org/10.1108/TLO-02-2017-0025.

Marozau, R. (2015). *Factors conditioning the role of higher education institutions in transition economies: An exploratory study of the republic of Belarus* (Doctoral dissertation). Retrieved from ProQuest (10189376). https://search.proquest.com/docview/ 2039580791?accountid=134066.

Melnikova, J. and Zaščerinska, J. (2016). Integration of entrepreneurship into higher education (educational sciences) in Lithuania and Latvia: Focus on students' entrepreneurial competencies. *Regional Formation and Development Studies*, **18**(1), 87–98. http://dx.doi.org/10.15181/rfds.v18i1.1250.

Melnikova, J., Grunwald, N., Ahrens, A. and Zaščerinska, J. (2017). Integration of entrepreneurship into higher education (educational sciences) in Lithuania and Latvia: Students' and university teachers' opinion. Balkan Region Conference on Engineering and Business Education. *Sciendo*, 3(1), 159–166.

Mets, T. (2006). Creating a knowledge transfer environment: The case of Estonian biotechnology. *Management Research News*, **29**(12), 754–768.

Mets, T. (2010a). Privileged and not privileged academician: View on intellectual property management at university. In *6th International Scientific Conference "Business and Management 2014" Proceedings* (pp. 550–556). Vilnius: Gediminas Technical University.

Mets, T. (2010b). Entrepreneurial business model for classical research university. *Engineering Economics*, **21**(1), 80–90.

Mets, T., Andrijevskaja, J. and Varblane, U. (2008). The role of the University of Tartu in the development of entrepreneurship in the region of South Estonia. *International Journal of Entrepreneurship and Innovation Management*, **8**(6), 648–664.

Mets, T., Kozlinska, I. and Raudsaar, M. (2017). Patterns in entrepreneurial competences as the perceived learning outcomes of entrepreneurship education: The case of Estonian HEIs. *Industry and Higher Education*, **31**(1), 23–33. https://doi.org/10 .1177/0950422216684061.

Mets, T., Leego, M., Talpsep, T. and Varblane, U. (2007). The role of Intellectual Property protection in the business strategy of university spin-off biotech companies in a small transition economy. *Review of Central and East European Law*, **32**(1), 19–40.

Neave, G. (2003). The Bologna Declaration: Some of the historic dilemmas posed by the reconstruction of the community in Europe's systems of higher education. *Educational Policy*, **17**(1), 141–164.

Olsen, J. P. (2007). The Institutional Dynamics of the European University. In P. Maassen and J. P. Olsen (Eds.), *University dynamics and European integration* (pp. 25–54). Dordrecht: Springer.

Olsen, J. P. and Maassen, P. (2007). European debates on the knowledge institution: The modernisation of the university at European level. In J. P. Olsen and P. Maassen (Eds.), *University Dynamics and European Integration* (pp. 3–22). Dordrecht: Springer.

Paes, K., Raudsaar, M., Roigas, A. and Barkalaja, A. (2014). "Total entrepreneurship education" model for implementing entrepreneurial university concept: The case of Estonia in the field of creative industries. In *7th International Conference of Education, Research and Innovation (ICERI) Proceedings* (pp. 3091–3099).

Pervin, L. (1967). The college as a social system: A fresh look at three critical problems in higher education. *The Journal of Higher Education*, **38**(6), 317–322.

Poder, A., Kallaste, M., Raudsaar, M. and Venesaar, U. (2017). Evaluation of entrepreneurial capacity of universities: A case of Estonia. *European Proceedings of Social and Behavioural Sciences*, **31**, 966–977.

Rezaev, A. and Starikov, V. (2017). The transformation of higher education systems in six post-Soviet countries: Causes and consequences of organizational change. *Comparative Sociology*, **16**(1), 127–146.

Secundo, G., Perez, S. E., Martinaitis, Ž. and Leitner, K. H. (2017). An intellectual capital framework to measure universities' third mission activities. *Technological Forecasting and Social Change*, **123**, 229–239.

Slaughter, S. and Leslie, L. L. (1997). *Academic capitalism. Politics, policies and the entrepreneurial university*. Baltimore: The Johns Hopkins University Press.

Smirnova, Y. (2016). University–industry knowledge transfer in an emerging economy: Evidence from Kazakhstan. *Science and Public Policy*, **43**(5), 702–712. https://doi.org/10.1093/scipol/scv074.

Smolentseva, A., Huisman, J. and Froumin, I. (2018). Transformation of higher education institutional landscape in post-Soviet countries: From Soviet model to where? In J. Huisman, A. Smolentseva and I. Froumin (Eds.), *25 years of transformations of higher education systems in post-Soviet countries: Reform and continuity* (pp. 1–22). Cham: Palgrave Macmillan.

Stensaker, B. and Benner, M. (2013). Doomed to be entrepreneurial: Institutional transformation or institutional lock-ins of 'new' universities? *Minerva*, **51**(4), 399–416.

Taks, M., Tynjala, P. and Kukemelk, H. (2016). Engineering students' conceptions of entrepreneurial learning as part of their education. *European Journal of Engineering Education*, **41**(1), 53–69.

Varblane, U., Mets, T. and Ukrainski, K. (2008). Role of university–industry–government linkages in the innovation processes of a small catching-up economy. *Industry and Higher Education*, **22**(6), 373–386.

Voolaid, K. and Ehrlich, U. (2016). Learning university versus entrepreneurial university: The case of Tallinn University of Technology, Estonia. In *Proceedings of the International Conference on Intellectual Capital Knowledge Management and Organizational Learning* (pp. 259–265).

Williams, D. and Kluev, A. (2014). The entrepreneurial university: Evidence of the changing role of universities in modern Russia. *Industry and Higher Education*, **28**(4), 1–10.

Williams, D., Bedny, A. and Terlyga, N. (2015). Evaluation of institutional factors shaping entrepreneurial university: A tale of two universities and regional development in Russia. In *Proceedings of the 10th European Conference on Entrepreneurship and Innovation* (pp. 731–739). Sonning Common: Academic Conferences and Publishing International.

Yashin, A., Klyuev, A. and Bagirova, A. (2018). Designing entrepreneurial education in Russia: Hard and soft skills. *Ekonomiski Vjesnik*, **31**(2), 261–274.

Yegorov, I. and Ranga, M. (2014). Innovation, politics and tanks: The emergence of a Triple Helix system in Ukraine and the influence of EU cooperation on its development. *International Journal of Transitions and Innovations System*, **3**(3), 189–224.

5 Orchestrating affect at the entrepreneurial university

Saija Katila, Ari Kuismin, Pikka-Maaria Laine and Anu Valtonen

Introduction

Entrepreneurial university has become a key term within higher education research. This term refers to a university that seeks to adapt to changing societal and economic demands by constantly improving its operations (Clark, 1998; Guerrero et al., 2015; Slaughter and Leslie, 1997). Recently, these demands have pushed universities to develop infrastructures necessary to promote job and wealth creation beyond the tasks of teaching and research (Heinonen and Hytti, 2010; Foss and Gibson, 2015; Sam and van der Sijde, 2014). Consequently, universities have established a range of 'entrepreneurship promotion activities', including startup incubators, business accelerators, and extracurricular training programs (Etzkowitz, 2002; Guerrero et al., 2015; Heinonen et al., 2007; Farny and Kyrö, 2015; Sá and Kretz, 2015). These activities concentrate on fostering entrepreneurial mindset, skills, and competencies among students and faculty members as well as supporting the commercialization of academic research findings (Foss and Gibson, 2015; Slaughter and Leslie, 1997). Specifically, they represent entrepreneurship as a viable career option in an uncertain job economy, encourage risk taking, and seek to create positive and engaging 'buzz' around venture creation (e.g. Katila et al., 2019a; Heinonen and Hytti, 2010). Overall, existing studies hint that entrepreneurship promotion activities operate not only via specific policies or discourses but also through (the creation of) affective, bodily experiences that are difficult to capture verbally.

However, while much of the existing research on entrepreneurial university has focused on regime and institutional level analyses (Clark, 1998; Etzkowitz et al., 1998; 2008; Foss and Gibson, 2015; Sam and van der Sijde, 2014;

67

Slaughter and Leslie, 1997), affect and the body have attracted less scholarly attention in this area. By affect, we refer here to pre-conscious and bodily responses that highlight 'the passage from one experiential state of the body to another and implying an augmentation or diminution in that body's capacity to act' (Massumi 1987: xvii). In other words, affect is a pre-personal force that can trigger, for example, creative behavior or individuated emotions such as excitement or anxiety (Massumi, 2002; Blackman and Venn, 2010; Stewart, 2007). In this view, affect differs from 'entrepreneurial passion' or intense positive emotion that sustains entrepreneurial activity (Cardon et al., 2009; 2012). Although entrepreneurial passion carries the same energizing component as affect, it refers to a cognitively conscious experience of an individual (Cardon et al., 2009). In contrast, affect is an experience that does not reside within the individual; instead, it emerges in and through the flow of everyday (entrepreneurial) practices and relationships (Massumi, 2002). The power of affect rests in its social nature; it is contagious and moves from body to body with the potential to influence a large number of people simultaneously (Gherardi, 2017). Although some studies have shown that particular kinds of affective responses may enhance entrepreneurship, for example by fostering entrepreneurial learning and doing (Katila et al., 2019a; 2019b; Laine and Parkkari, 2017), we know little about how they are manipulated and capitalized in university-based entrepreneurship promotion activities.

In this chapter, we address this question. In particular, by drawing on the concept of affect we suggest that entrepreneurship promotion activities can be understood as 'orchestration of affect'. By this notion, we refer to a range of practices, strategies and design efforts through which (powerful) actors seek to generate particular kinds of affective responses in other people in order to achieve certain organizational, political, or economic ends (Thrift, 2008; 2004). In the context of entrepreneurial university, such orchestration may work, for example, to direct the behaviors and 'energies' of university members towards entrepreneurship and venture creation. Existing research proposes that orchestration of affect operates indirectly, through the manipulation of the social and material circumstances in which people live their everyday lives, including architectural arrangements, technologies, and atmospheres (Ash, 2012; Bille et al., 2015; Michels and Steyaert, 2017; Thrift, 2004). Importantly, the outcomes of this orchestration are not predetermined; instead, they can develop into unintended and even surprising directions (Michels and Steyaert, 2017). Overall, we propose that examining university-based entrepreneurship promotion activities as orchestration of affect helps us to better understand the ways in which higher education organizations regulate their participants' experiences on the level of precognitive forces.

To empirically demonstrate how orchestration of affect takes place in action, we build on a recent ethnographic study. This study was conducted by the first two authors of this chapter and focused on Helsinki Think Company (ThinkCo), which is a university-based startup incubator located in Helsinki, Finland. ThinkCo is established by the University of Helsinki and the City of Helsinki to foster entrepreneurship and commercialization of academic research findings in and around the university. Among other services and activities, ThinkCo offers four co-working spaces at the university campuses as well as organizing regular entrepreneurship events such as accelerator programs and sales pitch nights to create the culture of an entrepreneurial university. In the empirical section of this chapter, we identify and analyze the key practices in and through which ThinkCo orchestrates affect in order to create support for an entrepreneurial university: (1) inviting inspirational speakers, and (2) facilitating business idea development. In addition, we will highlight the positive as well as the negative outcomes of these practices.

The chapter is organized as follows. We will first discuss our affect theoretical perspective in detail. This will be followed by an empirical example of orchestrating affect for creating an entrepreneurial university. We conclude by arguing for a need to pay attention to affect and body in research on entrepreneurial university in general and in critical research on it in particular. Finally, we set forth an agenda that spells out ideas for future research on entrepreneurial university from the perspective on affect.

Theorizing affect

The concept of affect has recently emerged as an analytic construct within organizational research (e.g. Fotaki et al., 2017). In this area, there are multiple understandings of affect that emphasize partially different things (see Wetherell, 2012). In this chapter, we join a stream of research that draws on the works of Deleuze (1994) and Massumi (2002) on affect. In these works, affect refers to 'forces' and 'intensities' that shape (i.e. increase or diminish) our capacity of acting in the flow of day-to-day practices (Gherardi, 2017; Keevers and Sykes, 2016). Specifically, affect emerges and operates through relations between people and material elements, including technologies, discourses, architectural arrangements, and material artifacts. To highlight the affective quality of heterogeneous human and nonhuman actors, affect theorists often call them equally as 'bodies' (Blackmann and Venn, 2010; Massumi, 2002). When human and nonhuman bodies encounter, they are able 'to affect and be affected' by each other (Massumi, 2002: 5). Body's capacity of acting, in turn, should be understood as dependent on the affective, social and material relationships in and through which it operates (Massumi, 2002).

In this view, affect can be seen as a visceral force; something that can be felt in the body and something that occurs in variations in the state of action readiness before its translation to individuated emotion or visible action (Keevers and Sykes, 2016; Katila et al., 2019b). Importantly, while verbal or textual representations such as entrepreneurial narratives may be affective, affect does not follow the logic of codified language but rather works on the level of bodily sensations and resonances (Blackman and Venn, 2010; Massumi, 2002). From this perspective, affect is different from a personal emotion; emotion refers to a meaningful and differentiated signifier of affect that is domesticated by the symbolic system of language (Massumi, 2002). Importantly, while affect is something that can be sensed in and through the body it is always social in nature, that is, it resides in-between bodies (Massumi, 2002; Stewart, 2007). Affect is contagious, transmitting from body to body and becoming visible, for example, in facial expressions, high fives, laughter, tone of voice, breathing, sound, clapping and via other sensorial means (Blackman and Venn, 2010; Massumi, 2002). To illustrate, we may have been affected in an exciting football match, while watching the thrilling finals of *The X Factor* or while attending/observing the intensive last moments of a hectic hackathon weekend.

Affect is orchestrated in several ways in day-to-day organizational life. By such orchestration, we refer here to a range of practices, strategies and design efforts through which actors seek to generate particular kinds of affective responses in other people in order to achieve certain organizational, political, or economic ends (Ash, 2012; Bille et al., 2015; Karppi et al., 2016; Michels and Steyaert, 2017; Thrift, 2004). To illustrate, Thrift (2008) suggests that manipulation of affect has become increasingly common and important in a range of industries. Using the marketing of consumer goods as an example, he argues that 'increasingly, commodities are thought of as interfaces that can be actively engineered across a series of sensory registers in order to produce positive affective responses in consumers […] [s]ensory design and marketing has become key' (Thrift, 2008: 39). Jenkins (2003), in turn, calls orchestration of affect for economic purposes as 'affective economics' and suggests that companies are increasingly blending entertainment content with branding content to transform their brand identity into an engaging 'way of life'. Orchestration of affect is not, however, limited to consumer goods marketing but also takes place through design and development of organizational and urban spaces. In these settings, orchestration of affect responds to the demand of organizations and cities 'to have "buzz", to be "creative" and to generally bring forth powers of invention and intuition, all of which can be forged into economic weapons'

(Thrift, 2008: 172). The ideas of creativity, invention and intuition seem to lie at the heart of what is understood as entrepreneurial action as well (e.g. Hjorth, 2015), thus producing 'buzz' and 'creativity', which are commonly expected outcomes when establishing entrepreneurship promoting activities and spaces.

Entrepreneurship research offers various examples of how affect becomes orchestrated. To illustrate, Katila and colleagues (2019b) showed how strong affective intensities were created in and through the festival making practice of a major startup conference. Within this practice, connections between a dark conference site, the beat of techno music, flashing lights, flowing masses of bodies, business talks, and the scent of fog were attached with the meanings of fun, excitement, and energy of startup entrepreneurship (Katila et al., 2019b). In another study, Mauksch (2017) demonstrated the affective nature of the ideological politics through which social entrepreneurship is constructed as a viable option to solve societal problems. This study showed how social entrepreneurship is staged to appeal to the public via practices of enchantment work – the interplay of powerful spiritual speeches, rational business talk, bodily involvement, and the aestheticization of events through tactile and sensual elements like beautiful location, lighting, recycled furniture, and organic food and drinks that are symbolically related to social business. Other studies have further indicated that orchestration of affect may enforce normative rules of what is considered 'appropriate' entrepreneurial behaviors and identities thus attracting some actors, while alienating and de-energizing others (Katila and Kuismin, 2017; Katila et al., 2019a).

Although several studies in different areas demonstrate that affective responses may be more-or-less deliberately orchestrated to support the accomplishment of particular aims, the outcomes of such efforts are not predetermined (e.g. Michels and Steyaert, 2017). Instead, as affect highlights unpredictable, open-ended and mutable potential, these outcomes may develop into surprising directions and thus generate unexpected conditions for being and doing. For example, feminist scholars have examined how affective shift can provide judgmental knowledge about unequal power relations and enable resistance for transforming them (Hemmings, 2012; Pullen et al., 2017).

Orchestrating affect at the University of Helsinki

In this section, our purpose is to demonstrate how orchestration of affect unfolds in a higher education context to create support for entrepreneurial university. In particular, we draw on a recent ethnographic fieldwork conducted by the first two authors of this chapter in the setting of Helsinki Think Company (ThinkCo), a startup incubator established by the University of Helsinki and the City of Helsinki. The stated goal of ThinkCo is to promote entrepreneurship, entrepreneurial spirit, and commercialization of academic research results in and around the University of Helsinki.

The most visible part of ThinkCo are four co-working spaces that are centrally located in each of the four university campuses and available for university students and staff free of charge, 24/7. Although the venues vary in size, they all consist of an open plan workspace, a kitchen area, and toilets. In addition to chairs, tables, sofas, and armchairs, the spaces are equipped with artefacts essential for co-working such as white boards, a Wi-Fi hotspot, printers, video projectors, canvases, post-it notes, and markers. The spaces are operated by a team of student 'hosts' who are recruited to help the space users and take care of the premises and technical equipment. In addition to serving entrepreneurial co-workers, the ThinkCo spaces serve as event venues for various entrepreneurial events like workshops, pitch nights, accelerator programs, and parties organized by the hosts and external stakeholders such as companies, associations, and entrepreneurs. The focus of the entrepreneurial events is commonly on inspiring, encouraging and supporting students and researchers to see entrepreneurship as a potential career option and to develop new business ventures and skills needed to put the ventures forward (e.g. sales pitching and marketing).

The reasons for establishing the ThinkCo incubator were twofold: first, the University of Helsinki needed to react to the criticism that it was not contributing to society sufficiently through new firm foundation regardless of being the number one university in Finland. Second, the city of Helsinki as a close collaborator of the university wanted to support the project in the hope that it would create new ventures that would eventually boost the regional economy. Overall, ThinkCo can be seen as a manifestation of the University of Helsinki's commitment to becoming an entrepreneurial university. ThinkCo is a particularly interesting case to examine how the orchestration of affect takes place in and through the activities of entrepreneurship promotion, since becoming an entrepreneur is not traditionally seen as a potential or desirable career option at the University of Helsinki. For example, the University of Helsinki does not have a faculty of technology or business that fosters such career aspirations. Further, many university members, faculty and students alike, have found the increasing emphasis on commercial interests as a potential threat to the university's autonomy and traditional values.

In the following, we will focus on the two key practices in and through which affect is orchestrated in the context of ThinkCo to create support for entrepreneurship around the University of Helsinki: (1) inviting inspirational speakers, and (2) facilitating business idea development. In particular, we suggest that through these practices, ThinkCo seeks to orchestrate affect to direct the activities and 'energies' in and around the University of Helsinki towards entrepreneurial identity construction and entrepreneurial action such as opportunity discovery, venture creation, and competition.

Inviting inspirational speakers

'Inviting inspirational speakers' is a common practice in any entrepreneurship enhancing space and ThinkCo is no exception. At the time of setting up ThinkCo, the founding group conducted a field trip to Stanford University's d-school (an innovation hub) and was amazed at what could be achieved through creation of a physical space for entrepreneurial action. Excited by what the founding group saw and heard, one of the first event series ThinkCo launched was 'Been there, done that', where seasoned entrepreneurs narrated their entrepreneurial journeys. The aim of the events was to inspire and encourage University of Helsinki members, faculty, alumni and students alike to embark on an entrepreneurial career of their own. In the following we will illustrate how such events were designed to affect their participants in particular ways but also how their design failed for multiple reasons. Hence, the example highlights the precarious nature of orchestration of affect.

Arto, a business angel and an active supporter of the ThinkCo initiative is eager to invest his time and energy in setting up the 'Been there, done that' inspirational speaker events. In order to attract a large audience and create 'good buzz', he utilizes his large networks in Finland, Silicon Valley and beyond. The line-up is impressive: male IT millionaire, followed by another male IT millionaire, and then yet another one. 'Inspiring people with interesting career paths', the net pages state. 'If you have followed the startup scene, if you understand anything of what this is about, you would know that these were tough guys', Arto says (referring to the line-up).

Another 'Been there, done that' event is starting. The speaker, a fairly young successful male IT entrepreneur, is standing in front of the audience ready to start. He looks relaxed and self-confident in his jeans and sneakers. The space is made ready for him; the rather small room is full of rows of chairs and the keynote speaker is in front of the space facing the audience. He and his success story are there to create enthusiasm and inspiration […] but they seem to do neither. The room looks desolate; the empty chairs facing the presenter. There, where buzz was intended, is emptiness and silence.

'The thing was that pretty much no-one attended those events', Mary, the host explains later. 'Like this IT-millionaire, he's some sort of a rock star and that's not at all for us', a female student entrepreneur adds. 'Traditionally, becoming an entrepreneur has been understood rather critically here [at the City Center Campus of University of Helsinki], it has been seen as a way of selling "the true you"', says Maija (a student entrepreneur). 'There may have been a lack of attention on the interests of the community for whom the events were made for', notes Tiina, a ThinkTank consultant working with the university. 'The [University of Helsinki] community is motivated by the big problems of the world. That is why they have come to the university', she continues.

The vignette above demonstrates how ThinkCo made use not only of the common practice of using inspirational speakers to inspire, that is, to affect people towards entrepreneurship, but also the recipe on how to assemble such a practice. In this practice an attempt is made to orchestrate affective intensity in and through the relational connections between the university audience, celebrity entrepreneurs' young male bodies, jeans and sneakers, intimate space, IT-technology, and language, which draws from masculine entrepreneurship discourses. This discourse emphasizes that self-confidence, courage, toughness, and competitiveness are needed in order to succeed in the world of business. The practice constructs more-or-less implicitly masculine tech heroes and what they represent (growth, global scale of operations, money, power) as an aspired and appropriate way of being entrepreneurial, thus reproducing ideals already prevalent in Finnish media and society at large. The practice thus reproduces and underscores the entrepreneurial ideal while simultaneously revealing its narrow and exclusionary nature.

Prior research suggests that the way in which (organizational) practices are assembled shapes the affective 'vibes' or 'resonances' surrounding it (Thrift, 2008). In the case of ThinkCo, the practice of inviting inspirational speakers was assembled in ways that did not resonate among bodies as intended, since they were not aligned with the 'affective charge' (Anderson, 2014: 16) of the bodies of the audience, which is constituted through the repetitive actions in the context of the University of Helsinki. The inspirational speaker events were held at the City Centre Campus of the university where the majority of the students are women and where the faculties of social sciences and humanities are located. The way the inspirational speaker practice was assembled disregarded the values, interest and identities of the people it aimed to attract, thus creating negative affective energies manifested in the quotes above, as well as in people not showing up to the event. Hence, while the practice of inviting inspirational speakers did not manage to orchestrate desired enthusiasm around entrepreneurship as intended, it was affective. The practice had the power to alienate and demotivate students and faculty from entrepreneurial doing, i.e. it diminished their capacity to act, highlighting the fragile nature of orchestrating affect.

Our analysis, then, suggests that entrepreneurial universities should be mindful of what kind of elements their key practices are made up of and how the different elements gain transformative power through their entanglements. It might be small tweaks here and there that can make a huge difference in the orchestration of affect and the consequences thereof: How will the affective forces energize or demotivate different kinds of entrepreneurial doing? Who feels included and who feels excluded by the practices? For example, within the practices of ThinkCo the discourse of 'start-up entrepreneurship' was, over time, downplayed and replaced with the discourse of 'social entrepreneurship'. Furthermore, alongside the global male tech heroes, an emphasis was put on highlighting local female heroines. This made a huge difference on the affective forces circulating in ThinkCo practices, consequently attracting and engaging a whole new group of university students in entrepreneurial doing. As one of the ThinkCo hosts told us a year after opening the first ThinkCo co-working space: 'It's not entrepreneurship as such that people are interested in […] it is the idea that you can really change things and make the world better through entrepreneurship which makes people come and stay here [at ThinkCo].' Thus, different relations to dominant modes of entrepreneurship provided active forces that increased the students' capacities to act and constructed a subjectivity of an 'entrepreneur' (Hjorth, 2015: 48). In the following we invite the reader to sense the affective shift between the common practice of inviting inspirational speakers and a new practice of facilitating business idea development.

Facilitating business idea development

Given the failure in orchestrating positive affective energies around entrepreneurship through using inspirational speakers, new steps were taken to create events that would be more appealing to the University of Helsinki community. A new concept was launched, the '4UNI Solution competition', which no longer explicitly emphasized '(start-up) entrepreneurship', fierce competition, or individual success, but rather the idea of taking academic knowledge into action through collaboration. The competition has thus far highlighted among other things the big societal problems of inequality, sustainability, health as well as peace. Specifically, the competition materializes the second key practice of orchestrating affect for the support of entrepreneurial university in the context of ThinkCo.

The 4UNI Solution competition is an entrepreneurship accelerator for university students, faculty, alumni and other interested participants. Welcoming about 50 participants a time, 4UNI takes place over a two-month period and involves several facilitated workshops and training sessions with business professionals. In the workshops, business plans are iterated through tasks that follow each other in 15-minute interval. The repetitive pattern of task instructions and 15 minutes of intensive working creates a rhythmic flow of affective intensities following the order of birth–growth–peak–end, as the following extract illustrates.

> [At a 4UNI workshop] We have barely finished the previous business development task when the workshop facilitator shouts: 'Ok, let's move on people!' and gives us the next task while setting the timer in front of us. I can see the seconds running in the timer and know we have to hurry up in order to complete the task. We lean towards each other and start writing our ideas on the post-it notes immediately. The rhythmic bangs of the post-it notes slapped on the table entangle with trembling beat of the bass resonances in my body as the fast-beat background music is turned up. Our team works like a collective entity without saying a word. I write post-it notes like there is no tomorrow and ignore the pain in my arm, and the handwriting that is getting messier and messier by the minute. Everyone in our team and around us seem to be doing the same. It feels amazing. Time is running, and I can feel my heart bounding.

> We start quickly grouping the post-its, negotiating, writing new ones and slapping them on the table as fast as we can. The closer we get to the finishing of time the more furor there is in the room then the facilitator shouts: 'Time's up!' The intensive sense of thrill erupts into whistles, yells, high-fives, and hugs that can be bodily felt. 'Fantastic work! Amazing!', says the facilitator and waits a while for the crowd to calm down before setting the next 15-minute development task.

> After nine hours we stop. I suddenly realize that I am exhausted. My body feels heavy and brain feels fuzzy. I have not had time to eat much but I have not felt hungry either. I have been carried away by the work and the intensive atmosphere. I can't remember when I have been able to work on such energy levels all day, maybe never.

> Next morning most of us are back, looking and feeling tired but more than ready to continue as the intoxicating affective sensations from the previous day are fresh in our memory. However, some teams have lost their members. They did not come back. The intensity, the fast rhythms, the ticking clock, the load music, the level of noise, and the continuous pressure did not energize them. On the contrary, the intensity demotivated and discouraged them. They felt stressed and not able to think and act in such circumstances, often standing still, as if their bodies and brains were working in 'slow motion' compared to others. This created an uncomfortable feeling of always lagging behind.

The 4UNI Solution Competition brings together people with similar values and interests to work on a self-set problem. This vignette highlights how affect is carefully orchestrated within the competition by following a workshop script that rhythmically brakes up the workshop day into affective and rhythmic sequences. The affective sensations and energy emerge from the relational connections between bodies, pens, discourses, music, ticking clock, post-it notes, sounds, and other elements in the flow of practice. Toward the end of each development round, the connections between the elements are formed more and more quickly and the affective energy emerging becomes part of the practice, further intensifying its affective power. The vignette further high-lights how affect moves from body to body filling the room with energy that erupts when time is up. It is a collective and contagious experience. Affective sensations and energy emerge in a similar way in each development round, increasing the participants' capacity to work more intensively, collaboratively, and for a long period of time.

The vignette demonstrates that powerful (positive) affective sensations have the capacity to attach participants to the practice at hand and motivate them to try hard. Affect is thus increasing the capacity of the participants to work individually as well as collectively. As Keevers and Sykes (2016) have noted, the affective quality of organizational practices needs to be attended to in order to create recognition and regard for the 'other' and to promote collabo-ration. These authors further highlight that it is of importance how practices are orchestrated to create positive affective experiences that create a sense of belonging and the willingness to participate. The affect carries the participants through the day and through the moments of exhaustion and hunger. While affects are pre-linguistic bodily sensations and as such short lived, powerful affective experiences have long-standing effects, as Pullen and colleagues (2017) have noted. As the vignette demonstrates, affective experiences attach the participants to the accelerator practice beyond the workshop day through positive affective memories and the hope of reliving such moments (Katila et al., 2019a).

This kind of business idea development practice is different from classroom teaching in universities in multiple ways. The practice imposes a fast-paced rhythm in which things are to be done, compared to relatively slow-paced lecture rhythms. Earlier studies in classroom circumstances have specifically pointed out that changing the tempo and intensity of engagement in teaching activities creates affective sensations that can be felt in the body and in the brain, contributing to learning (Mulcahy, 2012; MacLure, 2010). The acceler-ator practice further replaces books with post-its and business model canvases as educational artefacts demanding active participation and experimentation instead of passive sitting and abstract reflection. Similarly, Mulcahy (2012) shows that abandoning textbooks as affective objects generated a change in the eagerness of students to learn. Further, the accelerator practice focuses on group rather than individual learning – you learn through participating in (collective) practice. In relation to each other, each of these elements of practice intensifies the affective and thus transformative power of the practice; they enhance entrepreneurial learning.

In addition to highlighting how affective responses increased the capacity of most of the participants to work and co-operate, the vignette above also points to the opposite direction; for some, the affective forces worked to diminish their capacity to participate in the accelerator practices and identify with entrepreneurship. These individuals were not able to engage in the business development assignments to the same degree and felt they could not cope with the demands. This suggests that the practices of entrepreneurial universities can also be alienating and exclusive in multiple ways. In the case of ThinkCo, the accelerator practice pushed participants to adopt 'appropriate' upbeat appearances and behaviors (Katila et al., 2019a) that not all participants were able or willing to learn. There are always two paradoxes here. First, the entangling of relations may also produce negative affective intensities. Also, while participation in the accelerator practice at ThinkCo was voluntary, negotiating how to perform the accelerator practice was not. Hence, the second paradox emerges out of the case that since the accelerator practices are normative in nature and possess regulative power, they may prevent 'the will to overcome the limits of the present, to open up for a new', which Hjorth (2015: 51) has described as an entrepreneurial modus operandi of learning to know one's knowledge and inventing beyond the customary (ibid.: 50–51).

Conclusion and agenda for future research

In this chapter, we have examined entrepreneurial university from an affect theoretical perspective. In particular, we have focused university-based entrepreneurship promotion activities and suggested that they can be understood as 'orchestration of affect' or efforts to generate particular kinds of affective responses, especially those that support certain organizational goals. To empirically illustrate how such orchestration of affect may work in action, we built on a recent ethnographic study of a university-based startup incubator, Helsinki Think Company (ThinkCo). Drawing on this study, we highlighted two key practices in and through which orchestration of affect unfolds in the case of ThinkCo: (1) inviting inspirational speakers and (2) facilitating business idea development. When discussing these practices, we emphasized how they orchestrate affect to direct the behaviors and 'energies' of bodies in and around the University of Helsinki towards entrepreneurial identity construction and entrepreneurial action. Overall, the study highlighted that participating in the university-based entrepreneurship promotion activities is not neutral; instead, it can either increase or diminish one's power to act.

While much of the existing studies on entrepreneurial university have concentrated on regime and institutional analyses (Clark, 1998; Etzkowitz et al., 1998; 2008; Foss and Gibson, 2015; Sam and van der Sijde, 2014; Slaughter and Leslie, 1997), our study shifts attention to affect and the body. We posit that this is important in order to better understand how the practices of entrepreneurial university function on the level of pre-personal and precognitive forces that, for example, attach bodies to each other in venture creation processes. Paying attention to affect and the body is further important for understanding the unintended consequences of entrepreneurial university practices. To illustrate, the study of ThinkCo illustrated how the practice of 'inviting inspirational speakers' was highly affective but did not manage to orchestrate desired enthusiasm around entrepreneurship as intended. Although these unintended effects may easily be seen as 'failures' of fostering entrepreneurship, they highlight how (surprising) affective responses can trigger new and alternative ways of being and doing in entrepreneurial university. Hence, they offer an interesting entry point for examining, among other things, how resistance to the commodification and entrepreneuralization of higher education (Slaughter and Leslie, 1997) may emerge.

Furthermore, on the basis of our theoretical and empirical approach, we want to offer ideas for future research on entrepreneurial doing and learning in universities from the perspective of affect. These include participating in affective capitalism, enabling variety of entrepreneurial identities, constructing radically new ways of entrepreneuring, and shifting the onto-epistemological starting points of research.

Participating in affective capitalism

According to Massumi (2002), affect is 'a real condition, an intrinsic variable of the late-capitalist system, as infrastructural as a factory'. Extant studies have acknowledged how various industries invest in affect production, for example through reality shows, social media sites and celebrity blogs (Karppi et al., 2016). The capitalization effect rests on the capture and transformation of affective energies into systems of value (Karppi et al., 2016). Our example of the practices of ThinkCo can be seen as part of an affective infrastructure, which appeals to many young people, since the uncertainty of labor markets and the emerging gig economy have provided a ground for comprehending entrepreneuring as a self-fulfilling project of life (Saari and Harni, 2016). Still, there is a paucity of knowledge regarding the role of entrepreneurial universities in affective capitalism. Future studies could lead to a more comprehensive and nuanced understanding of how affective capitalism is enhanced and/or resisted within the practices of entrepreneurial university.

Enabling variety of entrepreneurial identities

Prior research has critically examined the reproduction of dominant depiction of entrepreneurs as heroic (Anderson and Warren, 2011; Hytti and Heinonen, 2013) and masculine figures (e.g. Ahl, 2004; Ozkazanc-Pan, 2014). In our study of ThinkCo, the practice of using inspirational speakers privileged similar figures. Reproducing such a narrow understanding of entrepreneurs, which limits the pool of candidates who can assume the identity of an entrepreneur, often excludes women, non-whites, people with disabilities, and those who are no longer perceived as young (Katila and Kuismin, 2017; see also Meriläinen et al., 2015). However, there is a lack of analysis on the role of affect in the construction of entrepreneurial identities, especially in the context of entrepreneurial university. Such analysis could focus, on the one hand, on how affect binds people to the existing and dominant modes of entrepreneuring and entrepreneurial identity (Hemmings, 2005). On the other hand, future studies could examine how affect can drive persons to generate new and alternative entrepreneurial identities (Hemmings, 2012; Pullen et al., 2017) such as social and impact entrepreneurs. Furthermore, there is a need to scrutinize how affect pushes people to identify with even more radically new ways of entrepreneuring, referred to in the next section.

Constructing radically new ways of entrepreneuring

Given the ongoing environmental crisis, there is an urgent need for a radical rethinking of the prevalent economic growth-based mindset underpinning much of the approaches to entrepreneurship. Some studies have already examined how and under which conditions entrepreneurship could act as a force for creating more sustainable and ethical worlds (Dey and Steyaert, 2018; Hjorth and Steyaert, 2009; Osburg, 2014). Our empirical case demonstrates how the goal for thriving for a better world through social and impact entrepreneurship drives university students towards entrepreneurship. However, extant studies have also expressed hesitancy towards the transformative potential of entrepreneurship due to its market-based view of social change (Cálas et al., 2009; Dey and Mason, 2018). Future research could scrutinize how radically different forms of entrepreneuring could emerge at entrepreneurial universities, and what is the role of affect in this process. Instead of considering the natural world as a context for business activities, or as a resource to be exploited for human purposes, the very practice of entrepreneuring should be analyzed as a collaborative enactment with humans and various more-than-humans. Such an analysis could focus on how the agency is performed in and through the entanglings of human and more-than-humans, and how affect – created within these entanglings – could foster desire for (Dey and Mason, 2018) much-needed forms of entrepreneuring that take the environmental crisis seriously.

Shifting the onto-epistemological starting points of research

Finally, the research agenda we are putting forward entails that we reconsider how we conduct research on entrepreneuring and entrepreneurial universities. In order to detect and understand affective intensities in the field, affective ethnography offers paths forward. Within affective ethnography, researchers see and use their bodies differently as resonant materiality that is able to affect and be affected by both human and non-human bodies. This entails attuning to sensual knowing in the field that takes place through touching, hearing, seeing, smelling and tasting (Gherardi, 2019; Katila et al., 2019a; Stewart, 2007). Further, the active role of non-human bodies needs careful attention both in the production of affective intensities as well as in creating radically new ways of entrepreneuring that acknowledge the interdependence of humans and more-than-humans as the ontological ground for human relations with nature (see Graham and Roelvink, 2010). Thus, what we propose is a new onto-epistemological stance that takes note of the agentive power of materiality (Barad, 2003). From this perspective the starting point of studies on entrepreneurial university would be on connections-in-action and their consequences (Gherardi, 2019), rather than entrepreneurial behavior, university spin-offs, or accelerator success.

References

Ahl, H. (2004), The Scientific Reproduction of Gender Inequality. A Discourse Analysis of Research Texts on Women's Entrepreneurship, Malmö: Liber.

Anderson, A.R. and L. Warren (2011), 'The entrepreneur as hero and jester: Enacting the entrepreneurial discourse', International Small Business Journal, 29 (6), 589–609.

Anderson, B. (2014), Encountering Affect: Capacities, Apparatuses, Conditions, Ashgate: Farnham.

Ash, J. (2012), 'Attention, videogames and the retentional economies of affective amplification', Theory, Culture & Society, **29** (6), 3–26.

Barad, K. (2003), 'Posthumanist performativity: Toward an understanding of how matter comes to matter', Signs, **28** (3), 801–831.

Bille, M., P. Bjerregaard and T. F. Sørensen, (2015), 'Staging atmospheres: Materiality, culture, and the texture of the in-between', Emotion, Space and Society, **15** (1), 31–38.

Blackman, L. and C. Venn (2010), 'Affect', Body & Society, **16** (1), 7–28.

Cálas, M. B., L. Smircich, and K. A. Bourne (2009), 'Extending boundaries: Reframing "entrepreneurship as social change" from the feminist perspective', Academy of Management Review, **34** (3), 552–569.

Cardon, M. S., M. D. Foo, D. Shepherd and J. Wiklund (2012), 'Exploring the heart: Entrepreneurial emotion is a hot topic', Entrepreneurship Theory and Practice, **36** (1), 1–10.

Cardon, M. S., J. Wincent, J. Singh and M. Drnovsek (2009), 'The nature and experience of entrepreneurial passion', Academy of Management Review, **34** (3), 511–532.

Clark, B. R. (1998), 'The entrepreneurial university: Demand and response', Tertiary Education and Management, **4** (1), 5–16.

Deleuze, G. (1994), Difference and Repetition (P. Patton, Trans.), New York: Columbia University Press.

Deleuze, G. and F. Guattari (1987), A Thousand Plateaus: Capitalism and Schizophrenia (B. Massumi, Trans.), Minneapolis, MN: University of Minnesota Press.

Dey, P. and C. Mason (2018), 'Overcoming constraints of collective imagination: An inquiry into activist entrepreneuring, disruptive truth-telling and the creation of "possible worlds"', Journal of Business Venturing, **33** (1), 84–99.

Dey, P. and C. Steyaert (2018), Social Entrepreneurship. An Affirmative Critique, Cheltenham, UK and Northampton, MA, USA: Edward Elgar Publishing.

Etzkowitz, H. (2002), 'Incubation of incubators: Innovation as a triple helix of university–industry–government networks', Science and Public Policy, **29** (2), 115–128.

Etzkowitz, H., A. Webster and P. Healey (eds) (1998), Capitalizing Knowledge: New Intersections of Industry and Academia, Albany, NY: SUNY Press.

Etzkowitz, H., M. Ranga, M. Benner, L. Guaranys, A. M. Maculan and R. Kneller (2008), 'Pathways to the entrepreneurial university: Towards a global convergence', Science and Public Policy, **35** (9), 681–695.

Farny, S. and P. Kyrö (2015), 'Entrepreneurial Aalto: Where science and art meet technology and business', in Lene Foss and David V. Gibson (eds), The Entrepreneurial University: Context and Institutional Change, New York: Routledge, pp. 150–166.

Foss, L. and D. V. Gibson (2015), 'The entrepreneurial university: Context and institutional change', in Lene Foss and David V. Gibson (eds), The Entrepreneurial University: Context and Institutional Change, New York: Routledge, pp. 1–17.

Fotaki, M., K. Kenny and S. Vachhani (2017), 'Thinking critically about affect in organization studies: Why it matters', Organization, **24** (1), 3–17.

Gherardi, S. (2017), 'One turn … and now another one: Do the turn to practice and the turn to affect have something in common?', Management Learning, **48** (3), 345–358.

Gherardi, S. (2019) 'Theorizing affective ethnography for organization studies', Organization, **26** (6), 741–760.

Graham, J. G. and Roelvink, G. (2010), 'An economic ethics for the Anthropocene', Antipode, **41**, 320–346.

Guerrero, M., J. A. Cunningham and D. Urbano (2015), 'Economic impact of entre-preneurial universities' activities: An exploratory study of the United Kingdom', Research Policy, **44** (3), 748–764.

Heinonen, J. and U. Hytti (2010), 'Back to basics: The role of teaching in developing the entrepreneurial university', The International Journal of Entrepreneurship and Innovation, **11** (4), 283–292.

Heinonen, J., S-A Poikkijoki and I. Vento-Vierikko (2007), 'Entrepreneurship for bio-science researchers: A case study of an entrepreneurship programme', Industry and Higher Education, **21** (1), 21–30.

Hemmings, C. (2005), 'Invoking affect', Cultural Studies, **19** (5), 548–567.

Hemmings, C. (2012), 'Affective solidarity: Feminist reflexivity and political transfor-mation', Feminist Theory, **13** (2), 147–161.

Hjorth, D. (2015), 'Sketching a philosophy of entrepreneurship', in Ted Baker and Friederike Welter (eds), The Routledge Companion to Entrepreneurship, Routledge, Abingdon, Routledge Companions in Business, Management and Accounting, pp. 41–58.

Hjorth, D. and C. Steyaert (2009), 'Entrepreneurship as disruptive event', in Daniel Hjorth and Chris Steyaert (eds), The Politics and Aesthetics of Entrepreneurship, Cheltenham, UK and Northampton, MA, USA: Edward Elgar Publishing, pp. 1–12.

Hytti, U. and J. Heinonen (2013), 'Heroic and humane entrepreneurs: Identity work in entrepreneurship education', Education + Training, **55** (8/9), 886–898.

Jenkins, H. (2003), Convergence Culture: Where Old and New Media Collide, New York: New York University Press.

Karppi, T., L. Kähkönen, M. Mannevuo, M. Pajala and T. Sihvonen (2016), 'Affective capitalism', ephemera, **16** (4), 1–13.

Katila, S. and A. Kuismin (2017), 'Gendering entrepreneurship enhancing space', Academy of Management Proceedings, Vol. 2017, https://doi.org/10.5465/AMBPP .2017.13842abstract.

Katila, S., A. Kuismin and A. Valtonen (2019a), 'Becoming upbeat: Learning the affecto-rhythmic order of organizational practices', Human Relations, https://doi .org/10.1177/0018726719867753.

Katila, S., P-M. Laine and P. Parkkari (2019b), 'Sociomateriality and affect in insti-tutional work: Constructing the identity of start-up entrepreneurs', Journal of Management Inquiry, **28** (3), 381–394.

Keevers, L. and C. Sykes (2016), 'Food and music matters: Affective relations and prac-tices in social justice organizations', Human Relations, **69** (8), 1643–1668.

Laine, P-M. and P. Parkkari (2017), 'Implications of the strategic agency of sociomate-rial configurations for participation in strategy-making', in I. Onciou (ed.), Driving Innovation and Business Success in the Digital Economy, IGI Global, pp. 172–192.

MacLure, M. (2010), 'The offence of theory', Journal of Education Policy, **25** (1), 277–286.

Massumi, B. (1987), 'Foreword', in G. Deleuze and F. Guattari (eds), A Thousand Plateaus: Capitalism and Schizophrenia (B. Massumi, Trans.), Minneapolis, MN: University of Minnesota Press, p. xvii.

Massumi, B. (2002), Parables for the Virtual: Movement, Affect, Sensation, Durham: Duke University Press.

Mauksch, S. (2017), 'Managing the dance of enchantment: An ethnography of social entrepreneurship events', Organization, **24** (2), 133–153.

Meriläinen, S., J. Tienari and A. Valtonen (2015), 'Headhunters and the "ideal" execu-tive body', Organization, **22** (1), 3–22.

Michels, C. and C. Steyaert (2017), 'By accident and by design: Composing affective atmospheres in an urban art intervention', Organization, **24** (1), 79–104.

Mulcahy, D. (2012), 'Affective assemblages: Body matters in the pedagogic practices of contemporary school classrooms', Pedagogy, Culture & Society, **20** (1), 9–27.

Osburg, T. (2014), 'Sustainable entrepreneurship: A driver for social innovation', in Christina Weidinger, Franz Fischler and Rene Schmidpeter (eds), Sustainable Entrepreneurship. Business Success Through Sustainability, Berlin, Germany: Springer, pp. 103–115.

Ozkazanc-Pan, B. (2014), 'Postcolonial feminist analysis of high-technology entrepreneuring', International Journal of Entrepreneurial Behaviour & Research, **20** (2), 155–172.

Pullen, A., C. Rhodes and T. Thanem (2017), 'Affective politics in gendered organizations: Affirmative notes on becoming-woman', Organization, **24** (1), 105–123.

Sá, C. and A. Kretz (2015), The Entrepreneurship Movement and the University, New York: Springer.

Saari, A. and E. Harni (2016), 'Zen and the art of everything: Governing spirituality in entrepreneurship education', ephemera, **16** (4), 99–119.

Sam, C. and P. van der Sijde (2014), 'Understanding the concept of the entrepreneurial university from the perspective of higher education models', Higher Education, **68** (6), 891–908.

Slaughter, S. and L. L. Leslie (1997), Academic Capitalism. Politics, Policies, and the Entrepreneurial University, Maryland: The Johns Hopkins University Press.

Stewart, K. (2007), Ordinary Affects, Durham, NC: Duke University Press.

Thrift, N. (2004), 'Intensities of feeling: Towards a spatial politics of affect', Geografiska Annaler: Series B, Human Geography, **86** (1), 57–78.

Thrift, N. (2008), Non-representational Theory: Space, Politics, Affect, London: Routledge.

Wetherell, M. (2012), Affect and Emotion: A New Social Science Understanding, London: Sage Publications.

6

Agent or principal?
A discursive and rhetorical approach to changing stakeholder relations in the entrepreneurial university

Miira Niska and Kari Mikko Vesala

Introduction

The entrepreneurial university is a fuzzy and an ambiguous concept. On the one hand, the concept suggests that the contemporary university is much like a business enterprise: effective, productive and profitable. On the other hand, the concept suggests that the university has "opened up" to the world outside and now engenders and supports business enterprises. The former meaning brings forth changes in funding and management, the latter meaning brings forth changes in external stakeholder relations. Whereas the "ivory tower" university focuses on academic interests in abstract and theoretical knowledge (Mautner, 2005; Nybom, 2008; Shore and McLauchlan, 2012), the entrepreneurial university fosters relationships with numerous external actors, including business sector actors, to promote social and economic development (Jongbloed et al., 2008; Philpott et al., 2011; OECD, 2012; Redford and Fayolle, 2014; Laalo and Plamper, 2019).

Transformation from the "ivory tower" to the entrepreneurial university requires changes in university-business sector relations. Before there can be spin-offs, there must be interaction and collaboration between the academic community and the business sector actors. Since this interaction and collaboration does not emerge automatically, universities have started to implement entrepreneurship policy. Interaction and collaboration with business sector actors can be facilitated, for example, with the help of start-up incubators, science parks and entrepreneurship education (Gilbert et al., 2004; Lundström and Stevenson, 2005; Audretsch and Beckmann, 2007). In this chapter, we argue that a crucial research agenda consists of understanding how new stakeholder relations are facilitated within the entrepreneurial university and how they work in practice.

Previous research constitutes a rich literature about university-business sector relations (Perkmann et al., 2013). Researchers have mainly used network analysis and stakeholder theory to map and classify these relations (Jongbloed et al., 2008; Perkmann et al., 2013; Redford and Fayolle, 2014), and explain their existence (Martinelli et al., 2008; D'Este and Perkmann, 2011; Perkmann et al., 2013). Although these studies have engendered important information, they have largely been based on substantialist (Emirbayer, 1997) and realist (Burr, 2015) assumptions. Researchers have been interested to explain university-business sector relations with multi-level factors like actors' motives and organizational cultures (i.e., substantialism). Researchers have based their studies on questionnaires filled in by academics, and these studies have been concerned with the reliability and validity of the research findings (i.e., realism) (see e.g., Perkmann et al. 2013).

We argue that in addition to substantialist and realist perspectives, it is also worthwhile studying stakeholder relations and their facilitation from relational (Emirbayer, 1997) and constructionist (Burr, 2015) perspectives. From a relational perspective, stakeholder relations are constructed and legitimated in situated and dynamic interaction processes. To understand relations with numerous partners and collaborators, it is best to study the everyday interactions in which these relations are constructed, managed and legitimated (i.e., using qualitative data). From a constructionist perspective, researchers cannot judge constructed relations in terms of their "truthfulness" simply because they have no access to the world "as it is". The relational-constructionist perspective allows us to study the context-specific construction of relations that take place in everyday interaction at the entrepreneurial university. Instead of truthfulness, it is intriguing to study how legitimate relationships are produced and why they are produced the way they are (Potter, 1996).

In this chapter, we elaborate relational and constructionist perspectives with the help of discursive and rhetorical social psychology (Potter and Wetherell, 1987; Billig, 1996; Potter, 1996; Harré and van Langenhove, 1999). Discursive and rhetorical social psychology provide theoretically robust tools for the analysis of everyday interaction thorough which the entrepreneurial university's relations with partners and collaborators are constructed, authorized and legitimated – but also challenged and negotiated. The chapter is structured as follows. In the first section, we discuss the contribution of network analysis, stakeholder theory and agency theory to our understanding of relations at the entrepreneurial university. In the second section, we introduce a discursive and rhetorical approach to these relations. In the third section, we provide an empirical example and analysis of a speech of the rector of the University of Helsinki from a discursive and rhetorical perspective. Finally, in the last section, we discuss our empirical example and the implications of our approach on the analysis of relations at the entrepreneurial university.

Relations at the entrepreneurial university: network analysis, stakeholder theory and agency theory

Stakeholder theory, agency theory and related network analysis are all widely known in entrepreneurship and management studies (Aldrich and Zimmer, 1986; Ross, 1973; Mitchell et al., 1997; Alsos et al., 2011). They have also been applied in the higher education context to analyse universities' relationships to people, groups, organisations and institutions (Jongbloed et al., 2008; Martinelli et al., 2008; Siegel and Wright, 2015). Stakeholder theory focuses specifically on actors who have legitimate interests in a university's actions (Donaldson and Preston, 1995; Mitchell et al., 1997). The "ivory tower" universities acknowledge and serve internal, academic actors' interests in public knowledge promotion, excellence in teaching and research, respectable reputation and autonomy of knowledge (Mautner, 2005; Nybom, 2008; Shore and McLauchlan, 2012). The entrepreneurial universities, in turn, are also responsive to external non-academic actors' interests, and satisfy societal and market demands through knowledge transfer and academic entrepreneurship (Jongbloed et al., 2008; Philpott et al., 2011; Shore and McLauchlan, 2012).

A widely recognised problem at the entrepreneurial university is the academic community – students and faculty members – which does not always recognise the legitimacy of the new stakeholders. Previous research has demonstrated how the academic community impugns universities' collaboration with business sectors on the basis that commercial interests violate "pure academic values" or "traditional ethos" (Lee, 1996; Ylijoki, 2003; Philpott et al., 2011). According to Jongbloed et al. (2008: 317), faculty members define "their identity as characterized by an independence of thought and action and do not want to be driven by external demands". Unwillingness to serve the interests of the new external stakeholders highlights the fundamental difference between universities and enterprises. Employees of a company may not be allowed to act against the business owners' will (at least without being fired) but students and faculty members are not employees of a single company called University. Instead of a principal with unambiguous interests, universities consist of separate disciplines and departments. The existence of distinct cultures, values and interests between the disciplines and departments has been something of a truism (e.g., Rinne, 2019). Not all members of the academic community have traditionally been willing to serve the same principals and interests.

Siegel and Wright (2015) discuss problems with stakeholder relations referring to the agency theory (Ross, 1973; Kiser, 1999; Shapiro, 2005). Agency theory focuses on relationships in which one party is designated as the principal, and the other party is designated as the agent who serves the principal. In the classic version, the business owner is the principal and the paid manager is the agent. The classic agency problem arises when the principal suspects that the agent is serving his/her own interests instead of maximizing the interests of the principal (Jensen and Meckling, 1976). At the entrepreneurial university, the classic agency problem arises when business sector actors as stakeholders or principals suspect that faculty members (agents) collaborate with them in order to support their own academic research – not to transfer their knowledge to benefit the business (e.g., D'Este and Perkmann, 2011).

The original formulation of agency theory assumes that there is just one principal, whose interests the agent serves. However, as Siegel and Wright (2015) demonstrate, stakeholder relations may face problems because agents have multiple principals whose interests they need to serve. For example, technology transfer offices (TTOs) must serve the interests of their clients (i.e., academic entrepreneurs) and the interests of the universities that established the TTOs (Siegel and Wright, 2015). In such situations, agents need to figure out how to deal with multiple principals and their interests.

An interesting detail in Siegel and Wright's (2015) example is the fact that the entrepreneurial university is portrayed as the principal, not the agent. Researchers often take for granted that the entrepreneurial university is the agent who serves the interests of external stakeholders (e.g., Redford and Fayolle, 2014). The concept "third mission" highlights universities' responsiveness to new partners (Jongbloed et al., 2008) in the sense that universities are agents who serve new partners' interests – not in the sense that new partners become agents who serve universities' academic interests.

Despite the "third mission", the entrepreneurial university is not only an agent for external principals. It is also a principal that authorises agents to act on its behalf (see Meyer and Jepperson, 2000). For example, Laalo and Plamper (2019: 444) demonstrate how academic managers construct students and faculty members as effective agents for the entrepreneurial university. Unlike the assumption in the classic formulation of agency theory, agent and principal are not fixed positions. As Shapiro (2005: 267) notes: "actors are not just principals or agents, but often both at the same time – even in the same transaction or hierarchical structure". We argue that this complexity, or ambiguity, in stakeholder relations should be taken into consideration and relational-constructionist discursive and rhetorical social psychology provide theoretically robust tools for such research.

Discursive and rhetorical approach on stakeholder relations

Discursive approaches are widely used in entrepreneurship and management studies (Hjorth and Steyaert, 2004; Perren and Jennings, 2005; Anderson and Warren, 2011). In the higher education context, researchers have mainly adopted Foucauldian and critical discourse analysis to study, for example, universities' websites, job advertisements and rectors' speeches (Fairclough, 1993; Mautner, 2005; Krejsler, 2006). In these studies, researchers have taken a critical stand on the development of the entrepreneurial university. They have demonstrated how industrial and commercial ideas have penetrated and colonized universities, and they have argued for universities' emancipation from the hegemonic entrepreneurship discourse (e.g., Mautner, 2005). Research that focuses on power and subjugation at the entrepreneurial universities could be labelled as representing macro social constructionism (Burr, 2015) and radical or critical entrepreneurship research (Grant and Perren, 2002; see also Jennings et al., 2005; Berglund and Verduijn, 2018).

The discursive approach we adopt – discursive and rhetorical social psychology (Potter and Wetherell, 1987; Billig, 1996; Potter, 1996; Harré and van Langenhove, 1999) – could be labelled as representing micro social constructionism (Burr, 2015) and interpretive entrepreneurship research (Grant and Perren, 2002; see also Jennings et al., 2005). Instead of focusing on the macro level linguistic structures (i.e., the entrepreneurship discourse or the managerial discourse) that frame actions at the entrepreneurial university, discursive and rhetorical social psychology focuses on language use in everyday interaction. The purpose is to understand the construction of phenomena such as interests or agent-principal relations at the entrepreneurial university. In line with Burr (2015: 17), these "phenomena become things we do rather than things we have". The purpose is not to take a stand on the overall goodness or badness of the entrepreneurship discourse or development of the entrepreneurial university.

From discursive and rhetorical perspectives, stakeholders and agents who serve these stakeholders are constructed and legitimated in daily interaction processes. This construction and legitimation takes place, for example, in the interaction processes of positioning (Harré and van Langenhove, 1999), and stake and accountability management (Potter, 1996). Researchers have demonstrated how actors construct themselves as principals of numerous agents (e.g., Niska and Vesala, 2013), and agents for numerous principals (e.g., Jarzabkowski and Sillince, 2007).

From the discursive and rhetorical perspective, stakeholders' attributes – including their power and legitimacy (Mitchell et al., 1997) – are effects of discourse and thus negotiated in daily interactions. In the same way, agents' attributes – including their ability and willingness to serve the stakeholders – are negotiable. This constructed nature means that legitimate positions of agent and principal can also be called into question, challenged or even rejected (Niska and Vesala, 2013). The discursive and rhetorical perspective engenders new research questions. How do actors construct themselves as legitimate stakeholders (i.e., principals) of the entrepreneurial university? How do actors construct the entrepreneurial university as an efficient agent for the legitimate stakeholders (i.e., principals)? How do actors construct the entrepreneurial university as a legitimate principal and authorise actors to serve its interests?

Empirical excursion: authorizing agents to engage in relations with business sector actors

As a demonstration of discursive and rhetorical approach on stakeholder relations, we analyzed a case of entrepreneurship policy implementation at an entrepreneurial university. The case is a speech given by Jukka Kola, the rector of the University of Helsinki (2013–2018).[1] This speech was an opening speech in an event called How to Change the World (Miten maailmaa muutetaan, in Finnish). The event was organised by the central campus Helsinki Think Company. The central campus Helsinki Think Company, established in 2013, is a body that hosts and promotes entrepreneurship for the faculties of Arts, Educational Sciences, Law, Social Sciences and Theology (see also Chapter 5 in this book).

The purpose of this event was to promote entrepreneurship with the help of inspirational speeches from experts like Bruce Oreck, an American diplomat and entrepreneur (Helsinki Think Company, 2016). Inspirational speeches from inspirational people are a widespread practice in entrepreneurship promotion in university contexts (see also Chapter 5 in this book). The event took place in the 700-seat Great Hall of the university main building on 22 September 2016 and it clearly targeted the university community members, especially students and staff members. Representatives of the Helsinki Think Company hosted the event and the Great Hall was crowded. The event was recorded and it is available in YouTube.[2] We have added punctuation and capital letters to the transcription for ease of reading (see e.g., Reynolds et al., 2007).

Previous research has demonstrated that compared to other faculties, the attitudes to entrepreneurship are especially negative in faculties of Arts, and Social and Behavioural Sciences (e.g., Philpott et al., 2011; Neittaanmäki et al., 2017). The rector of the University of Helsinki was thus opening an event to promote entrepreneurship to an audience known to be critical of entrepreneurship. From discursive and rhetorical perspectives, an interesting question is: what is the rector doing in this situation? How is he constructing and legitimating (a) entrepreneurship and (b) relations between the university and stakeholders?

The rector begins his speech with a greeting "good afternoon" and invites the audience to reply by pushing his ear forward (line 1). He thanks the audience for attending the event: "quite splendid to see so many of you in here" (lines 2–3). This acknowledgement is followed by an interesting remark: "I guess it was a small surprise that the hall is so crowded in this kind of event" (line 3). What does the rector mean with "this kind of an event" and why is it surprising that the event turned out to be popular? One reasonable interpretation is that the rector implies that previously the university community at the central campus has not been that interested in entrepreneurship or inspirational speeches given by entrepreneurs (see Chapter 5 of this book).

The rector continues by stating that the popularity of the event is a good thing because changing the world is an essential part of what the University of Helsinki does (lines 4–7). One might of course wonder why the university institution is aiming to change the world – should not the institution focus on academic education and research. The rector legitimises the world-changing mission by referring to the Universities Act: "in the university law it is stated very clearly that the mission of the university is to educate the youth to serve the fatherland and humankind" (lines 8–9). The rector thus refers to the

Table 6.1   The speech of the rector (recorded 22 September 2016)

1   Good afternoon (pushes his ear towards audience). Well yes, interactivity, please,

2   that is what we need also this evening right here. Quite splendid to see so many of you

3   here. I guess it was a small surprise that the hall is so crowded in this kind of event

4   but that's how it should be. Now we are close to very essential issues what we are going

5   to do and what we have already done in this university. This, how to change the world and

6   it starts actually if we have the desire to change it, which takes us into the question that if

7   we have the desire, so do we have the ability to change that world. And as a matter of fact,

8   now a little bureaucratic mention, in the university law it is stated very clearly that the

9   mission of universities is to educate youth to serve the fatherland and humankind. And now

10 many of you who are people from the University of Helsinki know that I have said this so

11 many times, but it is not enough, at least for the University of Helsinki. We educate youth,

12 our young students, and also more experienced students, we educate youth to change the

13 world into a better place to live in, for everybody in this country and in the world. And it

14 takes lots more than just to serve and adjust oneself. Changing is the driving force, it is the

15 factor into which we invest in our training. And that training is based on top research

16 through which our students always have available the latest knowledge, even earlier than

17 many others who don't even know about it because our teachers deliver it there and because

18 they are researchers as well. In this way that special expertise is built, that special know-

19 how, and that special desire and ability to change the world into a better place to live. Our

20 Think Company, these young people here, and many others have acted before, are in

21 particular an example of how we involve our youth early enough in these activities. And it

22 is in particular these youngsters who make the future. And when they also look at it from

23 the perspective of this kind of enterprise, entrepreneurship, creating new. One of our ideas

24 was exactly that the first Think Company came into the central campus in particular, where

25 perhaps there was not necessarily the readiness to see these things. And now we have gone

26 already to the Viikki campus, Meilahti campus and Kumpula campus is coming as well. In

27 other words, each of our four campuses will have a Think Company. A system driven by

28 students, pushed by students, and of student origin, with the help of which we do this thing

29 and through which we make the world a better place. Based on research but those ideas can

30 be such that there is also something that has not been researched yet. Young people have
31 some new, and often even many new thoughts. And as a matter of fact as a university rector
32 this is a special workplace you could say when working at the university not only as rector,
33 when every year new people come in. Also this year, a couple of weeks ago, about four
34 thousand new students came into this community, all at once just like that. Think about how
35 much that changes that community within a blink of an eye. Many new ideas thoughts
36 coming in. And they will be tested and then one starts to consider how things are taken
37 forward. It happens through the young people. Universities are forerunners, leading the
38 way. But in particular in that way that we have those young people here. It can be that us
39 older people will get stuck every now and then but those young people spar with us. They
40 make us think that where are we heading actually. In other words Think Company is such a
41 thing that is very important to us. Its impact starts to be pretty much what it should be but
42 one can build much more of it. Let's give one example, this morning there was Helsinki
43 innovation aquarium there at Luomus, the natural science central museum. And there were
44 many investors who also read, read and watch what kind of new moves come through our
45 science based ideas into business world, start-ups, spin-offs and so on. So this supports all
46 that young ones, utilize thoughts, be brave, take forward, change the world, that is one of
47 the main tasks of University of Helsinki. To change the world into a better place to live,
48 thanks so much.

Universities Act to point out that the University of Helsinki is acting as an agent for two legitimate principals: Finland and humankind.

The construction of the two stakeholders, Finland and humankind, includes an interesting particular. On lines 9–13, the rector positions himself as an authority, who interprets critically the Universities Act, who can redefine the mission of the University of Helsinki. According to the rector, the University of Helsinki does not educate students to serve Finland and humankind by adjusting themselves but instead by changing Finland and the world for the better (lines 8–14). Thus, besides arguing that the university serves two legitimate principals, the rector also actively defines how the university and its students should serve these principals. While highlighting change agency as the university's mission, the rector also highlights his own position as a person with authority to define the mission of the university and thereby manage or interpret the interests of the principals.

The rector also connects education and research (first and second missions) to the world-changing mission. According to the rector, research forms the basis of university education and the university education forms the basis of the world-changing action (lines 14–18). Following this interpretation, the third mission is really the main mission of the university; in the end, academic research and teaching inevitably also serve the interests of Finland and humankind.

From education and research, the rector moves into talking about the Helsinki Think Company and students who take part in Helsinki Think Company activities. He presents these two as an example of "how we involve our youth early enough in these activities" (line 21). One might ask, who are "we" and what are "these activities" in the rector's account. One reasonable interpretation is that according to the rector, the University of Helsinki involves its students at an early stage into serving the legitimate stakeholders as change-agents. The rector thus positions the Helsinki Think Company and students as agents for external principals.

The term "entrepreneurship" is first used when the rector continues that students "make the future and when they look at it also from the perspective of this kind of enterprise, entrepreneurship, creating new" (lines 22–23). He invokes entrepreneurship not only as something that has to do with business enterprises but also as a vehicle of change – a construction familiar from Schumpeterian entrepreneurship theories and discourses. In this sense, entrepreneurship appears as a desirable way to serve the legitimate stakeholders. The rector adds that the Helsinki Think Company was established on the central campus of the University of Helsinki because the faculties located on the central campus did not necessarily have "the readiness to see these things" (line 25). One reasonable interpretation of this argument is that according to the rector, the Helsinki Think Company was needed because the academic community at the central campus struggled to see entrepreneurship as a vehicle through which they could serve Finland and humankind.

The rector makes the point that the Helsinki Think Company is not a top-down institution but a bottom-up institution run by the students: "Think Company, a system driven by students, pushed by students, and of student origin" (lines 27–28). This is an interesting claim considering that previous studies have highlighted the role of the university administration in the establishment of the Helsinki Think Company (e.g., Siitonen, 2016). Nevertheless, the argument supports at least two impressions. First, the Helsinki Think Company and its students are portrayed as dynamic agents. Even if their ideas are based on academic research (line 29), they still represent young people who are not "stuck" (lines 29–39). Presumably, the "stuck ones" here refer to the faculty members. Second, the Helsinki Think Company is portrayed as an agent serving students' interests – not only university politics or external actors' interests. The portrayal of the Helsinki Think Company as a bottom-up institution aligns students' interests with the interests of the external stakeholders.

The final part of the rector's speech starts with an affirmation of the importance of the Helsinki Think Company: "In other words Think Company is such a thing that is very important to us" (lines 40–41). One might ask who "we" are in this account. The rector might refer to the University of Helsinki, to the Finns, or to humankind. Although the rector expresses that he is pleased with the impact of the Helsinki Think Company (line 41), he also envisions a future in which the impact is even higher. Assessments like these obviously construct the rector as a representative of a principal who is monitoring the agent.

As an example of wanted future actions, the rector narrates another event in which he had participated that morning. In this event, investors considered making investments in science-based ideas that came from the University of Helsinki (lines 42–45). Here the rector adopts the discourse commonly known as the entrepreneurship discourse and talks about start-ups and spin-offs (line 45). He also introduces a new stakeholder: investors who are interested in science-based ideas (line 44). Here, entrepreneurship is associated with business enterprises and dynamic business activities. Again, the rector appears as a representative of a principal who outlines the expected direction of the agent's activities.

The end of the speech is almost like the great commission: "utilize thoughts, be brave, take forward, change the world, that is one of the main tasks of the University of Helsinki. To change the world into a better place to live" (lines 46–47). This encouragement illustrates well the overall nature of the rector's speech. The rector is authorizing students and the Helsinki Think Company to act as agents who will seek to change the world for the better, create contacts and cooperate with the business sector, in the name of the University of Helsinki, Finland, and humankind.

The answer to the questions about how the rector of the University of Helsinki is constructing and legitimating entrepreneurship, and relationships between the university and the stakeholders, is tripartite. First, the rector constructs the University of Helsinki as an agent that serves two main stakeholders: Finland and humankind. According to him, the Universities Act legitimates these stakeholders, yet he reinterprets the mission stated in the Act. Furthermore, a third legitimate stakeholder – investors – comes up when the rector adopts the entrepreneurship discourse. Second, in line with the third mission discussions, the rector constructs entrepreneurship as a vehicle of change through which the University of Helsinki can serve the external stakeholders: Finland and humankind, but also investors and the business sector. Third, besides an agent for external principals, the rector constructs the University of Helsinki as a principal that authorises the Helsinki Think Company and the academic community as agents for not three but four principals. The rector implies that students' interests align with the stakeholders' interests but faculty members are a reluctant group, which – unlike students – "has not seen the light". The speech ends with the rector authorizing the Helsinki Think Company and the audience to act as agents for Finland, humankind, the business sector – and the University of Helsinki.

Discussion and conclusions: ways to move forward

New stakeholder relations are an important feature of the entrepreneurial university. In this chapter, we have emphasized that these relations and their facilitation and legitimation can be viewed from a relational-constructionist perspective as dynamic and situationally negotiated. While we acknowledge that discursive and rhetorical social psychology are not the only possible approaches, they provide theoretically robust tools for the analysis of everyday interaction in which the relations between the academic community and external stakeholders are constructed and legitimated.

Based on discursive and rhetorical perspective, we argue that a crucial research agenda consists of understanding (a) how entrepreneurship is constructed and (b) how these constructions facilitate or impair stakeholder relations at the entrepreneurial university. Hytti et al. (2017) call for a more refined understanding of local interpretations of entrepreneurship. Discursive and rhetorical social psychology are oriented to situationally constructed interpretations but also note that these interpretations are constructed to do things like facilitate – or impair – relationship building (Potter and Wetherell, 1987; Billig, 1996; Potter 1996).

In the empirical example, we analysed a speech made by the rector of the University of Helsinki, in which he constructed entrepreneurship in two distinct ways. First, the rector constructed entrepreneurship as "more than business making". Entrepreneurship equals heroic action that changes the world for better. This image of an entrepreneur as a saviour has also been identified in other contexts (e.g., Sørensen, 2008). Second, the rector constructed entrepreneurship as dynamic business making that is manifested in spin-offs and start-ups, which attract investors. The speech demonstrates that entrepreneurship is a fuzzy and ambiguous concept. It is by no means self-evident how entrepreneurship is interpreted in the local contexts of the entrepreneurial university.

The speech is an example of entrepreneurship policy implementation; in the speech, the rector activated and authorized students and faculty members to relate to the business sector and become entrepreneurial agents for the legitimate stakeholders: Finland, humankind, investors and the University of Helsinki. Public speeches represent a specific type of formal and unidirectional interaction, which does not allow for disagreements. Analysis of a public speech cannot reveal how the audience, academic community members, reacted to the rectors' constructions. However, the entrepreneurial university is also filled with informal and bidirectional communication through which entrepreneurship and relations between academic community members and external stakeholders are constructed but also challenged and negotiated. These interaction situations, such as consultation and counselling situations and advisory board meetings, make an interesting context for empirical research.

Considering that disciplines and departments have not traditionally shared cultures, values or interests (e.g., Rinne, 2019), it is important to study the construction of entrepreneurship and stakeholder relations in local contexts. In the speech, for example, the rector acknowledges the unwillingness of some academic community members to embrace entrepreneurship and business sector relations. Opposition to the entrepreneurial university has mainly been studied from Foucauldian and macro constructionist perspectives (e.g., Fairclough, 1993; Mautner, 2005; Krejsler, 2006). We argue that researchers should also take a discursive and rhetorical perspective on the counter talk, in which constructions of entrepreneurship are used to challenge new stakeholder relations.

Michael Billig (1996), a key author in discursive and rhetorical social psychology, has reflected on the transition from the "ivory tower" to the entrepreneurial university. According to Billig (1996), a major change in the university contexts is that funding is no longer sought in order to do research, but research is done in order to get funding. Economic interests no longer serve academic interests but academic interests serve economic interests. We argue that an important research agenda consists of studying who serves whom in the local contexts of the entrepreneurial university.

Notes

1.   After working at the University of Helsinki, Kola was appointed as the rector of the University of Turku (2019–).
2.   https://www.youtube.com/watch?v=h6UU8NMzAS8 (accessed 13 November 2019). Note: it is mainly in Finnish, translated by the second author of this chapter. The rector's speech starts at 5.15.

References

Aldrich, H. and Zimmer, C. (1986). Entrepreneurship through social networks. In D. L. Sexton and R. W. Smilor (eds.), *The Art and Science of Entrepreneurship*. Cambridge: Ballinger.

Alsos, A. G., Hytti, U. and Ljunggren, E. (2011). Stakeholder theory approach to technology incubators. *International Journal of Entrepreneurial Behaviour and Research*, **17** (6), 607–625.

Anderson, A. R. and Warren, L. (2011). The entrepreneur as hero and jester: Enacting the entrepreneurial discourse. *International Small Business Journal*, **29** (6), 589–609.

Audretsch, D. B. and Beckmann, I. A. M. (2007). From small business to entrepreneurship policy. In D. B. Audretsch, I. Grilo and A. R. Thurik (eds.), *Handbook of Research on Entrepreneurship Policy*. Cheltenham, UK and Northampton, MA, USA: Edward Elgar Publishing.

Berglund, K. and Verduijn, K. (2018). Introduction: Challenges for entrepreneurship education. In K. Berglund and K. Verduijn (eds.), *Revitalizing Entrepreneurship Education. Adopting a Critical Approach in the Classroom*. London: Routledge.

Billig, M. (1996). *Arguing and Thinking* (2nd ed.). Cambridge: Cambridge University Press.

Burr, V. (2015). *Social Constructionism* (3rd ed.). London: Routledge.

D'Este, P. and Perkmann, M. (2011). Why do academics engage with industry? The entrepreneurial university and individual motivations. *Journal of Technology Transfer*, **36**, 316–339.

Donaldson, T. and Preston, L. E. (1995). The stakeholder theory of the corporation: Concepts, evidence, and implications. *The Academy of Management Review*, **20** (1), 65–91.

Emirbayer, M. (1997). Manifesto for a relational sociology. *American Journal of Sociology*, **103** (2), 281–317.

Fairclough, N. (1993). Critical discourse analysis and the marketization of public discourse: the universities. *Discourse and Society*, **4** (2), 133–168.

Gilbert, B. A., Audretsch, D. B. and McDougall, P. P. (2004). The emergence of entrepreneurship policy. *Small Business Economics*, **22** (3–4), 313–323.

Grant, P. and Perren, L. (2002). Small business and entrepreneurial research. Meta-theories, paradigms and prejudices. *International Small Business Journal*, **20** (2), 185–211.

Harré, R. and van Langenhove, L. (eds.) (1999). *Positioning Theory*. Oxford: Blackwell.

Helsinki Think Company (2016). Miten maailmaa muutetaan. [How to change the world?] Facebook event. Available: https://www.facebook.com/events/helsingin-yliopiston-p%C3%A4%C3%A4rakennus-aleksanterinkatu-5/miten-maailmaa-muutetaan/919755894817610/ (accessed 26 March 2019).w

Hjorth, D. and Steyaert, C. (eds.) (2004). *Narrative and Discursive Approaches in Entrepreneurship. A Second Movements in Entrepreneurship Book*. Cheltenham, UK and Northampton, MA, USA: Edward Elgar Publishing.

Hytti, U., Eriksson, P., Montonen, T. and Peura, K. (2017). Making sense of entrepreneurship at the universities – Absolutely fabulous? Paper at the RENT Conference in Lund, Sweden, 16–17 November 2017. Available: https://research.utu.fi/converis/portal/Publication/27688756?lang=fi_FI (accessed 26 March 2019).

Jarzabkowski, P. and Sillince, J. (2007). A rhetoric-in-context approach to building commitment to multiple strategic goals. *Organization Studies*, **28** (11), 1639–1665.

Jennings, P., Perren, L. and Carter, S. (2005). Alternative perspectives on entrepreneurship research. *Entrepreneurship Theory and Practice*, **29** (2), 145–152.

Jensen, M. C. and Meckling, W. H. (1976). Theory of the firm: Managerial behavior, agency costs and ownership structure. *Journal of Financial Economics*, **3** (4), 303–360.

Jongbloed, B., Enders, J. and Salerno, C. (2008). Higher education and its communities: Interconnections, interdependencies and a research agenda. *Higher Education*, **56** (3), 303–324.

Kiser, E. (1999). Comparing varieties of agency theory in economics, political science, and sociology: An illustration from state policy implementation. *Sociological Theory*, **17** (2), 146–170.

Krejsler, J. (2006). Discursive battles about the meaning of university: The case of Danish university reform and its academics. *European Educational Research Journal*, **5** (3–4), 210–220.

Laalo, H. and Plamper, R. (2019). Rehtorit managereina – Yritysyliopistoparadigma ja managerialistinen hallintatapa lukuvuoden avajaispuheissa. In H. Nori, H. Laalo and R. Rinne (eds.), *Kohti oppimisyhteiskuntaa – Koulutuspolitiikan uusi suunta ja korkeakoulutuksen muuttuva maisema*. Turun yliopiston kasvatustieteiden tiedekunnan julkaisuja A:217. Turun yliopisto.

Lee, Y. S. (1996). Technology transfer and the research university: A search for the boundaries of university-industry collaboration. *Research Policy*, **25**, 843–863.

Lundström, A. and Stevenson, L. A. (2005). *Entrepreneurship Policy. Theory and Practice. International Studies in Entrepreneurship*. New York: Springer.

Martinelli, A., Meyer, M. and von Tunzelmann, N. (2008). Becoming an entrepreneurial university? A case study of knowledge exchange relationships and faculty attitudes in a medium-sized, research-oriented university. *Journal of Technology Transfer*, **33**, 259–283.

Mautner, G. (2005). The entrepreneurial university: A discursive profile of a higher education buzzword. *Critical Discourse Studies*, **2** (2), 95–120.

Meyer, J. W. and Jepperson, R. L. (2000). The "actors" of modern society: The cultural construction of social agency. *Sociological Theory*, **18** (1), 100–120.

Mitchell, R. K., Agle, B. R. and Wood, D. J. (1997). Towards a theory of stakeholder identification and salience: Defining the principle of who and what really counts. *Academy of Management Review*, 22 (4), 853–886.

Neittaanmäki, P., Mononen, L. and Kinnunen, P. (2017). Innovaatiot ja yrittäjyys osana yliopisto-opintoja (Innovations and entrepreneurship as part of university studies). Available at: https://www.jyu.fi/it/tutkimus/infjulk36 (accessed 12 November 2020).

Niska, M. and Vesala, K. M. (2013). SME policy implementation as a relational challenge. *Entrepreneurship and Regional Development*, 25 (5–6), 521–540.

Nybom, T. (2008). University autonomy: A matter of political rhetoric? In L. Engwall and D. Weaire (eds.), *The University in the Market*. Wenner-Gren International Series, 84. Stockholm.

OECD (2012). A guiding framework for entrepreneurial universities. Available at: https://www.oecd.org/site/cfecpr/EC-OECD%20Entrepreneurial%20Universities %20Framework.pdf (accessed 12 November 2020).

Perkmann, M., Tartari, V., McKelvet, M., Autio, E., Broström, A., D'Este, P., Fini, R., Geuna, A., Grimaldi, R., Hughes, A., Krabel, S., Kitson, M., Llerena, P., Lissoni, F., Salter, A. and Sobrero, M. (2013). Academic engagement and commercialisation: A review of the literature on university–industry relations. *Research Policy*, 42, 423–442.

Perren, L. and Jennings, P. L. (2005). Government discourses on entrepreneurship: Issues of legitimization, subjugation, and power. *Entrepreneurship Theory and Practice*, 29 (2), 173–184.

Philpott, K., Dooley, L., O'Reilly, C. and Lupton, G. (2011). The entrepreneurial university: Examining underlying academic tensions. *Technovation*, 31, 161–170.

Potter, J. (1996). *Representing Reality. Discourse, Rhetoric and Social Construction.* London: Sage.

Potter, J. and Wetherell, M. (1987). *Discourse and Social Psychology. Beyond Attitudes and Behaviour.* London: Sage.

Redford, D. T. and Fayolle, A. (2014). Stakeholder management and the entrepreneurial university. In A. Fayolle and D. T. Redford (eds.), *Handbook on the Entrepreneurial University*. Cheltenham, UK and Northampton, MA, USA: Edward Elgar Publishing.

Reynolds, J., Wetherell, M. and Taylor, S. (2007). Choice and chance: Negotiating agency in narratives of singleness. *The Sociological Review*, 55 (2), 331–351.

Rinne, R. (2019). Suomalaisen yliopiston tila: Rahan, vallankäytön ja hallinnan uudet muodot. In H. Nori, H. Laalo and R. Rinne (eds.), *Kohti oppimisyhteiskuntaa – Koulutuspolitiikan uusi suunta ja korkeakoulutuksen muuttuva maisema*. Turun yliopiston kasvatustieteiden tiedekunnan julkaisuja A:217. Turun yliopisto.

Ross, S. A. (1973). The economic theory of agency: The principal's problem. *The American Economic Review*, 63 (2), 134–139.

Shapiro, S. (2005). Agency theory. *Annual Review of Sociology*, 31, 263–284.

Shore, C. and McLauchlan, L. (2012). "Third mission" activities, commercialization and academic entrepreneurs. *Social Anthropology*, 20 (3), 267–286.

Siegel, D. S. and Wright, M. (2015). Academic entrepreneurship: Time for a Rethink? *British Journal of Management*, 26, 582–595.

Siitonen, J. (2016). "Synnytetään semmonen pöhinäpaikka". Unpublished master's thesis, University of Helsinki, Finland.

Sørensen, B. M. (2008). "Behold, I am making all things new": The entrepreneur as savior in the age of creativity. *Scandinavian Journal of Management*, **24**, 85–93.

Ylijoki, O. H. (2003). Entangled in academic capitalism? A case-study on changing ideas and practices of university research. *Higher Education*, **45**, 307–335.

7 Entrepreneurial university business models: core drivers, challenges and consequences

James A. Cunningham and Kristel Miller

Introduction

The knowledge-based economy has resulted in fundamental drivers for change within universities impacting both their mission and activities (Audretsch, 2014; Hayter et al., 2018; Marzocchi et al., 2019). Traditionally, universities' mission was predominantly to teach and to conduct research (Hayter et al., 2018). However, intense national and international competition for students and faculty, a changing income base and increased need for universities to demonstrate their impact within the societies where they reside, have required universities to become more entrepreneurial in order to ensure their long-term sustainability (Guerrero et al., 2014). This has resulted in a 'third mission', which emphasises the important role of knowledge transfer from universities as a source of innovation (Audretsch et al., 2015; Etzkowitz, 2002; Fayolle and Redford, 2014; Mascarenhas et al., 2017). Universities are now expected to contribute directly to the economic development of regions (Guerrero et al., 2016). This third mission has given rise to the advent of 'entrepreneurial universities' (Clark, 1998; 2004). An entrepreneurial university is one that performs 'entrepreneurial' activities such as licences, collaborative research with private firms and spinoffs, and engages in different knowledge transfer activities that have an impact on society (Siegel et al., 2007; Guerrero et al., 2016; Kalar and Antoncic, 2015) and acts as a catalyst for academic entrepreneurship (Shane, 2004).

To be 'entrepreneurial' requires not only the transformation of the core value activities of a traditional university but also greater engagement with external

103

stakeholders such as industry, government and wider society (Mascarenhas et al., 2017; Clauss et al., 2018). Indeed, research has highlighted the economic impact that entrepreneurial universities have beyond their own institutional boundaries (see Guerrero et al., 2015; Guerrero et al., 2016; Howlett, 2010). Within an entrepreneurial university the focus is not only on new knowledge production but on knowledge dissemination, which has an impact on wider society (Goddard and Vallance, 2013). Therefore, engaging more in 'entrepreneurial' activities requires changes to the core dominant logic of the university. The dominant logic of an organisation reflects the norms of how they operate (Roessler et al., 2019). Universities' traditional dominant logic is to provide high quality education, the creation of new knowledge and scientific advancement. However, the 'third mission' of universities puts emphasis on the commercialisation of knowledge. Whilst these activities can be and should be complementary, scarce resources and capabilities require trade-off decisions to be made regarding what mission and activities universities prioritise. Many universities want to maintain their core traditional mission and need to ensure they can react to changes in their external environment (Passaro et al., 2017). However, universities are limited by the path dependency of their structures, practices and identity concepts (Krucken, 2003). Consequently, scholars and policy makers alike have become increasingly interested in how universities' business models can react to the external drivers for change and become more entrepreneurial. Teece (2010) identifies that a business model 'describes the design or architecture of the value creation, delivery, and capture mechanisms it employs'. All organisations, either explicitly or implicitly, employ a business model, where a business model is designed to help an organisation realise its overall strategy (Casadesus-Masanell and Ricart, 2010). Yet research and understanding of university business models is limited (McAdam et al., 2017).

Organisations need to innovate and change their business model in response to changes in their environment (Demil and Lecocq, 2010; Schneider and Spieth, 2013). Therefore changes to the core mission of universities requires changes to their respective business model to reflect new value creating and capture activities (Miller et al., 2014; McAdam et al., 2017). However, there is a lack of understanding of how to design entrepreneurial university business models (Etzkowitz et al., 2019) and the challenges and consequences that being more entrepreneurial may have for universities (Cunningham et al., 2017a). This chapter aims to arrive at a research agenda focused on furthering theory and practice on the development of entrepreneurial university business models.

Literature review

Understanding and designing the entrepreneurial university business model

There has been increased interest in the entrepreneurial university business model as a mechanism for value creation and economic growth within regions (Guerrero et al., 2016; McAdam et al., 2017; Miller et al., 2018a). Despite research and policy stressing the need for university business models to become more entrepreneurial (e.g. see Audretsch et al., 2015; Etzkowitz, 2002; Fayolle and Redford, 2014; Mascarenhas et al., 2017), the concept of the entrepreneurial university business model is often discussed theoretically and superficially with a lack of understanding of its defining design features and complexity (Foss and Saebi, 2017; Clauss et al., 2018). The business model of the entrepreneurial university is usually described through discussion of the drivers for change discussed in the next section. However, only a few studies have empirically attempted to understand the components and design of the entrepreneurial university business model.

Research by Miller et al. (2014) was the first empirical study to attempt to understand the core changes required to the design of university business models to transition to become entrepreneurial. They draw upon Amit and Zott (2001) to view the university business model as comprising of (1) business model content, comprising the daily activities performed, (2) business model structure, comprising the ways in which activities are linked and (3) business model governance, which identifies the actors involved with each activity. They suggest that the entrepreneurial business model can be mapped out in relation to the change in activities, structures and external stakeholders (see Table 7.1 where the extension to the traditional business model is in italics). Miller et al. (2014) suggest that to be entrepreneurial, a university needs to open up its business model. The design of the entrepreneurial business model is negotiated with both internal and external stakeholders. Furthermore, power relationships between internal and external stakeholders can limit the ability of universities to be entrepreneurial. Whilst their research helps to map the activities involved, they do not explore how different types of universities may negotiate different types of business model designs or the challenges that universities encounter in implementing more entrepreneurial business models.

Research by McAdam et al. (2017) builds on work by Miller et al. (2014) to suggest that the transition to an entrepreneurial business model can take years for a university to achieve. The authors' research on how two universities of different types made changes to the design of their business model over time

Table 7.1 Activity-based view of the university business model

Activity-based view	Traditional university business model	Entrepreneurial university business model
Content	Teaching, research, knowledge dissemination, providing a skilled workforce	Teaching, research, knowledge dissemination, providing a skilled workforce, *entrepreneurship education, internationalisation, university-industry collaboration, developing intellectual property, spin outs, licences, new venture creation*
Structure (how activities are linked)	Academic registry, admissions, research office, schools for specific faculties	Academic registry, admissions, research office, departments for specific faculties, *TTOs, research and impact centers, international offices, business development staff, technology transfer procedures/ mechanisms, incubators, science parks*
Governance (who performs the activities)	University (academics, administrative staff, strategic staff members) government, industry	University (academics/*principal investigators, TTO staff, industry liaison staff,* administrative staff, strategic staff members); government (*regional development agencies, national government*), industry

Source: Adapted from Miller et al. (2014).

suggests that universities need to have a clear strategy regarding how their entrepreneurial activities will complement and align with their core traditional mission, otherwise this will result in a hybrid business model design. A hybrid business model design emerges when an organisation has competing dominant logics (Furr, 2016). McAdam et al. (2017) stress that university stakeholders need to agree upon which missions and activities they wish to prioritise and ensure alignment across all departments and faculties, otherwise this can lead to both temporary and permanent business model disequilibrium (Demil and Lecocq, 2010; Pache and Santos, 2010). Business model disequilibrium occurs when there are multiple and conflicting stakeholder objectives that compete for legitimacy and scarce resources. Pache and Santos (2010) highlight that disequilibrium can be permanent or temporary and is the result of hybridity in the business model. Hybrid business model designs are not always negative if strategically managed. However, universities are bureaucratic organisations bound by path dependency, making it difficult for them to change their business model. Consequently, McAdam et al. (2017) found that universities seeking to transition to become an entrepreneurial university often encounter a transient period where they inadvertently operate hybrid business models in an attempt to balance their traditional and entrepreneurial missions. This then leads to conflicting objectives between stakeholders where individuals compete for legitimacy and scarce resources. Whilst their research provides interesting insights, it was focused only on the technology transfer remit of universities and did not consider the interdependency between the different remits of a university.

Gaus and Raith (2016) appear to be the only study to date that attempts to understand the holistic design of a university business model. They demonstrate how the processes of value creation, delivery and capture have changed across the varying remits with the emergence of entrepreneurial university business models based on Osterwalder and Pigneur's (2010) business model canvas. The different remits of teaching, research and technology transfer are separate models of value creation within the overarching university business model. They also map out the different designs of university business models of different types showing that public and private universities need different incentives and governance structures to stimulate more entrepreneurial activities. Their research identifies the different components of an entrepreneurial university business model; however, they do not empirically explore the challenges of aligning the different value propositions across a university.

From the literature, it is evident that the design of the university business model can be viewed in different ways. The first is to view a university as one business model with different value propositions or alternatively to focus on the individual value creation activities, i.e. either teaching, research or technology transfer (third remit) as being separate business models. The ambiguity in understanding how the entrepreneurial business model is conceptualised and designed gives rise to its complexity and adds to the challenges universities face in developing more entrepreneurial business models.

More research is needed on understanding the design of entrepreneurial university business models and the intrinsic factors that influence their design. To help this, the core drivers for change will now be delineated in order to understand the challenges and consequences these may have for entrepreneurial university business models.

Core drivers, challenges, consequences and implications for university business models

A vast amount of literature has emerged over the past decade on entrepreneurial universities (see Etzkowitz 2002; Philpott et al., 2011; Guerrero and Urbano, 2012; Audretsch, 2014; Centobelli et al., 2019). There are systematic and fundamental drivers for change that are influencing the nature of the academia as well as how universities are organised, managed and led. These drivers are influencing all the activities of universities, from the programmes on offer, to the research that is being undertaken, and to levels of engagement that individual faculty members have with business and society. Through a review of the most pertinent literature, five core drivers that have significant challenges and consequences for universities business models have been identified (see Table 7.2), which forms the basis for opportunities for future research. Reacting to these drivers and challenges has consequences for the strategic direction of universities and consequently on the design of their business models.

Driver 1 – changing income and funding model

Challenge: Research conceptualises the entrepreneurial business model through their discussion of the changing income and funding model (Lapovsky, 2018). This research identifies that universities are starting to behave like businesses due to experiencing changes in their income base as public investment in supporting their activities is declining (Buchbinder and Newson, 1988; Geuna, 1998; Rolfe, 2003; Gaus and Raith, 2016). It is feared that entrepreneurial income-seeking activities will come at the expense of dedicating resources at furthering pure science (Philpott et al., 2011). Furthermore, rising costs of providing education along with increasing competition both nationally and internationally has meant that universities have had to examine other sources of income. In essence they have to diversify, protect and grow their income stream.

Consequence: Universities have sought to implement a range of initiatives that enables them to survive and thrive. This has meant for example changes in organisation structures (Guerrero et al., 2016), increased internationalisation of student cohorts (Minola et al., 2016), an expansion of engagement with industry to support research activities (Perkmann et al., 2013; Fan et al., 2019), creation of university foundations and the reconfiguration of programme offerings, developing new academic departments and changing the roles and responsibilities of academic staff (Geuna, 1998; Hedgepeth, 2000; Knight, 2013; Warwick, 2014).

Universities have become leaner organisations with the outsourcing of non-core activities such as IT (Allen et al., 2002), reduction in administrative support to support the university community and an increasing investment in systems and interfaces that are user self-service centric (Gupta et al., 2005; Russell, 2010). This has also led to more financially orientated planning within universities to ensure that they have the financial resources to invest in activities that enhance their competitive position (Pilbeam, 2012). Diversifying the entrepreneurial university income and funding model is essential for survival and meeting current and anticipated demands from the various stakeholders (see Estermann and Pruvot, 2011). Universities have invested in setting up and growing technology and knowledge transfer offices and putting in place policies and procedures to support faculty and industry engagement (see Baglieri et al., 2018; Fitzgerald and Cunningham, 2016; Sideri and Panagopolos, 2018). This has led to the development of university-based or supported research centres/institutes, incubators, accelerators and science parks (see Phan et al., 2005; Link and Scott, 2017; Stayton and Mangematin, 2019; Dolan et al., 2019).

Implications for the university business model: Universities need to extend their range of value creation activities, make changes to their revenue model, seek operational efficiencies and include additional stakeholders in both the governance and operational levels of their business models. They also need to ensure effective management of any hybrid business models and mitigate against any business model disequilibrium.

Driver 2 – corporatism and managerialism

Challenge: Universities are primarily organised around disciplines and departments. Traditionally, such units held significant decision making autonomy over their own activities and future direction. However, what has changed significantly is how these departments and faculties are managed and led (Musselin, 2013; Parker, 2011; White et al., 2011). Universities have centralised decision making, which has lessened the automony of units and individual faculty members with respect to their activities and future directions (Martin, 2016; Salancik and Pfeffer, 1974; Jarzabkowski, 2002).

Consequence: Restructuring of universities and departments to maintain overall university performance and competitiveness has resulted in a growing managerialism within universities (see Deem, 2001; Kolsaker, 2008; Lawrence and Sharma, 2002). In some universities there has been a retrenchment of mission and activities. Some universities have closed or merged disciplines and moved to a more centralised approach to annual planning (Gates 1997; Parker, 2011). Deans and heads of departments are not only responsible for managing academic affairs but also for planning and delivering activities as set out in annual operational and financial plans across teaching, research and knowledge engagement (Davis et al., 2016) including delivery of technology and knowledge transfer performance targets (see Newson, 1994). Overall, these structural changes have created additional tensions in aligning overarching university missions to the strategic ambition and operational plans at local levels within academic units. These tensions have consequences for individual faculty members in terms of their priorities, resources, rewards and incentives (see Mangematin et al., 2014). Therefore, there is a need for universities to develop talent management systems and career paths for academics and administrators. A further consequence is the development of new mechanisms to allocate activities, resources and workloads within faculties to ensure delivery of activities against annual operational plans (see Philpott et al., 2011; Winter and O'Donohue, 2012). Universities are increasingly using performance management systems to manage all staff and align this to operational planning within faculties/departments (see Taylor and Baines, 2012). However, simultaneously, universities are more becoming more centralised regarding decision making relating to core functions, thereby reducing the actual decision making autonomy of deans, heads of department and individual faculty members.

Implications for the university business model: This driver is leading to the need for interdependency across value creation activities in different disciplines. This requires new structures and organisational units, such as technology transfer offices, to align value creation activities within a more entrepreneurial business model. Furthermore, a focus on maximising efficiency requires university-wide systems to manage teaching, research and finances.

Driver 3 – competition

Challenge: Depending on national government policy and the regulatory environment within national markets, there is increasing and often intense competition among universities for students, research funding and faculty (see Brankovic, 2018; Frank and Gowar, 2019; Grewal et al., 2008).

Consequence: Universities increase their societal visibility through marketing campaigns aimed at students and their parents/guardians. Competition has also forced universities to articulate the unique or distinctive aspects of their university (see Maringe, 2006). Therefore, universities use different ranking systems to affirm their competitive position and distinctiveness (Hazelkorn, 2007; Johnes, 2018; Rindova et al., 2018). The changing financial model of universities means that they are now competing internationally. International student fee income is becoming an important income stream (Cantwell, 2019). To succeed in international markets, the distinctiveness of a university needs to pervade many nationalities and countries, and be credible and evidenced. National and international university rankings systems are used by universities as evidence of their standing, eminence and performance (Fowles et al., 2016; Elken et al., 2016). To compete internationally, some universities have established campuses off-shore (e.g. Escriva-Beltran et al., 2019; Smith, 2009; Healey, 2020), while others have entered different strategic alliances typically centred on academic programmes (Clarke and Hermens, 2001; Saffu and Mamman, 1999). Moreover, universities are not only competing for students but are also seeking to develop closer relationships with businesses and sectors that are important to local, regional and national environments (see Stevens and Bagby, 2001; Howlett, 2010). This has led to the creation of new units and the recruitment of professional staff to support technology and knowledge transfer between universities and business.

Implications for the university business model: Universities need to redefine their value propositions for diverse stakeholders and these need to be evidenced by impact and be communicated more widely outside and within the university environment. This also means the need for new structures and organisational units, where a more entrepreneurial business model should be designed around more effective international and industry engagement and co-value creation with an expanded set of stakeholders.

Driver 4 – economic imperative

Challenge: Increasingly, policy makers are viewing universities and their academic staff as key actors in economic development and contributing to economic growth (Cunningham et al., 2017b). The economic imperative centres on knowledge transfer, skill development and employability. Research has demonstrated the economic impact that entrepreneurial universities can have on all missions (Carroll and Smith, 2006; Guerrero et al., 2016; Siegfried et al., 2007).

Consequences: Globally, universities are expanding their mission to what is termed third mission activities – which encompasses both knowledge transfer and commercialisation activities such as spin-outs, spin-ins, licences, incubation, business plan competitions, etc. (Benneworth et al., 2015; Pinheiro et al., 2015). Universities have put in place policies and incentives to encourage the university community to pursue such activities (Bruneel et al., 2010; Cunningham and Harney, 2006; Cunningham et al., 2020; Dooley and Kirk, 2007; Siegel et al., 2003). For example, universities are supporting initiatives designed to support student start-up by sponsoring and encouraging participation in business plan start-up competitions (Watson and McGowan, 2017; Watson et al., 2018) and providing student incubation space and support (Culkin, 2013).

To enhance skills development, universities are aligning programme content and learning objectives with the skills required by industry (Baker and Henson, 2010). Industry needs employment-ready graduates to have the knowledge, skills and capacity to contribute effectively to their operations and performance from the first date of employment. Consequently, this is influencing programme and module content, placement opportunities, patterns of delivery and assessment approaches within degree programmes (see Crebert et al., 2004). National and international placement opportunities are offered across undergraduate and postgraduate programmes to support the employability of their student cohorts (Crebert et al., 2004; Rezaei Zadeh et al., 2017). Within modules there is an increasing emphasis on skills development that is transferable to a work environment. Moreover, there is a growth of entrepreneurship, management and business modules across university faculties to further support knowledge acquisition, skills development and employability of students (Garavan and O'Cinneide, 1994; Nabi et al., 2017). In addition, some universities are launching niche degree programmes at undergraduate and postgraduate levels that blend business with other discipline areas. There are even instances of whole degrees where students become entrepreneurs, set up their own business and get a degree (Blackwood et al., 2015). In addition, universities have initiated and or are part of incubator and new venture creation programmes where participants can validate their business ideas, write business plans, and set up and launch their ventures (see Bennett et al., 2017; Gately and Cunningham, 2017; Munari et al., 2017; Piterou and Birch, 2016).

Implications for the university business model: Universities need to balance social and civic impact with economic value and returns. Therefore, value propositions need to be impact-centred and there needs to be a greater focus on activities, which generates impact. This requires new value-creation activities and new internal organisational structures and units to support more entrepreneurial activities.

Driver 5 – academic work and human capital development

Challenge: The nature and demands of academic work have changed significantly (see Cannizzo and Osbaldiston, 2016; Cunningham et al., 2019; Leišytė, 2016) as well as the expectations required from academic staff (Cunningham et al., 2016a and 2016b; O'Kane et al., 2020). These expectations focus on all aspects of the academic work role – i.e. teaching, researching and service contributions as well as making an impact outside the university to relevant stakeholders (Miller et al., 2018b). The nature of academic work is constantly changing, alongside the conditions of employment for academics (see Allen and Gupta, 2016; Kenny, 2017). International mobility of academic talent combined with intense demand for academic talent means that academics are becoming more discerning about choosing universities that will support their career aspirations and research ambitions (Cantwell, 2011).

Consequence: Universities are investing more resources in career development particularly for early career academics (Ackers and Gill, 2005). For example, universities are putting in place specific career paths and supports for early career academics so that they transition to a tenured academic track position. In tandem with this, universities are now more formally recognising engagement with industry and entrepreneurial activities as part of performance, promotional and rewards systems (O'Gorman et al., 2008; Link et al., 2017; Nicolaou and Souitaris, 2016). This has seen a growth in academic entrepreneurship within universities (Audretsch et al., 2015; Link et al., 2015) and has shaped different types of academic entrepreneurship, i.e. academic entrepreneurs and entrepreneurial academics (see Miller et al., 2018b). Moreover, universities are attempting to adopt a more entrepreneurial culture among faculty and students (Bienkowska et al., 2016; Guerrero et al., 2016; Laskovaia et al., 2017) and provide institutional entrepreneurial supports (see Dolan et al., 2019; Saeed et al., 2015; Soetanto and Jack, 2016; Meoli and Vismara, 2016).

Implications for the university business model: Universities need to meaningfully support human capital management, extend value-creation activities, invest in entrepreneurial education and support and engage with a wider range of stakeholders to ensure equity and diversity.

A research agenda

Universities globally are undergoing fundamental changes, driving new activities and changing the structure and governance mechanisms of universities. This chapter has identified five key drivers for change for universities to become more entrepreneurial. However, how universities are able to effectively respond to the identified challenges and consequences presents a research agenda. There is a paucity of research that specifically addresses entrepreneurial university business models despite both researchers and policy makers' acknowledgement of the need for change. Therefore, adopting a business model lens can help researchers to advance understanding of business models and entrepreneurial universities. To this end we suggest five main research avenues to pursue.

Table 7.2   Core drivers, challenges, consequences and implications for university business models

Core Drivers	Challenges	Consequences	Implications for the University Business Model
Changing income and funding model	• Public funding declining • Rising costs of education • Need to balance research, teaching and impact	• Balancing traditional and entrepreneurial activities for long-term sustainability • Strategic alignment across all activities • Intense and scaling of industry engagement and value co-creation • Multiple business models required	• Extend range of value creation activities • Changing revenue model • Scope and scale • Operational efficiencies • Additional stakeholders and governance
Corporatism and managerialism	• Fostering interdisciplinary activities • Enhancing institutional and individual performance management	• Over centralisation stifles creativity, entrepreneurship and innovation • Longer decision making • Multiple business models needed	• Interdependency across value creation activities in different disciplines • New structures and organisational units • Efficiency • Investment in organisation systems • Talent management development

Core Drivers	Challenges	Consequences	Implications for the University Business Model
Competition	• Development of new teaching models and programmes • Expand internationalisation to maintain sustainability • Deeper and wider collaborations with industry • Effective marketing strategies and brand positioning	• Recalibration of balance between domestic and international markets • Multiple business models needed	• Clear, defined value propositions focused on impact • Communicating the value activities of the university • New business models for internationalisation and industry engagement • Extending governance stakeholders to enhance value co-creation • New structures and organisational units

Core Drivers	Challenges	Consequences	Implications for the University Business Model
Economic imperatives	• Contribute to economic development and growth • Foster entrepreneurship in both staff and students • Increasing skills development and employability	• Extensive staff support for extended activities • Staff confusion on which activities to focus on and prioritise • Lack of strategic alignment across activities • Multiple business models needed	• Need to balance social and economic value • Extended range of value creation activities • Value propositions focused on impact • Entrepreneurial education for staff and students to aid entrepreneurship and innovation • New structures • New business models for economic value
Academic work and human capital development	• Extended remit • Global demands for academic talent • Need for entrepreneurship support and skills • Gender disparity	• Performance mechanisms which give recognition to entrepreneurial and traditional activities • Entrepreneurial culture • Entrepreneurial supports • Different business models require different types of academics (entrepreneurial academics and academic entrepreneurs)	• Extended range of value creation activities • Entrepreneurial education • Need to engage with a wider range of stakeholders

Design of the entrepreneurial university business model

A lot remains unknown about the different business model designs that entrepreneurial universities use to maintain their long-term sustainability in light of changing funding mechanisms, increasing societal challenges such as climate change and to mitigate shocks in the external environment (such as Covid-19 and political shocks like Brexit). This involves the need to explore different contexts where universities adopt singular, multiple and hybrid models. This will extend the work of Miller et al. (2014), McAdam et al. (2017) and Gaus and Raith (2016) through unravelling the nature, scope, purpose, multitude, interconnectivity and alignment of different types of entrepreneurial university business models. This is important because universities increasingly need to address competing missions – both economic and societal – as they seek to secure their long-term sustainability and societal relevance. Some key research questions include: How are the tensions between economic and societal-orientated business models managed? How are the boundaries between business models delineated and what organisational mechanisms, organising principles and process are used to support and mediate internal competition or enhance complementarities? Do separate but interdependent business models help limit the chances of business model hybridity, aid resources allocation and improve strategic alignment across their extended range of value-creating activities within an entrepreneurial university?

Future studies should also examine how universities design entrepreneurial business models that are responsive to the changing external environments and internal pressures through the deployment of a variety of resource-allocation models. However, in designing new business models that attempt to balance competing interests, a strand of research needs to focus on what impact multiple business models have on the autonomy of individual academics. This may explore to what extent they change the institutional support structures and how they influence teaching, research and academics' mission activities. Research is also needed on the implications of changes to the business model design in relation to gender, equality and diversity.

Moreover, it is unclear how business models are developed and implemented within an entrepreneurial university. What processes and artifacts are used and who and/or what units drive business model creation? To develop a more entrepreneurial business model, existing organisational structures need to be aligned to such business models to support implementation and consistent execution. Research is needed to understand if entrepreneurial universities create new organisational units, or take a centralised and decentralised approach in the management of business models. At a micro level, we still have limited knowledge of how entrepreneurial universities attempt to balance individual unit autonomy and responsiveness while maintaining overall institutional coherency with respect to institutional purpose. Moreover, research is needed on how the design of the entrepreneurial university business model may have implications for performance, particularly with respect to culture, structures, processes and their engagement within the local region, national context and internationally.

Antecedent factors and the operationalisation of university business models

There is a need for further research on how entrepreneurial university business models operationalise different income and funding models, which enable a university to support economic and societal-orientated missions. In particular, micro level comparative studies would enable in-depth exploration of factors that influence the actual design of entrepreneurial university business models. In exploring this agenda, research questions that could be pursued include: Who designs entrepreneurial universities' business models and what institutional and structural barriers do they face in their design and implementation? Does the adaption of business model thinking and approaches radically change income and funding models, managerialism and how university employees are nurtured, developed and supported? How can university business models balance and mediate economic imperatives against societal and civic responsibilities? What antecedent factors prevent business model disequilibrium within university business models?

Stakeholder engagement and types of entrepreneurial university business models

Universities through formal and informal mechanisms at individual and at institutional level are constantly engaging with stakeholders from industry, government and society through their three missions. Moreover, such stakeholders are placing greater demands on universities to respond to their agendas, such as the decarbonisation of industry, reducing waste, etc. A lot remains unknown on what types of entrepreneurial university business models enhance and expand stakeholder engagement both internally and externally to address societal grand challenges as well as individual stakeholder interests. Appropriate design of an entrepreneurial university business model offers the potential to engage with stakeholders in a more dynamic, collaborative and sustainable manner, resulting in shared value creation. Some future research questions should focus on how entrepreneurial universities use different types of business models to engage with stakeholders. What complexities arise from embedding diverse stakeholders into different processes? Does developing processes for external stakeholders' engagement change the business models of entrepreneurial universities? Research is needed on the evolution and transformation of business models to further understand the types of entrepreneurial university business models that support long-term stakeholder engagement. Research is also needed on how universities overcome tensions associated with economic and social goals of external stakeholders. How do entrepreneurial universities define, create and capture value for stakeholders? Finally, research should explore how adaptive entrepreneurial universities become as a result of using a business model approach.

Business modeling to meet economic, social and policy demands

There is a need to explore how entrepreneurial universities' business models can become more flexible to respond to a variety of economic and social public policy demands. Entrepreneurial universities need to be discerning with respect to what demands they need to address, and to allocate appropriate resources. Some of these demands are outside the mission and scope or there is no discernable value for the university. They also need to decide what economic, social and policy demands not to respond to that would potentially create business model disequilibrium. Key questions include: How can entrepreneurial university business models be designed to make them better able to adapt to short-term public policy demands and pressures placed by national, regional and local policy makers and institutional political structures? To what extent do the demands placed on entrepreneurial universities influence stakeholder engagement, university and department level dominant logics? How do entrepreneurial universities use business modeling to anticipate and respond to economic, social and policy demands? What are the process and structures that support the alignment of business models meeting these demands with entrepreneurial university resource allocation and decision-making processes?

Entrepreneurial university business models to support academic work

The entrepreneurial university business model has implications for the nature of academic work. This will involve taking a micro level perspective to explore key research questions such as: How can academic staff develop the skills and capabilities to deliver upon and balance value creation and capture activities across the range of remits? For example, do academics have the necessary skills to engage with industry and society? If not, how can they develop these skills? How do entrepreneurial university business models shape the measurement of value capture and value logics of academic work? What challenges do academics face in engaging in a wider set of activities, which may expand disciplines and involve a wider set of stakeholders? How can academics manage these demands and what implications will this have for entrepreneurial university business model creation? Do the changing entrepreneurial university business models demand different types of academics such as practice-orientated academics versus traditional academics? What challenges would more practice-orientated academics face in embedding themselves into university institutional systems? How will reward and promotional systems change to reflect an extended range of activities within a more entrepreneurial business model?

Conclusion

Universities play an important role in the evolution of economies and societies. In times of national and international crisis such as Covid-19 and Brexit, universities remain the anchors within regions, where their human capital and infrastructure are used to address immediate societal and economic pressures. Scientific communities through national and international research collaborations are addressing grand societal challenges and new educational offerings are developed by universities to respond to specific industry needs and broader societal demands. Consequently, universities need to become more entrepreneurial due to evolving external pressures.

University communities have the human capital capabilities to instigate, contribute and lead complex industry and societal problems and challenges. Over many centuries universities have been adept at evolving while holding onto their core values and purpose, which sets them apart from other institutions. Using a business model lens provides researchers with opportunities to unearth how universities are evolving to embrace the entrepreneurial university agenda serving the economic as well as the broader societal and common good agendas. Expanding and deepening the research agenda on entrepreneurial university business models will open up new empirical and theoretical avenues, but can also provide much needed evidence-based practical and policy insights. The overall intention of our contribution is to provide some research directionality to this emergent research agenda.

References

Ackers, L. and Gill, B. (2005) Attracting and retaining 'early career' researchers in English higher education institutions. *Innovation*, **18** (3), 277–299.

Allen, D., Kern, T. and Mattison, D. (2002) Culture, power and politics in ICT outsourcing in higher education institutions. *European Journal of Information Systems*, **11** (2), 159–173.

Allen, R. and Gupta, S. (2016) 'Academic Leadership' and the Conditions of Academic Work. In *Academic Labour, Unemployment and Global Higher Education* (pp. 81–102). Palgrave Macmillan UK.

Amit, R. and Zott, C. (2001) Value creation in e-business. *Strategic Management Journal*, **22**, 493–520.

Audretsch, D.B. (2014) From the entrepreneurial university to the university of the entrepreneurial society. *The Journal of Technology Transfer*, **39** (3), 313–321.

Audretsch, D.B., Lehmann, E.E. and Paleai, S. (2015) Academic policy and entrepreneurship: A European perspective. *The Journal of Technology Transfer*, **40** (3), 363–368.

Baker, G. and Henson, D. (2010) Promoting employability skills development in a research-intensive university. *Education + Training*, **52** (1), 62–75.

Baglieri, D., Baldi, F. and Tucci, C.L. (2018) University technology transfer office business models: One size does not fit all. *Technovation*, **76**, 51–63.

Bennett, D., Yábar, D.P.B. and Saura, J.R. (2017) University Incubators may be Socially Valuable, but How Effective are They? A Case Study on Business Incubators at Universities. In *Entrepreneurial Universities* (pp. 165–177). Springer International Publishing.

Benneworth, P., de Boer, H. and Jongbloed, B. (2015) Between good intentions and urgent stakeholder pressures: Institutionalizing the universities' third mission in the Swedish context. *European Journal of Higher Education*, **5** (3), 280–296.

Bienkowska, D., Klofsten, M. and Rasmussen, E. (2016) PhD students in the entrepreneurial university-perceived support for academic entrepreneurship. *European Journal of Education*, **51** (1), 56–72.

Blackwood, T., Round, A., Pugalis, L. and Hatt, L. (2015) Making sense of learning: Insights from an experientially-based undergraduate entrepreneurship programme. *Industry and Higher Education*, **29** (6), 445–457.

Brankovic, J. (2018) The status games they play: Unpacking the dynamics of organisational status competition in higher education. *Higher Education*, **75** (4), 695–709.

Bruneel, J., d'Este, P. and Salter, A. (2010) Investigating the factors that diminish the barriers to university–industry collaboration. *Research Policy*, **39** (7), 858–868.

Buchbinder, H. and Newson, J. (1988) Corporate-university linkages in Canada: Transforming a public institution. *Higher Education*, **20** (4), 355–379.

Cannizzo, F. and Osbaldiston, N. (2016) Academic work/life balance: A brief quantitative analysis of the Australian experience. *Journal of Sociology*, **52** (4), 890–906.

Cantwell, B. (2011) Transnational mobility and international academic employment: Gatekeeping in an academic competition arena. *Minerva*, **49** (4), 425–445.

Cantwell, B. (2019) Are international students cash cows? Examining the relationship between new international undergraduate enrolments and institutional revenue at public colleges and universities in the US. *Journal of International Students*, **5** (12), 512–525.

Carroll, M.C. and Smith, B.W. (2006) Estimating the economic impact of universities: The case of Bowling Green State University. *The Industrial Geographer*, **3** (2), 1.

Casadesus-Masanell, R. and Ricart, J.E. (2010) From strategy to business models and onto tactics. *Long Range Planning*, **43** (2–3), 195–215.

Centobelli, P., Cerchione, R., Esposito, E. and Shashi (2019) Exploration and exploitation in the development of more entrepreneurial universities: A twisted learning path model of ambidexterity. *Technological Forecasting and Social Change*, **141**, 172–194.

Clark, B.R. (1998) *Creating Entrepreneurial Universities: Organizational Pathways of Transformation. Issues in Higher Education*. Pergamon.

Clark, B.R. (2004). Delineating the character of the entrepreneurial university. *Higher Education Policy*, **17** (4), 355–370.

Clarke, T. and Hermens, A. (2001) Corporate developments and strategic alliances in e-learning. *Education + Training*, **43** (4/5), 256–267.

Clauss, T. (2017) Measuring business model innovation: Conceptualization, scale development, and proof of performance. *R&D Management*, **47** (3), 385–403.

Clauss, T., Moussa, A. and Kesting, T. (2018) Entrepreneurial university: A stakeholder-based conceptualization of the current state and an agenda for future research. *International Journal of Technology Management*, **77** (1–3), 109–144.

Crebert, G., Bates, M., Bell, B., Patrick C.J. and Cragnolini, V. (2004) Developing generic skills at university, during work placement and in employment: Graduates' perceptions. *Higher Education Research & Development*, **23** (2), 147–165.

Culkin, N. (2013) Beyond being a student: An exploration of student and graduate start-ups (SGSUs) operating from university incubators. *Journal of Small Business and Enterprise Development*, **20** (3), 634–649.

Cunningham, J. and Harney, B. (2006) *Strategic Management of Technology Transfer, the New Challenge on Campus*. Oak Tree Press: Cork.

Cunningham, J.A., Guerrero, M. and Urbano, D. (2017a) Entrepreneurial Universities – Overview, Reflections, and Future Research Agendas. In *Entrepreneurial Universities Technology and Knowledge Transfer, The World Scientific Reference on Entrepreneurship: Volume 1* (pp. 3–19). World Scientific Press.

Cunningham, J.A., Menter, M. and Wirsching, K. (2019) Entrepreneurial ecosystem governance: A principal investigator-centered governance framework. *Small Business Economics*, **52** (2), 545–562.

Cunningham, J.A., Mangematin, V., O'Kane, C. and O'Reilly, P. (2016a) At the frontiers of scientific advancement: The factors that influence scientists to become or choose to become publicly funded principal investigators. *The Journal of Technology Transfer*, **41** (4), 778–797.

Cunningham, J.A., O'Reilly, P., O'Kane, P. and Mangematin, V. (2016b) Publicly Funded Principal Investigators as Transformative Agents of Public Sector Entrepreneurship. In *Essays in Public Sector Entrepreneurship* (pp. 67–94). Springer International Publishing.

Cunningham, J.A., O'Reilly, P., Dolan, B., O'Kane, C. and Mangematin, V. (2017b) Entrepreneurship: A Study of Scientists in the Principal Investigator Role. In *Gender and Entrepreneurial Activity* (pp. 221–251). Cheltenham, UK and Northampton, MA, USA: Edward Elgar Publishing.

Cunningham, J.A., O'Reilly, P., Hooper, D., Nepelski, D. and Van Roy, V. (2020) *The Role of Project Coordinators in European Commission Framework Programme Projects*. Results of the Innovation Radar PC Survey in FP R&I Projects (No. JRC120015). Joint Research Centre (Seville site).

Davis, A., Jansen van Rensburg, M. and Venter, P. (2016) The impact of managerialism on the strategy work of university middle managers. *Studies in Higher Education*, **41** (8), 1480–1494.

Deem, R. (2001) Globalisation, new managerialism, academic capitalism and entrepreneurialism in universities: Is the local dimension still important? *Comparative Education*, **37** (1), 7–20.

Demil, B. and Lecocq, X. (2010) Business model evolution: In search of dynamic consistency. *Long Range Planning*, **43**, 227–246.

Dolan, B., Cunningham, J.A., Menter, M. and McGregor, C. (2019) The role and function of cooperative research centers in entrepreneurial universities. *Management Decision*, **57** (12), 3406–3425.

Dooley, L. and Kirk, D. (2007). University-industry collaboration: Grafting the entrepreneurial paradigm onto academic structures. *European Journal of Innovation Management*, **10** (3), 316–332.

Elken, M., Hovdhaugen, E. and Stensaker, B. (2016) Global rankings in the Nordic region: Challenging the identity of research-intensive universities? *Higher Education*, **72** (6), 781–795.

Escriva-Beltran, M., Muñoz-de-Prat, J. and Villó, C. (2019) Insights into international branch campuses: Mapping trends through a systematic review. *Journal of Business Research*, **101**, 507–515.

Estermann, T. and Pruvot, E.B. (2011) *European Universities' Diversifying Income Streams*. European University Association.

Etzkowitz, H. (2002) Incubation of incubators: Innovation as a triple helix of university-government relationships. *Science and Public Policy*, **29** (2), 115–128.

Etzkowitz, H., Germain-Alamartine, E., Keel, J., Kumar, C., Smith, K.N. and Albats, E. (2019) Entrepreneurial university dynamics: Structured ambivalence, relative deprivation and institution-formation in the Stanford innovation system. *Technological Forecasting and Social Change*, **141** (C), 159–171.

Fan, H.-L., Huang, M.-H. and Chen, D.-Z. (2019) Do funding sources matter? The impact of university-industry collaboration funding sources on innovation performance of universities. *Technology Analysis and Strategic Management*, **31** (11), 1368–1380.

Fayolle, A. and Redford, D.T. (2014) *Handbook on the Entrepreneurial University*. Cheltenham, UK and Northampton, MA, USA: Edward Elgar Publishing.

Fitzgerald, C. and Cunningham, J.A. (2016) Inside the university technology transfer office: Mission statement analysis. *The Journal of Technology Transfer*, **41** (5), 1235–1246.

Foss, N.J. and Saebi, T. (2017) Fifteen years of research on business model innovation: How far have we come, and where should we go? *Journal of Management*, **43** (1), 200–227.

Fowles, J., Frederickson, H.G. and Koppell, J.G. (2016) University rankings: Evidence and a conceptual framework. *Public Administration Review*, **76** (5), 790–803.

Frank, J. and Gowar, N. (2019) *English Universities in Crisis: Markets without Competition*. Policy Press.

Furr, N. (2016) Hybrid business models look ugly but they work. *Harvard Business Review*, March, 30.

Garavan, T.N. and O'Cinneide, B. (1994) Entrepreneurship education and training programmes: A review and evaluation – Part 1. *Journal of European Industrial Training*, **18** (8), 3–12.

Gately, C. and Cunningham, J. (2017) Technology entrepreneurs; Relational capital; New venture formation; Start-ups; Social context; Networks; Relationship building; Leveraging knowledge experts. *Journal of Intellectual Capital*, **15** (4), 516–536.

Gates, G.S. (1997) Isomorphism, homogeneity, and rationalism in university retrenchment. *The Review of Higher Education*, **20** (3), 253–275.

Gaus, O. and Raith, M.G. (2016) Commercial transfer: A business model innovation of the entrepreneurial university. *Industry and Higher Education*, **30**, 103–201.

Geuna, A. (1998) The internationalisation of European universities: A return to medieval roots. *Minerva*, **36** (3), 253–270.

Goddard, J. and Vallance, P. (2013) *The University and the City*. Routledge.

Grewal, R., Dearden, J.A. and Lilien, G.L. (2008) The university rankings game: Modeling the competition among universities for ranking. *The American Statistician*, **62** (3), 232–237.

Guerrero, M. and Urbano, D. (2012) The development of the entrepreneurial university. *The Journal of Technology Transfer*, **37** (1), 43–74.

Guerrero, M., Cunningham, J.A. and Urbano, D. (2015) Economic impact of entrepreneurial universities' activities: An exploratory study of the United Kingdom. *Research Policy*, **44** (3), 748–764.

Guerrero, M., Urbano, D. and Cunningham, J. (2014) Entrepreneurial universities in two European regions: A case study comparison. *The Journal of Technology Transfer*, **39** (3), 415–434.

Guerrero, M., Urbano, D., Fayolle, A., Klofsten, M. and Mian, S. (2016) Entrepreneurial universities: Emerging models in the new social and economic landscape. *Small Business Economics*, **47** (3), 551–563.

Gupta, A., Kanthi Herath, S. and Mikouiza, N.C. (2005) Outsourcing in higher education: An empirical examination. *International Journal of Educational Management*, **19** (5), 396–412.

Hayter, C.S., Nelson, A.J., Zayed, S. and O'Connor, A.C. (2018) Conceptualising academic entrepreneurship ecosystems: A review, analysis and extension of the literature. *The Journal of Technology Transfer*, **43** (4), 1039–1082.

Hazelkorn, E. (2007) The impact of league tables and ranking systems on higher education decision making. *Higher Education Management and Policy*, **19** (2), 1–24.

Healey, N.M. (2020) The end of transnational education? The view from the UK. *Perspectives: Policy and Practice in Higher Education*, **24** (3), 102–112.

Hedgepeth, R.C. (2000) *How Public College and University Foundations Pay for Fund-Raising*. Association of Governing Boards of Universities and Colleges.

Howlett, R.J. (2010) Knowledge Transfer between UK Universities and Business. In *Innovation through Knowledge Transfer* (pp. 1–14). Springer.

Jarzabkowski, P. (2002) Centralised or decentralised? Strategic implications of resource allocation models. *Higher Education Quarterly*, **56** (1), 5–32.

Johnes, J. (2018) University rankings: What do they really show? *Scientometrics*, **115** (1), 585–606.

Kalar, B. and Antoncic, B. (2015) The entrepreneurial university, academic activities and technology and knowledge transfer in four European countries. *Technovation*, **36**, 1–11.

Kenny, J. (2017) Academic work and performativity. *Higher Education*, **74** (5), 897–913.

Knight, J. (2013) The changing landscape of higher education internationalisation – For better or worse? *Perspectives: Policy and Practice in Higher Education*, **17** (3), 84–90.

Kolsaker, A. (2008) Academic professionalism in the managerialist era: A study of English universities. *Studies in Higher Education*, **33** (5), 513–525.

Krucken, G. (2003) Learning the 'new, new thing'. On the role of path dependency in university structures. *Higher Education*, **46** (3), 315–339.

Lapovsky, L. (2018) The changing business model for colleges and universities. *Forbes*, 6 February.

Laskovaia, A., Shirokova, G. and Morris, M.H. (2017). National culture, effectuation, and new venture performance: Global evidence from student entrepreneurs. *Small Business Economics*, **49** (3), 687–709.

Lawrence, S. and Sharma, U. (2002) Commodification of education and academic labour – Using the balanced scorecard in a university setting. *Critical Perspectives on Accounting*, **13** (5–6), 661–677.

Leišytė, L. (2016) New public management and research productivity – A precarious state of affairs of academic work in the Netherlands. *Studies in Higher Education*, **41** (5), 828–846.

Link, A.N. and Scott, J.T. (2017) US University Research Parks. In *Universities and the Entrepreneurial Ecosystem*. Cheltenham, UK and Northampton, MA, USA: Edward Elgar Publishing.

Link, A.N., Siegel, D.S. and Bozeman, B. (2017) An empirical analysis of the propensity of academics to engage in formal university technology transfer. In *Universities and the Entrepreneurial Ecosystem*. Cheltenham, UK and Northampton, MA, USA: Edward Elgar Publishing.

Link, A.N., Siegel, D.S. and Wright, M. (Eds.) (2015) *The Chicago Handbook of University Technology Transfer and Academic Entrepreneurship*. University of Chicago Press.

Mangematin, V., O'Reilly, P. and Cunningham, J. (2014) PIs as boundary spanners, science and market shapers. *The Journal of Technology Transfer*, **39** (1), 1–10.

Maringe, F. (2006) University and course choice: Implications for positioning, recruitment and marketing. *International Journal of Educational Management*, **20** (6), 466–479.

Martin, B.R. (2016) What's happening to our universities? *Prometheus*, **34** (1), 7–24.

Marzocchi, C., Kitagawa, F. and Sánchez-Barrioluengo, M. (2019) Evolving missions and university entrepreneurship: Academic spin-offs and graduate start-ups in the entrepreneurial society. *Journal of Technology Transfer*, **44** (1), 167–188.

Mascarenhas, C., Marques, C., Galvão, A. and Santos, G. (2017) Entrepreneurial university: Towards a better understanding of past trends and future directions. *Journal of Enterprising Communities: People and Places in the Global Economy*, **11** (3), 316–338.

McAdam, M., Miller, K. and McAdam, R. (2017) University business models in equilibrium – Engaging industry and end users within university technology transfer processes. *R&D Management*, **47** (3), 458–472.

Meoli, M. and Vismara, S. (2016) University support and the creation of technology and non-technology academic spin-offs. *Small Business Economics*, **47** (2), 345–362.

Miller, K., McAdam, M. and McAdam, R. (2014) The changing university business model: A stakeholder perspective. *R&D Management*, **44**, 265–287.

Miller, K., McAdam, R. and McAdam, M. (2018a) A systematic literature review of university technology transfer from a quadruple helix perspective: Toward a research agenda. *R&D Management*, **48** (1), 7–24.

Miller, K., Alexander, A., Cunningham, J.A. and Albats, E. (2018b) Entrepreneurial academics and academic entrepreneurs: A systematic literature review. *International Journal of Technology Management*, **77** (1–3), 9–37.

Minola, T., Donina, D. and Meoli, M. (2016) Students climbing the entrepreneurial ladder: Does university internationalisation pay off? *Small Business Economics,* **47** (3), 565–587.

Munari, F., Sobrero, M. and Toschi, L. (2017) Financing technology transfer: Assessment of university-oriented proof-of-concept programmes. *Technology Analysis and Strategic Management,* **29** (2), 233–246.

Musselin, C. (2013) How peer review empowers the academic profession and university managers: Changes in relationships between the state, universities and the professoriate. *Research Policy,* **42** (5), 1165–1173.

Nabi, G., Liñán, F., Fayolle, A., Krueger, N., and Walmsley, A. (2017) The impact of entrepreneurship education in higher education: A systematic review and research agenda. *Academy of Management Learning and Education,* **16** (2), 277–299.

Newson, J.A. (1994) Subordinating democracy: The effects of fiscal retrenchment and university-business partnerships on knowledge creation and knowledge dissemination in universities. *Higher Education,* **27** (2), 141–161.

Nicolaou, N. and Souitaris, V. (2016) Can perceived support for entrepreneurship keep great faculty in the face of spinouts? *Journal of Product Innovation Management,* **33** (3), 298–319.

O'Gorman, C., Byrne, O. and Pandya, D. (2008) How scientists commercialise new knowledge via entrepreneurship. *The Journal of Technology Transfer,* **33** (1), 23–43.

O'Kane, C., Mangematin, V., Zhang, J.A. and Cunningham, J.A. (2020) How university-based principal investigators shape a hybrid role identity. *Technological Forecasting and Social Change,* **159**, 120–179.

Osterwalder, A. and Pigneur, Y. (2010) *Business Model Generation: A Handbook for Visionaries, Game Changers and Challengers.* Wiley.

Pache, A.C. and Santos, F. (2010) When worlds collide: The internal dynamics of organizational responses to conflicting institutional demands. *Academy of Management Review,* **35**, 455–476.

Parker, L. (2011) University corporatisation: Driving redefinition. *Critical Perspectives on Accounting,* **22** (4), 434–450.

Passaro, R., Quinto, I. and Thomas, A. (2017) The impact of higher education on entrepreneurial intention and human capital. *Journal of Intellectual Capital,* **19** (1), 135–156.

Perkmann, M., Tartari, V., McKelvey, M., Autio, E., Brostrom, A., D'Este, P., Fini, R., Geuna, A., Grimaldi, R., Hughes, A., Krabel, S., Kitson, M., Llerena, P., Lissoni, F., Salter, A. and Sobrero, M. (2013) Academic engagement and commercialisation: A review of the literature on university industry relations. *Research Policy,* **42** (2), 423–442.

Phan, P.H., Siegel, D.S. and Wright, M. (2005) Science parks and incubators: Observations, synthesis and future research. *Journal of Business Venturing,* **20** (2), 165–182.

Philpott, K., Dooley, L., O'Reilly, C. and Lupton, G. (2011) The entrepreneurial university: Examining the underlying academic tensions. *Technovation,* **31** (4), 161–170.

Pilbeam, C. (2012) Pursuing financial stability: A resource dependence perspective on interactions between pro-vice chancellors in a network of universities. *Studies in Higher Education,* **37** (4), 415–429.

Pinheiro, R., Langa, P.V. and Pausits, A. (2015) The institutionalization of universities' third mission: Introduction to the special issue. *European Journal of Higher Education,* **5** (3), 227–232.

Piterou, A. and Birch, C. (2016) The role of higher education institutions in supporting innovation in SMEs: University-based incubators and student internships as knowledge transfer tools. *Impact: The Journal of Innovation Impact*, 7 (1), 72.

Rezaei Zadeh, M., Hogan, M., O'Reilly, C., Cunningham, J. and Murphy, E. (2017) Core entrepreneurial competencies and their interdependencies: Insights from a study of Irish and Iranian entrepreneurs, university students and academics. *International Entrepreneurship and Management Journal*, 13 (1), 35–73.

Rindova, V.P., Martins, L.L., Srinivas, S.B. and Chandler, D. (2018) The good, the bad, and the ugly of organizational rankings: A multidisciplinary review of the literature and directions for future research. *Journal of Management*, 44 (6), 2175–2208.

Roessler, M., Schneckenberg, D. and Velamuri, V. (2019) Situated entrepreneurial cognition in corporate incubators and accelerators: The business model as a boundary object. *IEEE Transactions in Engineering Management*, doi: 10.1109/TEM.2019.2955505.

Rolfe, H. (2003) University strategy in an age of uncertainty: The effect of higher education funding on old and new universities. *Higher Education Quarterly*, 57 (1), 24–47.

Russell, A. (2010) *Outsourcing Instruction: Issues for Public Colleges and Universities. Policy Matters: A Higher Education Policy Brief*. American Association of State Colleges and Universities.

Saeed, S., Yousafzai, S.Y., Yani-De-Soriano, M. and Muffatto, M. (2015) The role of perceived university support in the formation of students' entrepreneurial intention. *Journal of Small Business Management*, 53 (4), 1127–1145.

Saffu, K. and Mamman, A. (1999) Mechanics, problems and contributions of tertiary strategic alliances: The case of 22 Australian universities. *International Journal of Educational Management*, 13 (6), 281–286.

Salancik, G.R. and Pfeffer, J. (1974). The bases and use of power in organizational decision making: The case of a university. *Administrative Science Quarterly*, 453–473.

Schneider, S. and Spieth, P. (2013) Business model innovation: Towards an integrated future research agenda. *International Journal of Innovation Management*, 17, 1–34.

Shane, S. (2004). *Academic Entrepreneurship: University Spinoffs and Wealth Creation*. Cheltenham, UK and Northampton, MA, USA: Edward Elgar Publishing.

Sideri, K. and Panagopoulos, A. (2018) Setting up a technology commercialization office at a non-entrepreneurial university: An insider's look at practices and culture. *The Journal of Technology Transfer*, 43 (4), 953–965.

Siegel, D.S., Wright, M. and Lockett, A. (2007) The rise of entrepreneurial activity at universities: Organizational and societal implications. *Industrial and Corporate Change*, 16 (4), 489–504.

Siegel, D.S., Waldman, D.A., Atwater, L.E. and Link, A.N. (2003) Commercial knowledge transfers from universities to firms: Improving the effectiveness of university–industry collaboration. *The Journal of High Technology Management Research*, 14 (1), 111–133.

Siegfried, J.J., Sanderson, A.R. and McHenry, P. (2007) The economic impact of colleges and universities. *Economics of Education Review*, 26 (5), 546–558.

Smith, L. (2009) Sinking in the sand? Academic work in an offshore campus of an Australian university. *Higher Education Research and Development*, 28 (5), 467–479.

Soetanto, D. and Jack, S. (2016). The impact of university-based incubation support on the innovation strategy of academic spin-offs. *Technovation*, 50, 25–40.

Stayton, J. and Mangematin, V. (2019) Seed accelerators and the speed of new venture creation. *The Journal of Technology Transfer*, 44 (4), 1163–1187.

Stevens, J.M. and Bagby, J.W. (2001) Knowledge transfer from universities to business: Returns for all stakeholders? *Organization*, **8** (2), 259–268.

Taylor, J. and Baines, C. (2012) Performance management in UK universities: Implementing the balanced scorecard. *Journal of Higher Education Policy and Management*, **34** (2), 111–124.

Teece, D.J. (2010) Business models, business strategy and innovation. *Long Range Planning*, **43**, 172–194.

Warwick, P. (2014) The international business of higher education – A managerial perspective on the internationalisation of UK universities. *The International Journal of Management Education*, **12** (2), 91–103.

Watson, K. and McGowan, P. (2017) Technology Nascent Entrepreneur Experiences of Start-up Competition Participation. In *Technology-Based Nascent Entrepreneurship* (pp. 279–308). Palgrave Macmillan.

Watson, K., McGowan, P. and Cunningham, J.A. (2018) An exploration of the business plan competition as a methodology for effective nascent entrepreneurial learning. *International Journal of Entrepreneurial Behavior and Research*, **24** (1), 121–146.

White, K., Carvalho, T. and Riordan, S. (2011) Gender, power and managerialism in universities. *Journal of Higher Education Policy and Management*, **33** (2), 179–188.

Winter, R.P. and O'Donohue, W. (2012) Academic identity tensions in the public university: Which values really matter? *Journal of Higher Education Policy and Management*, **34** (6), 565–573.

8 Calling for student engagement in an entrepreneurial university

Katja Lahikainen, Kati Peltonen, Lenita Hietanen and Elena Oikkonen

Introduction

Universities desire to become entrepreneurial (Rae et al., 2009). This change in mentality can be traced back to the early 1980s when universities started to create stronger links with industry and take a more active role in regional development (Mascarenhas et al., 2017). As a result, the vision and mission of entrepreneurial universities has become a broadly researched topic (e.g. Urbano and Guerrero, 2013; Rubens et al., 2017). In recent years, the stakeholder approach to entrepreneurial universities has raised more interest among entrepreneurship scholars; as a result, students have begun to be recognized as an important internal stakeholder group within an entrepreneurial university (Clauss et al., 2018; Redford and Fayolle, 2014). This reflects the adaptation of the wider perspective of the entrepreneurial university, which emphasizes the development of an entrepreneurial culture at all levels of the university (Urbano and Guerrero, 2013).

Subsequently, discussions on universities as entrepreneurial ecosystems have emerged (Hayter, 2016). In successful entrepreneurial university ecosystems, all stakeholders should be involved in entrepreneurial activities (Greene et al., 2010). Hence, all members should be invited to develop the community (Greene et al., 2010; O'Brien et al., 2019). However, research conducted among university actors tends to focus on the university management or academic staff's point of view (Guerrero and Urbano, 2012), while the student perspective remains neglected. As the literature review conducted by Clauss et al. (2018) reveals, only six out of 108 papers published between 1900 and

2015 addressed students as stakeholders in entrepreneurial universities. This is a somewhat perplexing result considering that one of the key dimensions of the entrepreneurial university is to create an environment that encourages and supports the development of entrepreneurial behaviour and mindsets of students and university staff (Guerrero and Urbano, 2012; Hannon, 2013). One reason for this may be that students are not necessarily seen as equal stakeholders in community development (Clauss et al., 2018).

Acknowledging that students are an important, but often neglected, stakeholder group in entrepreneurial universities, there is a need to strengthen discussions and research on the role of students and to explore how this approach has been studied in the existing research on entrepreneurial universities. Further, as Guerrero and Urbano (2012, 55) underline, an entrepreneurial university should be seen as 'an instrument that not only provides a workforce and value added with the creation or transformation of knowledge but also improves the individual's values and attitudes towards these issues'. Nonetheless, there seems to be a lack of research focusing on student engagement in extra-curricular activities that would allow students' voices to be heard in the university community (Trowler, 2010). This calls for us to address the knowledge gap that exists in understanding students' engagement in entrepreneurial universities. Therefore, this chapter participates in this discussion and applies a critical approach to the predominant administration-centred approach that has focused more on the technology transfer discussion (Mascarenhas et al., 2017). In this chapter, we address the following questions: Why should student engagement in entrepreneurial universities be studied? How can student engagement in entrepreneurial universities be studied? This chapter first introduces entrepreneurial university as a research topic and conceptual construct. Drawing from higher education research, the following section addresses different viewpoints on student engagement. Finally, the chapter ends with a research agenda for the future.

Entrepreneurial universities as a research topic

Universities

An entrepreneurial university is a multifaceted concept and it can be studied from different perspectives. Furthermore, it is important to clarify what we mean when talking about entrepreneurial universities. The different conceptualizations reflect the emergent nature of entrepreneurial universities. According to Hannon (2013), an entrepreneurial university is an agile organization adapting its actions, due to new challenges and under pressure, in order to find new solutions to address the demands presented by unpredictable and uncertain environments. Etzkowitz (2013) states that entrepreneurial universities evolve through three different phases, starting from (1) setting their own strategic priorities and seeking and negotiating funding accordingly; (2) commercializing the intellectual property and establishing their own technology transfer capabilities; and further (3) taking a proactive role in regional development. Furthermore, entrepreneurial universities are shifting from the narrow elitist view of entrepreneurship education focusing on start-ups and moving towards universities that provide entrepreneurship education that is relevant for everybody and that acknowledges a broader range of entrepreneurial behaviour and entrepreneurial activities (O'Brien et al., 2019).

Occasionally, the definition of an entrepreneurial university arises from the university's third mission (Wissema, 2009; Etzkowitz, 2016), where the university's core missions of teaching and research are crucial, and the third mission, societal interaction, is tackled as an all-embracing concept and solution for a majority of societal challenges, competitiveness problems and unemployment (Lahikainen et al., 2018; Rubens et al., 2017). Moreover, the concept of academic entrepreneurship is used as a partial synonym for entrepreneurial universities, where commercialization, spin-offs, patenting and licensing are all embraced (Bronstein and Reihlen, 2014; Grimaldi et al., 2011). According to the systematic literature review by Mascarenhas et al. (2017), research on entrepreneurial universities is strongly associated with academic entrepreneurship and the creation of technology-based companies. This is not surprising, because entrepreneurial universities are seen as an answer to the need for economic growth by transferring knowledge and to fulfilling the needs for increasing global academic competition (Wissema, 2009).

As can be seen above, the emphasis on studies concerning entrepreneurial universities has been on technology-transfer and commercialization-related activities. However, in this chapter we take a broader view and build our approach on a holistic perspective of entrepreneurial universities. That is, in addition to the aforementioned aspects, in a holistic view entrepreneurship and an entrepreneurial approach are embedded in all the activities of the higher education institution (HEI), starting from the strategy and followed by appreciating an entrepreneurial mindset in the students and faculty members (Lahikainen et al., 2018; 2019; Greene et al., 2010). In this chapter, we focus on the student perspective, and especially on student engagement in entrepreneurial universities.

Students in entrepreneurial universities

As highlighted in the previous chapter, entrepreneurial university research is strongly focused on academic entrepreneurship and the creation of technology-based companies (Mascarenhas et al., 2017). The few studies that include a student perspective mainly explore the involvement of students in the venture creation process of university-based spin-offs (Boh et al., 2016; Hayter et al., 2017; Jansen et al., 2015; Lundqvist and Williams Middleton, 2013). Further, in those studies, the students seem to play only an indirect role in the technology transfer and development of university-based spin-offs (Boh et al., 2016; Rasmussen and Wright, 2015). Additionally, universities' entrepreneurship initiatives, such as entrepreneurship programmes and curricula, have been separate for the students and faculty (Huang-Saad et al., 2017).

Students are recognized as a potential resource that could be stimulated in order to get them involved more systematically in the commercialization actions of university-based inventions (Jansen et al., 2015). Although students are recognized as a potential resource, the current studies tend to take a commercialization approach towards entrepreneurial universities. According to the study by Åstebro et al. (2012), university graduates establish more start-ups than faculty members, and consequently graduate students could play a similar role as individual faculty member entrepreneurs in university-based spin-offs. The development and success of student-led spin-offs are, however, closely linked to the availability of and connections to relevant contacts and their resources in the surrounding ecosystem. Furthermore, support mechanisms and programmes, as well as networks, can be unknown to graduate students (Hayter et al., 2017). This means that, in addition to offering new study programmes that foster student entrepreneurship, smooth information flows between all stakeholders are essential to the functioning of entrepreneurial universities and in their ecosystems (Ferreira et al., 2018).

However, some studies apply a broader perspective, by considering the involvement of students in commercialization of technology within a university entrepreneurial ecosystem (Levie, 2014), different types of entrepreneurship education programmes (Culkin and Mallick, 2011; Rasmussen and Sørheim, 2006; Ribeiro et al., 2018) or venture creation programmes combining entrepreneurship education and technology transfer (Lackéus and Williams Middleton, 2015). Siegel and Wright (2015) called for a wider perspective on academic entrepreneurship that would involve more stakeholders, including students. Some studies that have applied student perspectives have investigated the university's support for academic entrepreneurship from the PhD students' points of view (Bienkowska et al., 2016) and the influence of research and teaching activities on graduate start-ups (Marzocchi et al., 2019). Based on a survey conducted among all PhD students in a Swedish university, Bienkowska et al. (2016) suggest that PhD students should especially be put in a central position when attempting to create a more entrepreneurial university, since they are more receptive to communication about the commercialization of results than senior academics. Further, the studies based on the Global University Entrepreneurial Spirit Students' Survey (GUESSS) investigating the university's influence on student entrepreneurship and student involvement, highlight the importance of cross-disciplinary learning opportunities and social networking among students (e.g. Bergmann et al., 2016; Morris et al., 2017)

Taking into consideration the social context of student entrepreneurship, it is important to enhance the social networking opportunities of students in the university community by integrating different programmes and activities, as well as enhancing the inter-relationships between different actors (Boh et al., 2016; Morris et al., 2017). This means that universities should offer programmes and practices for cross-disciplinary teams, such as training and education for faculty members and students (Bergmann et al., 2016), as well as informal opportunities such as mentoring programmes, business accelerators/ incubation programmes and business plan competitions (Boh et al., 2016; Wright et al., 2017). Universities should also involve students in venture creation with scientists through action-based education (Lundqvist and Williams Middleton, 2013). Additionally, student-led entrepreneurial clubs or societies can act as vehicles for engaging students in an entrepreneurial community and can offer them extra-curricular learning opportunities (Pittaway et al., 2015). These clubs and societies can also increase the interaction between students and the stakeholders of a surrounding entrepreneurial ecosystem and enhance the proactive formulation of an entrepreneurship agenda for mutual benefit and synergy (Björklund and Krueger, 2016).

As can be seen, the current literature is strongly built on commercialization and technology-transfer processes of universities, with the assumption that if students are involved, they have an indirect role in entrepreneurial processes, e.g. through thesis and projects related to university spin-offs (Rasmussen and Wright, 2015). Furthermore, if students are not aware of alternative positions available for them, the students may see themselves more like customers of the university (Niemi and Tuijula, 2011). If so, their involvement and engagement in the university community may be a challenge. Therefore, we combine views from entrepreneurial university literature and student engagement literature. Thus, the next section outlines the existing research on student engagement focusing on helping students achieve positions in which they are seen as an equal stakeholder group in an entrepreneurial university. It is important that students can interact with other students, staff and other stakeholders in ways that allow their voices to be heard.

Student engagement

Viewpoints on student engagement

The modern student engagement literature has its historic roots in higher education studies (e.g. Astin, 1984) concerned with student involvement and it has received increasing academic attention since the mid-1990s (Trowler, 2010). Student engagement is a fuzzy concept with multiple meanings depending on the context (Vuori, 2014) and object of engagement (Ashwin and McVitty, 2015). Fredricks and McColskey (2012) defined engagement as a multidimensional construct, including behavioural, emotional and cognitive dimensions. Behavioural engagement includes extra-curricular and other social activities, for example. The emotional dimension relates to the sense of belonging and the connectedness to the educational institution, while the cognitive dimension refers to students' investments in their learning (Fredricks et al., 2004; Fredricks and McColskey, 2012).

Student engagement does not take place in isolation, and therefore it cannot be separated from its environment (Fredricks and McColskey, 2012). According to Trowler (2010), student engagement is the responsibility of both students and their institutions. Coates (2005, 26) emphasized that 'Learning is seen as a "joint proposition" […], which also depends on the institutions and staff providing students with conditions, opportunities and expectations to become involved. However, individual learners are ultimately the agents in discussions of engagement […]'. Consequently, recent discussion on student engagement has focused more on finding different ways in which educational institutions are fostering student engagement (Budd, 2005; Hockings et al., 2007; Mandernach, 2015; Masika and Jones, 2016) and involving students in shaping the learning societies of which they are a part (Vuori, 2014; Ashwin and McVitty, 2015). Pike and Kuh (2005) captured a social view of student engagement as part of the concept of institutional engagement. This means that when intellectually stimulated, students are engaged in a variety of academic activities. Additionally, by being interpersonally supportive, students may have many contacts with faculty members inside and outside the lessons (Pike and Kuh, 2005). Hockings et al. (2007) and Koro-Ljungberg (2007) point out that the teacher's role in engaging students in their studies and environment is important by emphasizing each student's rights and allowing different students' voices to be equally heard. This supports involving the teaching staff as informants in studies focusing on student engagement in entrepreneurial universities. Furthermore, Kuh (2009) and Magolda (2005) point out that students may engage themselves in extra-curricular activities and impact the university community by participating in different committees or groups, as an example. Referring to Lizzio and Wilson (2009) the students should be functionally involved in decision making processes at the university level to benefit the university.

As can be seen above, student engagement is a widely used concept in educational research and student engagement is seen as one of the key ingredients in developing learning communities in higher education (Ashwin and McVitty, 2015). This developmental characteristic, as Ashwin and McVitty (2015) further explain, means that student engagement entails the aspect of change. Yet, student engagement, involving the idea of student agency in learning communities, has not received much attention in entrepreneurial university research. Thus, in the following we link the student engagement perspective with discussion on entrepreneurial universities.

The need for student engagement in entrepreneurial universities

According to the stakeholder approach (Clauss et al., 2018), students are considered not only as 'consumers' of higher education, but significant actors in entrepreneurial universities and in wider entrepreneurial ecosystems. Seeing students as one of the core stakeholder groups within an entrepreneurial university also calls us to look for the different ways that students are engaged with entrepreneurial university structures and activities (Clauss et al., 2018). Drawing on higher education research, student engagement means much more than simple participation in courses and extra-curricular activities, as it also incorporates feelings and sense-making as well as activity (Trowler, 2010). According to Planas et al. (2013, 578), one of the main reasons for low participation is that students perceive the university as an institution that is 'not their own' and one that they are only 'passing through'.

Increasing student engagement in entrepreneurial universities requires supportive initiatives from different hierarchical levels within the university. For example, the study by Bienkowska et al. (2016) on PhD students indicated that implementing policies on the university governance level is not enough, but that perceived support coming from the faculty level is also needed. Similarly, a study by Kahu (2013) emphasizes that relationships with staff and feelings of being part of a learning community have a positive influence on student engagement.

Furthermore, student engagement and participation in the university and wider entrepreneurial ecosystems require resources and flexibility from the university management in order to legitimize the internal initiatives at the university. For this reason, it could be likely that such programmes would be implemented without formal connections to study programmes (Rasmussen and Sørheim, 2006). Moreover, universities aiming at developing student entrepreneurship need to interconnect the 'traditional' model based on the commercialization of research with a 'student-based' entrepreneurship model and develop them in parallel, as well as implement internal changes to increase cooperation within the university and focus more on behavioural transformation than on venture creation (Matt and Schaeffer, 2018).

Research agenda for the future

Why to study student engagement?

We chose students' engagement as a key concept for our methodology. We see students as an important, but neglected, stakeholder group in entrepreneurial universities. Studying student engagement in entrepreneurial universities is a complex theme, which calls for pertinent methodological choices. Thus, in this chapter, drawing from student engagement research combined with a holistic entrepreneurial university approach, we outline new potential topics and methodological approaches to study student engagement. The existing research on students tends to focus on the involvement of students in technology transfer and the commercialization actions of the university, thus limiting the positions available for students (Boh et al., 2016; Hayter et al., 2017; Jansen et al., 2015; Lundqvist and Williams Middleton, 2013). Venture creation programmes (Lackéus and Williams Middleton, 2015), action-based entrepreneurship education (Rasmussen and Sørheim, 2006) and student-led entrepreneurial clubs (Lahikainen et al., 2018; Pittaway et al., 2015) seem to be prominent ways to engage students in the university community. In the context of entrepreneurial universities, behavioural and emotional dimensions are interesting aspects to examine, since they offer lenses to investigate student engagement as a social construct, which can include various formal and informal activities (Fredricks et al., 2004; Fredricks and McColskey, 2012) and incorporate feelings and a sense of belonging (Trowler, 2010).

Instead of considering students merely as 'customers' passing through the university (Niemi and Tuijula, 2011; Planas et al., 2013), they need to be seen as significant actors (Clauss et al., 2018) and equal stakeholders in the university community, who should be engaged in developing the university community and actively involved in informal and formal activities and decision-making processes (Lizzio and Wilson, 2009; Pike and Kuh, 2005; Rasmussen and Sørheim, 2006). To increase the students' entrepreneurial engagement in formal university activities, more attention could be given, for example, to examining different ways in which lecturers' possibilities, abilities and resources to make students' voices heard could be increased. Furthermore, students' engagement could also be studied through an entrepreneurial lens by focusing on the students' ways to participate in their extra-curricular activities and student clubs. Conducting research, for example on these different student-led initiatives, through the lens of student engagement would contribute to the current literature on entrepreneurial university.

We set our focus on students; however, there might also be other interesting but, as of yet, understudied stakeholders in the entrepreneurial university ecosystem. Therefore, in the future, researching the involvement of other understudied stakeholder groups within and outside the university, such as political initiatives, competitor universities, and press, could generate more understanding of the topic, especially how they possibly impact students' experiences and their engagement with the university (Clauss et al., 2018).

How to study student engagement?

Owing to the multidimensional nature of student engagement, multiple ways of studying and assessing the focus, level and nature of engagement, capturing all dimensions, are needed. Student engagement can be assessed at both the institutional and course levels. Institutional-level assessment methods include student self-reports, experience sampling, interviews, observations and focused case studies (Fredricks and McColskey, 2012; Mandernach, 2015; Vuori, 2014), for example. When studying student engagement in their own environment, which in this case would be an entrepreneurial university, using behavioural and emotional approaches, self-reporting survey measures may be used, as these are the most common methods in student engagement studies; whereas, observation better suits behavioural engagement (Fredricks and McColskey, 2012). To study student engagement in the class or educational institution, it is possible to exploit experience sampling (ESM) or different interview techniques (Fredricks and McColskey, 2012). Narrative and descriptive techniques may be better suited than pre-specified coding categories for measuring the multidimensional construct of engagement (Fredricks and McColskey, 2012).

Methodologically, this means that a mixed-methods approach needs to be more rigorously applied. For future studies, we suggest using mixed methods based on large quantitative surveys on student engagement at the institutional level. The results of the quantitative study could be deepened by micro- or meso-level qualitative data, based on elements such as student self-reports or thematic interviews. Further, it would be very ambitious to create a longitudinal data-gathering setting, focusing on students' engagement and experiences of entrepreneurial universities. It would be captivating to analyze and compare the data gathered at the beginning of the studies, in the middle, at the end and some years after graduation.

Teachers' checklists or rating scales may also be useful methods for studying student engagement (Fredricks and McColskey, 2012). Observational methods are recommended in order to better discover variations in student engagement relating to affordances in contexts. However, as noticed in student engagement studies (Fredricks and McColskey, 2012), in entrepreneurial education-related studies (Blenker et al., 2014), and in business ecosystem studies (Järvi and Kortelainen, 2017), the obviously dynamic nature of student engagement in an entrepreneurial university would benefit from a wide range of methods, connecting both quantitative and qualitative approaches. As an example, Hockings et al. (2007) studied higher education students' academic engagement using questionnaires, focus groups, and finally to gain deeper insight into the students' lives, through interviews. To investigate the perceptions of business management students regarding their engagement in learning together, Masika and Jones (2016) utilized Wenger's (2009) social theory of learning, which advances a multi-dimensional view of learning, and this fits with a multi-faceted nature of engagement. Finally, as Lawson and Lawson (2013) suggest, more nuanced intervention research, interdisciplinary research design, and research conducted by teams are needed. Interestingly, similar findings on research methodology have been presented in the research field of entrepreneurship education. This is in line, for instance, with Fayolle's (2013) findings about a lack of variation in methodological approaches. In the same vein, Blenker et al. (2014) call for methodological triangulation to bring more depth and width into findings. They claim that research would benefit from combining the empirical sensitivity of qualitative techniques and the strict rigour of quantitative measuring.

Adopting a wider perspective of the entrepreneurial university requires that instead of concentrating only on one stakeholder group, more attention needs to be put on the linkage and interplay of the stakeholders. However, here we have deliberately focused on students' perspective as this stakeholder group has been understudied (Clauss et al., 2018). We consider this a limitation, and therefore challenge ourselves and other researchers to broaden the view to be more holistic. For example, the concepts and challenges of entrepreneurial universities, as well as the university's entrepreneurial ecosystem, entrepreneurship education and entrepreneurial learning, could all be studied at the same time.

References

Ashwin, P. and McVitty, D. (2015), 'The meanings of student engagement: Implications for policies and practices', in Adrian Curaj, Liviu Matei, Remus Pricopie, Jamil Salmi and Peter Scott (eds), *The European Higher Education Area*, Cham: Springer, pp. 343–359.

Åstebro, T., Bazzazian, N. and Braguinsky, S. (2012), 'Startups by recent university graduates and their faculty: Implications for university entrepreneurship policy', *Research Policy*, **41**, 663–667.

Astin, A.W. (1984), 'Student involvement: A development theory for higher education', *Journal of College Student Development*, **40**, 518–529.

Bergmann, H., Hundt, C. and Sternberg, R. (2016), 'What makes student entrepreneurs? On the relevance (and irrelevance) of the university and the regional context for student start-ups', *Small Business Economics*, **47** (1), 53–76.

Bienkowska, D., Klofsten, M. and Rasmussen, E. (2016), 'PhD Students in the entrepreneurial university: Perceived support for academic entrepreneurship', *European Journal of Education*, **51** (1), 56–72.

Björklund, T.A. and Krueger, N.F. (2016), 'Generating resources through co-evolution of entrepreneurs and ecosystems', *Journal of Enterprising Communities, People and Places in the Global Economy*, **10** (4), 477–498.

Blenker, P., Elmholdt, S.T., Frederiksen, S.H., Korsgaard, S. and Wagner, K. (2014), 'Methods in entrepreneurship education research: A review and integrative framework', *Education + Training*, **56** (8/9), 697–715.

Boh, W., De-Haan, U. and Strom, R. (2016), 'University technology transfer through entrepreneurship: Faculty and students in spinoffs', *The Journal of Technology Transfer*, **41** (4), 661–669.

Bronstein, J. and Reihlen, M. (2014), 'Entrepreneurial university archetypes: A meta-synthesis of case study literature', *Industry and Higher Education*, **28** (4), 245–262.

Budd, H. (2005), 'The value of student engagement for higher education quality assurance', *Quality in Higher Education*, **11** (1), 25–36.

Clauss, T., Moussa, A. and Kesting, T. (2018), 'Entrepreneurial University: A stakeholder-based conceptualisation of the current state and an agenda for future research', *International Journal of Technology Management*, **77** (1/2/3), 109–144.

Coates, H . (2005), 'The value of student engagement for higher education quality assurance', *Quality in Higher Education*, **11** (1), 25–36.

Culkin, N. and Mallick, S. (2011), 'Producing work-ready graduates: The role of the entrepreneurial university', *International Journal of Market Research*, **53** (3), 347–368.

Etzkowitz, H. (2013), 'Anatomy of the entrepreneurial university', *Social Science Information*, **52** (3), 486–511.

Etzkowitz, H. (2016), 'The entrepreneurial university: Vision and metrics', *Industry and Higher Education*, **30** (2), 83–97.

Fayolle, A. (2013), 'Personal views on the future of entrepreneurship education', *Entrepreneurship and Regional Development*, **25** (7–8), 692–701.

Ferreira, J.J., Fayolle, A., Ratten V. and Raposo M. (2018), 'Conclusion: Future suggestions for entrepreneurial universities', in João J. Ferreira, Alain Fayolle, Vanessa Ratten and Mário Raposo (eds), *Entrepreneurial Universities: Collaboration, Education and Policies*, Cheltenham, UK and Northampton, MA, USA: Edward Elgar Publishing, pp. 263–270.

Fredricks, J.A. and McColskey, W. (2012), 'The measurement of student engagement: A comparative analysis of various methods and student self-report instruments', in Sandra L. Christensen, Amy L. Reschly and Cathy Wylie (eds), *Handbook of Research on Student Engagement*, New York, USA: Springer.

Fredricks, J.A., Blumenfeld, P.C. and Paris, A.H. (2004), 'School engagement: Potential of the concept, state of the evidence', *Review of Educational Research*, **74**, 59–109.

Greene, P.G., Rice, M.P. and Fetters M.L. (2010), 'University-based entrepreneurship ecosystems: Framing the discussion', in Michael L. Fetters, Patricia G. Greene, Mark P. Rice and John S. Butler (eds), *The Development of University-Based Entrepreneurship Ecosystems: Global Practices*, Cheltenham, UK and Northampton MA, USA: Edward Elgar Publishing, pp. 1–11.

Grimaldi, R., Kenney, M., Siegel, D.S. and Wright, M. (2011), '30 years after Bayh–Dole: Reassessing academic entrepreneurship', *Research Policy*, **40** (8), 1045–1057.

Guerrero, M. and Urbano, D. (2012), 'The development of an entrepreneurial university', *The Journal of Technology Transfer*, **37** (1), 43–74.

Hannon, P. (2013), 'Why is the entrepreneurial university important?', *Journal of Innovation Management*, **1** (2), 10–17.

Hayter, C. (2016), 'A trajectory of early-stage spinoff success: The role of knowledge intermediaries within an entrepreneurial university ecosystem', *Small Business Economics*, **47** (3), 1–24.

Hayter, C., Lubynsky, R. and Maroulis, S. (2017), 'Who is the academic entrepreneur? The role of graduate students in the development of university spinoffs', *The Journal of Technology Transfer*, **42** (6), 1237–1254.

Hockings, C., Cooke, S. and Bowl, M. (2007), '"Academic engagement" within a widening participation context – A 3D analysis', *Teaching in Higher Education*, **12** (5–6), 721–733.

Huang-Saad, A., Fay, J. and Sheridan, L. (2017), 'Closing the divide: Accelerating technology commercialization by catalyzing the university entrepreneurial ecosystem with I-Corps™', *Journal of Technology Transfer*, **42**, 1466–1486.

Jansen, S., Van De Zande, T., Brinkkemper, S., Stam, E. and Varma, V. (2015), 'How education, stimulation, and incubation encourage student entrepreneurship: Observations from MIT, IIIT, and Utrecht University', *International Journal of Management Education*, **13** (2), 170–181.

Järvi, K. and Kortelainen, S. (2017), 'Taking stock of empirical research on business ecosystems: A literature review', *International Journal of Business and Systems Research*, **11** (3), 215–228.

Kahu, E.R. (2013), 'Framing student engagement in higher education', *Studies in Higher Education*, **38** (5), 758–773.

Koro-Ljungberg, M. (2007), '"Democracy to come": A personal narrative of pedagogical practices and "Othering" within a context of higher education and research training', *Teaching in Higher Education*, **12** (5–6), 735–747.

Kuh, G.D. (2009), 'What student affairs professionals need to know about student engagement', *Journal of College Student Development*, **50** (6), 683–706.

Lackéus, M. and Williams Middleton, K. (2015), 'Venture creation programs: Bridging entrepreneurship education and technology transfer', *Education + Training*, **57** (1), 48–73.

Lahikainen, K., Pihkala, T. and Ruskovaara, E. (2018), 'European approaches to enterprise education', in Jason J. Turner and Gary Mulholland (eds), *International Enterprise Education: Perspectives on Theory and Practice*, London, UK: Routledge, pp. 1–22.

Lahikainen K., Kolhinen, J., Ruskovaara, E. and Pihkala, T. (2019), 'Challenges to the development of an entrepreneurial university ecosystem: The case of a Finnish university campus', *Industry and Higher Education*, **33** (2), 96–107.

Lawson, M.A. and Lawson, Hal A. (2013), 'New conceptual frameworks for student engagement research, policy, and practice', *Review of Educational Research*, **83** (3), 432–479.

Levie, J. (2014), 'The university is the classroom: Teaching and learning technology commercialization at a technological university', *The Journal of Technology Transfer*, **39** (5), 793–808.

Lizzio, A. and Wilson, K. (2009), 'Student participation in university governance: The role of conceptions and sense of efficacy of student representatives on departmental committees', *Studies in Higher Education*, **34** (1), 69–84.

Lundqvist, T.M. and Williams Middleton, K. (2013), 'Academic entrepreneurship revisited – University scientists and venture creation', *Journal of Small Business and Enterprise Development*, **20** (3), 603–617.

Magolda, P. (2005), 'Promoting student success: What student leaders can do (Occasional paper No. 8)', National Survey of Student Engagement, Bloomington, Indiana: Indiana University Center for Postsecondary Research.

Mandernach, B.J. (2015), 'Assessment of student engagement in higher education: A synthesis of literature and assessment tools', *International Journal of Learning, Teaching and Educational Research*, **12** (2), 1–14.

Marzocchi, C., Kitagawa, F. and Sánchez-Barrioluengo, M. (2019), 'Evolving missions and university entrepreneurship: Academic spin-offs and graduate start-ups in the entrepreneurial society', *The Journal of Technology Transfer*, **44** (1), 167–188.

Mascarenhas, C., Marques, C.S., Galvão, A.R. and Santos, G. (2017), 'Entrepreneurial university: Towards a better understanding of past trends and future directions', *Journal of Enterprising Communities: People and Places in the Global Economy*, **11** (3), 316–338.

Masika, R. and Jones, J. (2016), 'Building student belonging and engagement: Insights into higher education students' experiences of participating and learning together', *Teaching in Higher Education*, **21** (2), 138–150.

Matt, M. and Schaeffer, V. (2018), 'Building entrepreneurial ecosystems conducive to student entrepreneurship: New challenges for universities', *Journal of Innovation Economics and Management*, **25** (1), 9–32.

Morris, M.H., Shirokova, G. and Tsukanova, T. (2017), 'Student entrepreneurship and the university ecosystem: A multi-country empirical exploration', *European Journal of International Management*, **11** (1), 65–85.

Niemi, M. and Tuijula, T. (2011), 'Sen tulee olla palveleva "yritys": Opiskelijoiden käsitykset yliopistosta oppimisympäristönä', *Kasvatus*, **42** (3), 210–221.

O'Brien, E., Cooney, T.M. and Blenker, P. (2019), 'Expanding university entrepreneurial ecosystems to under-represented communities', *Journal of Entrepreneurship and Public Policy*, DOI 10.1108/JEPP-03-2019-0025.

Pike, G.R. and Kuh, G.D. (2005), 'A typology of student engagement for American colleges and universities', *Research in Higher Education*, **46** (2), 429–454.

Pittaway, L.A., Gazzard, J., Shore, A. and Williamson, T. (2015), 'Student clubs: Experiences in entrepreneurial learning', *Entrepreneurship & Regional Development*, **27** (3–4), 127–153.

Planas, A., Soler, P., Fullana, J., Pallisera, M. and Vila, M. (2013), 'Student participation in university governance: The opinions of professors and students', *Studies in Higher Education*, **38** (4), 571–583.

Rae, D., Gee, S. and Moon, R. (2009), 'Creating an enterprise culture in a university: The role of an entrepreneurial learning team', *Industry and Higher Education*, **23** (3), 183–197.

Rasmussen, E.A. and Sørheim, R. (2006), 'Action-based entrepreneurship education', *Technovation*, **26** (2), 185–194.

Rasmussen, E. and Wright, M. (2015), 'How can universities facilitate academic spin-offs? An entrepreneurial competency perspective', *The Journal of Technology Transfer*, **40** (5), 782–799.

Redford, D. and Fayolle, A. (2014), 'Stakeholder management and the entrepreneurial university', in Alain Fayolle and Dana T. Redford (eds), *Handbook on the Entrepreneurial University*, Cheltenham, UK and Northampton, MA, USA: Edward Elgar Publishing, pp. 11–24.

Ribeiro, A., Uechi, J. and Plonski, G. (2018), 'Building builders: Entrepreneurship education from an ecosystem perspective at MIT', *Triple Helix*, **5** (1), 1–20.

Rubens, A., Spigarelli, F., Cavicchi, A. and Rinaldi, C. (2017), 'Universities' third mission and the entrepreneurial university and the challenges they bring to higher education institutions', *Journal of Enterprising Communities: People and Places in the Global Economy*, **11** (3), 354–372.

Siegel, D. and Wright, M. (2015), 'Academic entrepreneurship: Time for rethink?', *British Journal of Management*, **26** (4), 582–595.

Trowler, V. (2010), *Student Engagement Literature Review*. York: The Higher Education Academy.

Urbano, D. and Guerrero, M. (2013), 'Entrepreneurial universities socioeconomic impacts of academic entrepreneurship in a European region', *Economic Development Quarterly*, **27** (1), 40–55.

Vuori, J. (2014), 'Student engagement: Buzzword or fuzzword?', *Journal of Higher Education Policy and Management*, **36** (5), 509–519.

Wenger, E. (2009), 'A social theory of learning', in Knud Illeris (ed.), *Contemporary Theories of Learning: Learning Theorists … in Their Own Words*, Abingdon and New York: Routledge, pp. 209–218.

Wissema, J.G. (2009), *Towards the Third Generation University*, Cheltenham, UK and Northampton, MA, USA: Edward Elgar Publishing.

Wright, M., Siegel D.S. and Mustar, P. (2017), 'An emerging ecosystem for student start-ups', *The Journal of Technology Transfer*, **42** (4), 909–922.

9 The entrepreneurial university in the digital era: looking into teaching challenges and new higher education trends

Maribel Guerrero and David Urbano

Introduction

The 2008 financial recession represented a strategic game-changer for most organizations and severe resource constraints with unpredictable conditions creating significant challenges for organizational survival (Guerrero et al., 2016). After this socio-economic event, higher educational organizations are facing more pressures as higher rates of unemployment, the reduction of public budgets, reduction in the demand of traditional higher education studies, rising tuition costs, and competing in environments that have become global (Guerrero and Urbano, 2019).The COVID-19 pandemic has also represented an unprecedented challenge for education that affects more than 1.5 billion students that are no longer able to go to school physically (Kandri, 2020). In response to this health emergency, universities have been resilient to move physical activities into new online activities (i.e., open access online training, hubs with courses, webinars, conferences, expert videos, multimedia materials, and others). However, post-pandemic, universities will face many challenges at all organizational dimensions (i.e., managerial, operational, functional, relational, financial) to satisfy their stakeholders' needs (i.e., students, employers, government, society).

The digital economy allows understanding the new ways of communications and the technologies that have produced profound organizational transformations on internal processes, strategic organizational decisions, and new versatility for doing any type of activity in real-time across many locations (Brynjolfsson and Kahin, 2002, p. 2). For universities, the digital economy has represented a competitive environment because it introduces new rules in the delivery of higher education services across traditional borders (Teece, 2018). Initially, the procurement from analogic to digital transformed essential university functions like registration, purchasing learning resources, administering classes, and accessing knowledge in the format now accessible by way of personal devices (Carter, 2016). Subsequently, digitalization has transformed the university's core activities, evidenced the need for dynamic entrepreneurial capabilities[1] for being competitive, as well as opened new market opportunities for providing educational services aligned with the needs of digital workplaces (OECD, 2016; CISCO, 2018; WEF, 2018). One plausible explanation is related to those students' generations – for example, students born in an online era demand continual digital access to social networks, multimedia resources, and flexible learning experiences (Amphlet, 2018). In this view, traditional learning models are unlikely to inspire new students' generations (or 'digital natives'). Another plausible explanation is the aging diversity in workplaces (Guerrero et al., 2019) – for example, older generations are demanding long-life courses or training to acquire such digital competence as data analytics, big data, social media, and others (Deloitte, 2017).

In reflective entrepreneurial and knowledge-based societies, university managers have been involved in the evolutionary process of higher education organizations. Traditional organizations tend to be rigid to change, take a narrow view of industry-university relations (Wright et al., 2007) and tend to believe that entrepreneurship and innovation are two different phenomena (Autio et al., 2014). In contrast, innovative and entrepreneurial universities tend to adopt an entrepreneurial orientation transversely and try to be resilient in their interaction with the university's stakeholders (Audretsch, 2014; Guerrero et al., 2015). In this assumption, higher education organizations are dichotomous, focusing on both innovation and entrepreneurship core activities that contribute to competitiveness and economic growth (Guerrero and Urbano, 2019). Therefore, entrepreneurial and innovative organizations (the so-called 'entrepreneurial universities') are more adaptable to the digitalization trends that are dramatically affecting the development of their core activities as well as transforming their stakeholders' expectations (students, industry, labor market). In this vein, entrepreneurial and innovative universities are looking for new digital opportunities to be exploited with restricted resources and considering students' needs and profiles.

Inspired by this argument, this chapter aims to discuss how entrepreneurial universities are managing new digital trends in order to be competitive in both the traditional and the digital higher education market. By exploring the current debates in academia and higher education policymakers, we identify several university challenges and higher education trends in the digital context. In this vein, we discuss how challenges and trends are converging into new opportunities for achieving teaching activities that are one of the core activities – teaching, research, and commercialization (Guerrero and Urbano, 2019). Based on this information, we include several implications for academics, university managers, and policymakers.

The chapter is organized as follows. The first section discusses the entrepreneurial university in the digital economy. The second section introduces how universities are transforming their digital teaching challenges with the implementation of new digital strategies. The third section discusses the main implications of the theory, practice, and policymakers. Finally, we present our conclusions.

Entrepreneurial universities in the digital economy

Since the publication of the first edition of Clark's book (1998), research on the phenomena of 'entrepreneurial universities' and their core activities has increased significantly (Guerrero and Urbano, 2019). The entrepreneurial university simultaneously fulfills three different activities – teaching, research, and entrepreneurship – while providing an adequate atmosphere in which the university community can explore and exploit ideas and contributing to the creation of a sustained competitive advantage that could be transformed into social and economic impacts (Guerrero and Urbano, 2012).

In the context of the digital economy, the core activities of entrepreneurial and innovative higher education organizations are also influenced by technological and digital revolutions. Internally, entrepreneurial universities should develop dynamic entrepreneurial capabilities to transform routines into new innovative and new digital ways of managing, teaching, learning, and working (Guerrero et al., 2020). However, the academic literature does not provide enough answers about how digitalization has influenced organizational processes, transformed paradigms and redefined core activities of both traditional and entrepreneurial universities (e.g., teaching, research, as well as fostering innovative, disruptive and entrepreneurial initiatives) (Guerrero and Urbano, 2019).

In our assumption, there are three gaps in the academic discussion about entrepreneurial universities' core activities in the digital era. First, for teaching core activities, digitalization represents a critical challenge of paradigm for traditional organizations given their routines and aversion to change. Regarding entrepreneurial universities, the implementation of new online and offline learning education programs to enhance students' digital capabilities (e.g., digital entrepreneurship[2] that implies digital marketing, digital technologies and digital operations, as is explained by Giones and Brem, 2017 and Nambisan, 2017), represents an opportunity for introducing new business models, entry into new international markets, and generating higher social impact via human capital (Guerrero and Urbano, 2019). For instance, the most entrepreneurial universities have implemented massive online open courses with short modules for updating digital entrepreneurship capabilities exploiting internal capabilities (Teece, 2018), as well as creating online platforms oriented to support entrepreneurial and innovative initiatives (Sussan and Acs, 2017; Nambisan et al., 2019; Allahar and Sookram, 2019). However, the entrepreneurship and management fields need further studies to understand how entrepreneurial universities are exploring and exploiting internal and external challenges linked with teaching activities in the digital era.

Second, in relation to research core activities, anecdotal evidence reveals that entrepreneurial universities have also promoted the exploration and exploitation of data science (Waller and Fawcett, 2013; Guerrero and Urbano, 2019), as well as promoting the generation and commercialization of digital technologies such as social media, business analytics, the Internet of Things, big data, advanced manufacturing, 3D printing, cloud and cyber-solutions (Rippa and Secundo, 2019). Nevertheless, the entrepreneurship and innovation fields demand more investigations to understand how entrepreneurial universities are managing internal and external challenges linked with research and knowledge transfer activities in the digital era.

Third, in relation to entrepreneurship core activities, anecdotal evidence shows how some entrepreneurial universities have also encouraged entrepreneurial initiatives at the university community level (students, graduates, alumni, academics) based on artificial intelligence, big data and digital technologies (Guerrero and Urbano, 2019; Obschonka and Audretsch, 2019). As a result, academic and student entrepreneurs focus on exploring and exploiting digital technologies or transforming paradigms in collaboration with multiple stakeholders to generate societal impacts (Rippa and Secundo, 2019). However, the entrepreneurship field needs more research to understand how entrepreneurial universities are exploring and exploiting internal and external challenges linked with entrepreneurial and knowledge commercialization activities in the digital era.

Given the complexity related to digital adoption across all entrepreneurial universities' core activities, this chapter focuses on the digitalization challenges of teaching core activities of entrepreneurial universities.

Linking teaching challenges with new digital trends

The digital economy has transformed the rules of the game in higher education trends, job market demands, low-cost business models, and global competition. In this vein, entrepreneurial university managers are facing several challenges that may be transformed into sustained competitive advantages. Table 9.1 shows a selection of challenges and digital trends that will be discussed in this section.

External challenges

New students' needs and hybrid learning approaches

Based on the standards and regulations, higher education systems have increasingly focused on the effectiveness of digital learning and its compatibility with job market requirements, as well as with students' learning expectations (Entwistle and Ramsden, 2015). This requires an in-depth understanding of the main characteristics of new generations, which, in turn, influence and enhance the design of digital learning activities. The design of teaching courses requires the co-creation and involvement of the university community with stakeholders in identifying the skills and technical knowledge necessary in a competitive job market (WEF, 2018). According to Amphlet (2018), the very nature of the target audience – mainly young and highly connected – means the higher education sector must adapt to accommodate their students' expectations. Current student generations have grown up online and will expect the same levels of technology in their learning environments as in their day-to-day lives (Amphlet, 2018). Therefore, traditional, rigid modes of classroom instruction are unlikely to inspire students whose online life outside the classroom is dynamic and evolutionary.

A hybrid of traditional and digital learning approaches could help to be more empathetic with students' needs, encourage high-level cognitive activities, and create appropriate learning environments. An example could be the insertion

Table 9.1   Selected teaching challenges and digital trends

Focus	Challenges	Digital trends	Example	Source
External	Students' need new engaging and flexible methodologies for learning	Digital learning approaches and environments	Effective digital learning environment using: a. Hybrid approaches: virtual reality + artificial intelligence + social media in classrooms + digital campus b. E-learning environments (MOOCs)	Bradley et al. (2015); CISCO (2018); Teece (2018); Guerrero and Urbano (2019)
	Labor market demands new digital competences	Digital skills framework	Mixing curricula: a. Soft skills like creativity, persuasion, collaboration, adaptability b. Hard skills like cloud computing, artificial intelligence, big data analytical reasoning c. Long-life e-learning partnerships with companies	OECD (2016); PWC (2018); WEF (2018); Guerrero et al., (2020)

Focus	Challenges	Digital trends	Example	Source
Internal	Teachers should develop new digital capabilities	Digital train-the-trainers	Development of digital skills and capabilities of new and existing university teachers: a. Basic training consists of developing general IT and internet skills with the implementation of tools b. The specific training consists of under-standing and applicability of e-commerce, e-banking, e-government, digital marking, digital entrepreneurship	European Union (2012); Murraya and Olcese (2011); Scuotto and Morellato (2013)
	University managers should develop dynamic, digital and entrepreneurial capabilities	Dynamic, digital, and entrepreneurial university capabilities	The development of dynamic, digital, and entrepreneurial capabilities focused on: a. Sensing new innovative and entrepreneur-ial opportunities in higher education digital trends b. Seizing resources and capabilities to exploit these opportunities c. Transforming these opportunities into new business models, new higher education paradigms that contribute to the society and democratization of technologies	Teece (2018); Guerrero et al. (2020)
COVID-19	University responses to the restriction of developing physical core activities	Open-access teaching and learning courses using digital platforms	a. During the pandemic, the replacement of classrooms by distance teaching and learning b. After the pandemic, universities should adapt their core activities to the new health and social reality	Kandri (2020); QS (2020); UNESCO (2020a, 2020b)

of real workplace experiences using simulations, experiments, real-time interventions, and digital workplace practices per subject, defining explicit pedagogic purposes, learning designs, skills, and competencies associated with each practice. More concretely, in this hybrid approach, the course delivery combines face-to-face classroom activities with lectures, plus online guided practices in work placements (Collins and Halverson, 2018), as well as connecting with outside experts – both national and international – that share ideas that increase students' learning process (Amphlet, 2018). As a result, students can be engaged in authentic, real, collaborative and experiential learning processes based on a variety of theories, approaches, and environments to enrich human capital, as well as making sense of the demands of students, university teaching missions and labor market needs (Gibb et al., 2013). These hybrid practices facilitate the development of learning models that work best for students as well as communication improvements to deliver exciting lectures and to provide more personalised feedback and mentoring using any device.

Hybrid practices are particularly relevant when at least four generations of adults are working together in current workplaces (European Union, 2012). New generations of graduates will be part of this diversified (digital) workforce characterized by multiple profiles, motivations, perspectives, and adapted to work design, objectives, incentives, and metrics of performance (King et al., 2017). Therefore, this challenge represents an opportunity to be more open to new methods and technologies that enhance students' professional development, facilitates new transformations of learning and professionalizes teaching experience, so achieving the requirements of the new labor market.

Despite the growth and potential of using devices (i.e., laptops, smartphones, tablets, mobile applications, wireless applications, games applications) in the learning process, the embryonic stage of this type of learning does not generalize the learning outcomes (Motiwalla, 2007). On the one hand, studies with positive outcomes have recognized that technology makes learning more adaptive, flexible, and easier for learners to boost their achievements (Grand-Clement, 2017). Concretely, Tiven et al. (2018) showed primary learning outcomes from digital learning such as digital literacy,[3] language communication, self-efficacy, academic engagement, and critical thinking. From the entrepreneurship perspective, the digital learning process also encourages creativity, appreciation for diversity, a cultural approach, global knowledge, and global engagement. On the other hand, studies with unfavorable outcomes for digital learning have shown a resilience for adopting technologies. Concretely, technologies are seen as expensive tools that only cause learner distraction (Douglas et al., 2012) and learner confusion (Arguel et al., 2017). As a consequence, learners capture adverse outcomes in their digital learning with respect to traditional learning.

To that end, there is no conclusive debate about the positive or negative impact of digitalization on learning outcomes.

New student needs and e-learning environments

The technological evolution has also influenced the method of teaching and learning. Although higher education organizations have rigid routines in the development of their core activities – teaching and research (Guerrero et al., 2016) – managers of entrepreneurial universities have implemented diverse strategies to be simultaneously competitive in the traditional and digital market. The most innovative and entrepreneurial implementation behind these strategies has been associated with the e-learning or digital learning revolution, such as the massive online open courses (MOOCs), the design of 'virtual classrooms' connecting students' devices to the learning process or the 'digital university campus' using virtual reality plus artificial intelligence. Given the embryonic stage of these research trends, we focused on the analysis of MOOCs.

Although MOOCs have not been the only mechanism used in the digital transformation of innovative and entrepreneurial universities, it is recognized that MOOCs have been considered the most significant technological advance in the pedagogic part of higher education in a millennium (Teece, 2018, p. 98). By contrasting traditional and digital environments, MOOCs have attracted substantially larger audiences in a relatively short period without formal requirements – fees, previous accreditations (Al-Atabi and DeBoer, 2014) – and voluntary depending on individual needs and interests (Hollands and Tirthali, 2015). These large audiences are demanding to learn something new using low-cost digital mechanisms to improve their competencies and careers to enhance salaries in better workplaces. Pioneer universities such as Stanford and MIT have implemented a business model that offers free digital courses with the possibility to obtain a paid certificate and diploma that could also represent credits in specific traditional courses. The world of MOOCs is very complex but provides a digital learning environment instead of merely traditional methodological foundations (Christensen et al., 2013). MOOCs play an essential role in the transition through new educational and pedagogical paradigms concerning an open way of learning, technological design of specific contents, and innovative learning methodologies using digital tools (Liyanagunawardena et al., 2013).

According to their feedback, students' main motivation in participating in MOOCs is the possibility of obtaining specialized knowledge in a short period of time and being able to access multimodal digital resources easily (image, videos, web resources, simulations, platforms, devices, etc.) (Knox, 2014). Unfortunately, the academic literature does not provide enough answers about innovative and disruptive teaching and learning tools associated with MOOCs that have increased students' recruiting and university visibility (Ospina-Delgado and Zorio-Grima, 2016; Guerrero et al., 2020). Indeed, there is no reliable evidence about the transformation process of hybrid teaching models (on-offline) or the resources required to create digital MOOCs platforms, or clarity about the requirements of collaborating with existing platforms that supply the link between the course and the students. Therefore, a critical research paradigm is the transformation of university routines into new entrepreneurial capabilities to survive and sustain performance in the digital context (Guerrero et al., 2016; Klofsten et al., 2019).

Regarding outcomes, the advantages of MOOCs are associated with access to free courses offered by professors at the top schools across the globe; the learners' performance is monitored across the courses; professors and learners get worldwide exposure; and MOOCs can be used as a tool in a blended learning program (Al-Atabi and DeBoer, 2014; Eesley and Wu, 2015; Guerrero et al., 2020). Furthermore, MOOCs' learners have highlighted favorable learning outcomes such as labor promotion, an increase of self-efficacy, and increment of salaries (Al-Atabi and DeBoer, 2014; Eesley and Wu, 2015; Guerrero et al., 2020). Intuitively, MOOCs are advantageous for those learners who need basic knowledge but also for those who want to improve knowledge obtained in previous educational training programs. On the other hand, the disadvantages of MOOCs are that there may be problems in providing personalized courseware, or a lack of proper support given to students. There may also be difficulties in keeping track of students' assignments and their involvement, and problems with learners who have a poor internet connection or who have disabilities and therefore cannot access to the courses. Language may also be a barrier. Finally, courses cannot be used as credit-earning courses in some universities (Eesley and Wu, 2015; Guerrero et al., 2020). Intuitively, MOOCs are advantageous for those learners with limited resources and not familiar with digital learning styles. Based on these views, university performance evaluations should be revised and analyzed to understand what these evaluations are measuring in both digital and non-digital learning environments (Bedggood and Donovan, 2012).

The challenges of the digital economy should be transformed into an opportunity for creating value-added into the current students' generations as well as for capturing an international presence to open doors to students and collaborations across the globe. It explains that an increasing number of universities have adopted MOOCs with different purposes such as internationalization strategy, international recognition, and to capture sustained competitive advantages. The success of MOOCs has positioned and legitimized new digital teaching and higher education learning environments (Guerrero et al., 2016). However, from a systemic point of view, the enormous limitation of MOOCs is recognition of their modalities by both higher education systems and the labor market.

Labor market demands and the new digital curricula

Automation and advanced digital technologies have transformed industries and corporate work, providing new opportunities to explore and posing significant threats to those across the globe that do not adapt to the times (Alcácer et al., 2016). Consequently, skills requirements have also changed across organizations, industries, and countries (Zysman and Kenney, 2018). For senior and elderly employees, the importance of acquiring digital skills is reflected in the wage returns for these skills compared to workers who can only perform the most basic skills. As a consequence, the demand for digital training programs has notably incremented during the last decade. For governments, the challenge is ensuring that everyone has the right skills for an increasingly digital and globalized world that is essential to promote inclusive labor markets and to spur innovation, productivity, and growth (OECD, 2016, p. 1). Therefore, governments have implemented several public actions[4] to support learners and educators during the acquisition of necessary digital skills. For traditional universities, the principal inhibitor to digital uptake is digital literacy and the resilience to acquire these internal capabilities. By adopting an entrepreneurial universities' perspective, this labor market challenge will be translated into the re-design of the curricula with digital contents that enhance digital skills using hybrid learning approaches and hybrid learning environments.

Entrepreneurial universities are challenging the labor market demands of human capital that should possess traditional mixed skills (e.g., creativity, persuasion, collaboration, adaptability) and digital skills (e.g., cloud computing, artificial intelligence, big data analytical reasoning) (WEF, 2018). In this respect, entrepreneurial universities have adapted their curricula by introducing contents according to the needs of their specific target groups, as well as digital tools like online platforms, e-books, simulations, virtual reality, and artificial intelligence (see Karpati, 2011; Conrads et al., 2017; Makarova and Makarova, 2018). For example:

- By focusing on new users, the curricula content has been oriented to provide generic skills that allow devices to be applied effectively (i.e., use of laptops, tablets, smartphones, digital artifacts), generic software tools to be utilized in users' lives or works (i.e., certification of specific software), and developing capabilities to adapt to current changes in infrastructures and applications (i.e., digital resilience).

- By focusing on business and engineering, the curricula content has been oriented to develop skills and competencies related to exploring and exploiting business opportunities using advanced digital technologies[5] (i.e., digital entrepreneurship, digital marketing), as well as efficient and effective performance in the new ways of conducting new and established business (e.g., cryptocurrency, digital banking, digital government, digital entrepreneurial ecosystems). Similarly, in engineering and technological developer fields, the curricula content has included high-level specialized knowledge for researching, developing, designing, managing, protecting, and selling technological tools, devices, and platforms (i.e., data science, advanced digital technologies). Besides, these curricula contents have been transversally introduced in all university faculties, departments, and schools.

Consequently, entrepreneurial universities have redefined their business models to provide higher education programs oriented to new generations of students (e.g., general diplomas with digital competencies or specialized digital diplomas) or for long-life learning students (e.g., specialized training and certifications in collaboration with experts and companies). In addition, entrepreneurial universities' academics and staff should be specialized experts in disruptive technologies, analyzers of enormous amounts of information, and improvers of digital educational tools (WEF, 2018).

Internal challenges

Teachers and researchers' digital capabilities and train-the-trainers

According to the PWC (2018, p. 6), many academics and staff may not be confident in using digital tools, as well as nervous about engaging in digital spaces where they may feel at a disadvantage to students or digital natives. This represents the highest obstacle for universities in delivering curricula that ensure the development of digital skills. According to Grand-Clement (2017), there is a general assumption that educators, trainers, and academics are familiar with and confident in the use of digital technologies in their teaching and research activities. However, this is disrupted when educators need to adapt their pedagogy to different generations of learners to reduce time-wasting by students' incorrect use of digital technologies in class or their lack of discrimination when using multiple sources of unreliable information on digital media. Two plausible explanations are associated with the barriers to educators, trainers, and academics.

The first barrier is the lack of digital and technological skills. Teachers and researchers are not always systematically well prepared to deal with the use of technologies. We need to consider that this collective is mostly integrated by older generations for whom continuing professional training to upskill digitally has not always been mandatory because of their outstanding expertise in their particular fields. Anecdotal evidence reveals how entrepreneurial universities (e.g., Cambridge[6]) have implemented continuous professional development options to support the role of digital educators, digital trainers, and digital academics by explaining their contribution to the university digital framework as well as providing full information about digital tools, techniques, and training (i.e., ensuring critical competencies for teaching effectively with technology covering the different components: the digital classroom, designing learning, delivery learning, evaluating learning). In more specialized fields, digital educators, digital trainers, and digital academics have implemented successful technological elements like interactive training simulations and digital storytelling for design, developing, and evaluating their educational programs (Dörner et al., 2002). In this case, these technological elements support teachers and learners in expressing their stories to ensure communication interfaces between technology, storytelling, and application domain (i.e., using artificial intelligence).

The second barrier is looking at the future tasks and roles of educators if learners can retrieve knowledge for themselves. On the one hand, some authors argue that universities will disappear because of technology (O'Donoghue et al., 2001; Vieira et al., 2019). On the other hand, some authors have argued that educators should be using digital technology as a 'weapon of mass stimulation' where knowledge can be shared in advance with the class so that educators can maximize the contact time they have with their students and focus on mentoring and coaching them (Grand-Clement, 2017). Although the role of technology cannot be overemphasized, traditional universities will not disappear but universities should transform their capabilities to be competitive in the digital economy (Dennis, 2019).

Consequently, entrepreneurial universities' human resource managers should internally ensure continuous professional digital development as well as considering these professional digital capabilities during the hiring processes (i.e., usually these universities attract talent and expect to generate digital entrepreneurs and digital intrapreneurs) (Scuotto and Morellato, 2013; Allahar and Sookram, 2019; Rippa and Secundo, 2019).

Transforming and generating universities' dynamic capabilities in the digital era[7]

Previous studies have focused on the development of university capabilities to achieve an entrepreneurial orientation (Kalar and Antonic, 2015), international orientation (Minola et al., 2016), diversification orientation (Guri-Rozenblit, 1993), value creation, and new business models (Abdelkafi et al., 2013). However, there are no studies that have discussed the relevance of digital capabilities in entrepreneurial universities (Teece, 2018; Guerrero et al., 2020). In this vein, strategic management studies consider dynamic capabilities such as higher-level competencies that determine the universities' ability to integrate, build, and reconfigure internal/external resources/ competencies to shape rapidly changing business environments (Teece, 2018). Entrepreneurship studies consider capability as part of the organizational resources that are durable and difficult to imitate, and differentiate the organization from its competitor (Antoncic and Hisrich, 2003). By merging theoretical foundations, dynamic capabilities are higher-level competencies to improve and to transform routines into entrepreneurial actions that allow reconfiguring internal and external resources to the refined core activities in the digital economy (Guerrero et al., 2020).

In the context of the digital economy, Teece (2018) argues that universities should exploit ordinary capabilities (i.e., teaching and research activities) to reconfigure the new core activities and to transform these ordinary capabilities into unique dynamic capabilities (i.e., exploiting their competitive advantages for sensing opportunities assuming risks, transforming routines by being innovative and seizing by being proactive). In this reconfiguration, ordinary capabilities are associated with the quality of universities' human capital (i.e., teachers, academics, researchers), the quality of research resources, and the quality of the administrative process. According to Guerrero et al. (2020), the expertise of university human capital, the quality of research, and the experience of administrative staff have contributed to building new and digital capabilities.

As a result, entrepreneurial universities will be able to generate sensing capabilities (i.e., scanning new opportunities to date digital educational strategies), seizing capabilities (i.e., open innovation practices for sharing resources/ technologies with providers and platforms), and transforming capabilities (i.e., renewal of higher education services both online and offline) (Guerrero and Urbano, 2019). As a result, these university capabilities are expected to capture sustained competitive outcomes in the digital era. Therefore, entrepreneurial university managers have the challenge to effectively transform, generate, and manage the existent resources and capabilities into new requirements and rules of the digital economy.

University response to COVID-19 pandemic

The global lockdown of education organizations has been the primary reason for classroom go-to distance teaching and learning (Kandri, 2020). It required a rapid response of teachers to adjust pedagogies into online assignments by using digital tools (i.e., Blackboard, Zoom, Moodle, CANVAS, MOOCs platforms, Skype, and others). According to UNESCO (2020b), the most common distance learning strategies in response to COVID-19 should include how students can access remotely delivered content and communicative support; how learners' rights and data privacy can be protected; how teachers are supported in the transition to remote teaching; and how financial and technological resources can be mobilized to sustain the provision for several months.

In the context of remote learning, to ensure sustainable teaching quality outcomes, universities should strengthen communication and cooperation among teachers, learners, and parents (UNESCO, 2020a). Teachers are investing extra hours to ensure curricula appropriateness, increase communication with students, and ensure the inclusion of minority groups (i.e., people with physical disabilities; those who do not have access to the internet). Entrepreneurial universities are exploiting their technical infrastructures, licenses, and capabilities to optimize distance learning and achieving stakeholder outcomes (Marinoni et al., 2020). Despite these efforts, many students have had their education and learning interrupted because they do not have access to the internet or to computers at home (Burges and Sievertsen, 2020). This issue is generating educational inequalities across the world. Similarly, many graduates have been affected by the interruption of final exams, as well as the weak labor conditions.

Discussion

This chapter has discussed how entrepreneurial universities are facing the current challenges of being competitive both in traditional and digital higher education markets. Our discussion highlights the implications for entrepreneurial university stakeholders, particularly since university stakeholders should be oriented to enhance, develop, and update the digital universities' capabilities required for developing their digital core activities (Teece, 2018; Guerrero et al., 2020). We identified several strategies implemented by universities to ensure digital learning approaches, digital learning environments, and curricula with digital components and competencies. However, our study was limited by the embryonic stage of the literature about digitalization, digital entrepreneurial universities, digital learning and training, and digital impacts. In this way, this limitation opens a window of research opportunities in multi-disciplinary fields.

Implications and opportunities for entrepreneurial universities in the digital era

Although some higher education organizations have tried to adapt to the challenges, most have needed to prioritize resource allocation, institutional intro-spection, proactive cultural change, and the development of effective processes for diagnosing teaching and learning problems and decision making (Teece, 2018). However, there are numerous reasons why these changes are likely to be difficult, and some stakeholders will inevitably feel short-changed by the process. In this section, we pay attention to the following four implications.

The first highest digital economy opportunity is transforming the rigid tertiary education system with 'un-updated rules of the game' that tend to evaluate new education and learning practices compared with the norms of the last century. Some prestigious higher educational bodies and agencies have been working together to ensure the quality of new teaching and learning courses as well as recognizing new digital modalities of education as a part of the education and training of individuals (OECD, 2016; WEF, 2018). However, the promise of generating new value for society could be the critical promoter of the configu-ration of an entrepreneurial higher education ecosystem. For a time, the reality is that every day the world is changing, and higher education organizations need to be aligned with this change in order to be competitive and sustainable. Therefore, collaboration with stakeholders as an entrepreneurial and inno-vative higher education ecosystem should be essential to co-design teaching and learning courses, tools, and delivery in a hybrid (traditional and digital) learning way that supports and enhances employability and work inclusivity (Tomlinson, 2017) – notably, 'growing skills instability' scenarios that are characterized by a rapid technology change, new digital skills, and workers' displacement by robot automation in many workplaces (Charlton, 2019).

The second highest digital economy opportunity is the engagement and motivation of new generations of students ('digital natives') who are living in a transformative world where every day is a new opportunity for learning and influencing their environments. Consequently, higher education organizations need not only to adapt curricula and learning environments but they should also foster an entrepreneurial and innovative culture that allows them to be more proactive instead of reactive in respect of learning and teaching activities (CISCO, 2018). This is only possible if higher education organizations work more like entrepreneurial ecosystems that encourage students to voice their opinions and requirements as well as bringing all university departments together in the definition and co-creation of sustained educational plans for generating an impact on society. It also demands the creation of a learning and training culture among academics, staff, and students to identify the best technological solutions for the growing digital campus imprint (Carter, 2016). In this regard, an eclectic collection of learning pedagogies, practices, and adequate learning environments will contribute to students' achievements, satisfactions, sustainable university objectives, academic standards defined by the educational system, labor market requirements, socio-economic development and well-being (Bradley et al., 2015).

The third highest digital economy opportunity is the transformation of university archetypes, new business models, and ensuring organizational sustainability (Teece, 2018). University managers should adopt an adequate university model to be competitive in traditional and digital markets according to their ordinary capabilities and dynamic capabilities. Sustainability is generally consistent with the development of goals that are, in turn, relevant for tackling fundamental societal challenges (Pacheco et al., 2010). For higher education organizations, sustainability could have two central angles: (a) at the organizational level, sustainability represents a new university business model that allows the moderation of funding based on restrictions and resource constraints; and (b) at the operational level, sustainability is associated with the generation of impacts in quality and outcomes of learning and teaching by strengthening responsibility, recognition, and rewards (e.g., affordable schemes to help students to participate in tertiary education as well as supporting and contributing to graduates' employability). Therefore, university digital economy actions should also be measured in terms of graduation rates, employability, students' and employers' satisfaction, awards, international students, the ratio of students per professor, etc. (Guerrero et al., 2015). By focusing on sustainability, new performance metrics should be implemented to capture the effect of universities' dynamic capabilities on achieving sustained organizational performance, as well as the contribution of teaching and research activities to building a sustainable society. By adopting an entrepreneurial ecosystem perspective, university managers must evaluate digital strategies in respect of the universities' measurements of performance, sustainability, digital entrepreneurial innovations rates, digital entrepreneurship initiatives, and students' employability (Nambisan, 2017; Klofsten et al., 2019).

Consequently, university managers should be oriented to explore the role of entrepreneurial universities in digital entrepreneurship ecosystems (Sussan and Acs, 2017).

The fourth highest digital economy opportunity is related to the COVID-19 pandemic. According to Marinoni et al. (2020), the move to distance learning represents a significant opportunity to explore mixing synchronous learning with asynchronous learning for multiple learners, as well as to increase innovations in teaching pedagogies and assessments. A recent report on the new higher education paradigms has highlighted the highest student interest in studying degrees online, but some overseas students have also stated their disinterest in online learning (QS, 2020). A plausible explanation for this is that these overseas students prefer face-to-face learning because of their motivation to travel abroad for academic purposes and to be immersed in different cultures. Therefore, post the COVID-19 pandemic, entrepreneurial university managers should (a) embrace distance learning by considering all participants' needs and interest, (b) estimate the cost-benefits analysis, (c) improve the overseas recruiting strategy, (d) update graduation and administrative procurements, (e) enhance cooperation among university stakeholders, and (f) ensure well-being across the university community. Similarly, public policy implications should emerge based on experiences and best practices across the world.

Research agenda

Based on the topics discussed above, it is evident that there is a need to extend the analysis of the role of entrepreneurial universities in the digital economy. Concretely, natural extensions for future research should be focused on the following four potential research gaps.

- To contribute to the strategic management literature by understanding the complexity of digital entrepreneurial university capabilities (Teece, 2018; Guerrero and Urbano, 2019; Guerrero et al., 2020). It needs an extensive analysis of the micro-foundations of digital entrepreneurial university capabilities (i.e. the role of existing routines, the transformation, or the development, of new ones), as well as how to manage these capabilities (i.e. management of conflicts, attitudes, cultures, and motivations experienced during conversion to digital capabilities). Given the nature of this phenomenon, it is necessary to explore longitudinal studies that allow understanding of the role of space and time in the digital transformation trajectory. In this regard, multiple theoretical approaches could be adopted such as RBV, dynamic capabilities, strategic management approaches, evolutionary approaches, agency theory, and others. Several research opportunities emerge in the pre-post COVID-19 pandemic analysis. The strategic management analysis is critical for understanding the relationship between university investments and university outcomes. In this way, it is possible to provide insights about the digital transformation of universities across the globe, as well as to identify the digital dynamic capabilities of universities across the globe. Another research opportunity should be teachers' work-life balance and productivity as a consequence of working remotely.

- To contribute to the entrepreneurship and innovation literature by understanding how advanced technologies are configuring entrepreneurship initiatives into the university community: digital graduates entrepreneurship, digital academic entrepreneurship, digital intrapreneurs (Nambisan, 2017; Rippa and Secundo, 2019; Obschonka and Audretsch, 2019; Guerrero et al., 2019). Given the nature of this phenomenon, it is necessary to explore both qualitatively and quantitatively the digital entrepreneurial process as well as the implementation of metrics to understand the benefits of digitalization for entrepreneurial universities' stakeholders. From the theoretical point of view, multiple approaches could be adopted like open innovation, entrepreneurial universities, digital entrepreneurship, knowledge spillover theory, and others. An interesting research question related to the pre-post COVID-19 pandemic should be the emergence of entrepreneurial students and academics involved in innovative projects and entrepreneurial initiatives associated with the COVID-19 pandemic.

- To contribute to the education and pedagogy literature by exploring the impacts of offline and online learning programs for diverse target groups (i.e., native digitals, elderly generations), the analysis of the digital learning process (i.e., including design, delivery, evaluation, and follow up), the effectiveness of higher education regulations, support regarding digitalization, and the pedagogy implementation in multiple learning settings (Motiwalla, 2007; Murray and Olcese, 2011; Grand-Clement, 2017; Guerrero et al., 2019). Given the nature of this phenomenon, it is necessary to adopt mixed methodologies, including experiments and simulations for capturing perceptions, outcomes, and tendencies. The COVID-19 pandemic also represents an open window for research related to the role of innovations and digitalization in distance learning, as well as the analysis of learning differences between minorities (i.e., students with and without internet access, male and female students, students with or without disabilities)

- To contribute to the national innovation and entrepreneurial ecosystems by exploring the role of entrepreneurial universities in the configuration of digital innovation and entrepreneurial ecosystems (Sussan and Acs, 2017;

Nambisan et al., 2019; Ahluwalia et al., 2020). Assuming the role of space/ time, researchers could analyze the systemic relationships in offline and online ecosystems in order to measure the efficiency and effectiveness in terms of the creation of digital entrepreneurs. In this vein, new metrics/ theoretical approaches should be implemented for testing the role of entrepreneurial universities as part of digital entrepreneurial ecosystems. By focusing on the COVID-19 pandemic, an interesting research question is related to the effectiveness of the digital entrepreneurial ecosystem in the creation of new ventures pre and post COVID-19 pandemic analysis.

Acknowledgments

David Urbano acknowledges the financial support from the Spanish Ministry of Economy and Competitiveness [project ECO2017-87885-P], the Economy and Knowledge Department – Catalan Government [project 2017-SGR-1056] and ICREA under the ICREA Academia Programme.

Maribel Guerrero acknowledges the Facultad de Economía y Negocios at the Universidad del Desarrollo (Chile), the Northumbria Centre for Innovation, Regional Transformation and Entrepreneurship based on Newcastle Business School at Northumbria University (UK), and the Centre for Innovation Research (CIRCLE) at Lund University (SE) for their invaluable support.

Notes

1. By dynamic entrepreneurial capabilities, we refer to higher-level competencies that determine universities' ability to integrate, build, and reconfigure internal and external resources and competencies to shape rapidly changing business environments like the digital economy (Guerrero et al., 2020). By assimilating Teece's (2018) ideas, these university capabilities should be oriented to seizing resources, sensing opportunities, and transforming these into new business models.
2. Digital entrepreneurship is understood as the intersection of entrepreneurship and digital technologies (e.g., digital artefacts, platforms and infrastructures) where entrepreneurial ideas emerge (Nambisan, 2017, p. 1031).
3. The knowledge, skills and confidence to use the technologies and devices to deliver the outcomes you want (PWC, 2018).
4. The US goverment has implemented a digital literacy program for supporting learners and educators (see https://digitalliteracy.gov/). Similarly, a support program called SELFIE (Self-reflection on Effective Learning by Fostering

Innovation through Educational technology) has been implemented in Europe for students and teachers (see https://ec.europa.eu/education/schools-go-digital).
5. More advanced digital technologies include the Internet of Things, additive manufacturing, big data, artificial intelligence, Cloud computing, virtual reality and blockchain technologies (Nambisan, 2017; Rindfleisch et al., 2017; Ahluwalia et al., 2020).
6. For further details, see https://thedigitalteacher.com/?_ga=2.8433717.165517393 .1575808033-453659041.1575808033.
7. In Europe, a good tool has been the HEInnovative project, which has supported university managers in the development of university capabilities for being more entrepreneurial, innovative and digital (https://heinnovate.eu/en).

References

Abdelkafi, N., Makhotin, S. and Posselt, T. (2013). Business model innovations for electric mobility – What can be learned from existing business model patterns? *International Journal of Innovation Management*, **17**(1), 1340003.

Ahluwalia, S., Mahto, R.V. and Guerrero, M. (2020). Blockchain technology and startup financing: A transaction cost economics perspective. *Technological Forecasting and Social Change*, 151. Doi: https://doi.org/10.1016/j.techfore.2019.119854.

Al-Atabi, M. and DeBoer, J. (2014). Teaching entrepreneurship using massive open online course (MOOC). *Technovation*, **34**(4), 261–264.

Alcácer, J., Cantwell, J. and Piscitello, L. (2016). Internationalization in the information age: A new era for places, firms, and international business networks? *Journal of International Business Studies*, **47**, 499. https://doi.org/10.1057/jibs.2016.22.

Allahar, H. and Sookram, R. (2019). A university business school as an entrepreneurial ecosystem hub. *Technology Innovation Management Review*, **9**(11), 15–25.

Amphlet, D. (2018). Digital evolution: A new approach to learning and teaching in higher education. CISCO: Public Sector Division. https://gblogs.cisco.com/uki/digital-evolution-a-new-approach-to-learning-and-teaching-in-higher-education/.

Antoncic, B. and Hisrich, R.D. (2003). Clarifying the intrapreneurship concept. *Journal of Small Business and Enterprise Development*, **10**(1), 7–24.

Arguel, A., Lockyer, L., Lipp, O.V., Lodge, J.M. and Kennedy, G. (2017). Inside out: Detecting learners' confusion to improve interactive digital learning environments. *Journal of Educational Computing Research*, **55**(4), 526–551.

Audretsch, D.B. (2014). From the entrepreneurial university to the university for the entrepreneurial society. *The Journal of Technology Transfer*, **39**(3), 313–321.

Autio, E., Kenney, M., Mustar, P., Siegel, D. and Wright, M. (2014). Entrepreneurial innovation: The importance of context. *Research Policy*, **43**(7), 1097–1108.

Bedggood, R.E. and Donovan, J.D. (2012). University performance evaluations: What are we really measuring? *Studies in Higher Education*, **37**(7), 825–842.

Bradley, J., Loucks, J., Macaulay, J., Noronha, A. and Wade, M. (2015). Digital vortex: How digital disruption is redefining industries. IMD and Cisco Initiative. https://www.cisco.com/c/dam/en/us/solutions/collateral/industry-solutions/digital-vortex-report.pdf.

Brynjolfsson, E. and Kahin, B. (Eds.) (2002). *Understanding the Digital Economy: Data, Tools, And Research*. MIT Press.

Burges, S. and Sievertsen, H. (2020). Schools, skills, and learning: The impact of COVID-19 on education. https://voxeu.org/article/impact-covid-19-education.

Carter, J. (2016). Tracking the digital evolution of higher education. https://www.educationdive.com/news/tracking-the-digital-evolution-of-higher-education/432555/.

Charlton, E. (2019). These are the 10 most in-demand skills of 2019, according to LinkedIn. WEF: Digital Economy and Society Agenda. https://www.weforum.org/agenda/2019/01/the-hard-and-soft-skills-to-futureproof-your-career-according-to-linkedin?fbclid=IwAR2JG9Z03ppEgPsjoAHBiyUtp-Qb-uLRNJKwX9k75Z-mnquWz7E1zQhut-yM.

Christensen, G., Steinmetz, A., Alcorn, B., Bennett, A., Woods, D. and Emanuel, E.J. (2013).*The MOOC Phenomenon: Who Takes Massive Open Online Courses and Why?* University of Pennsylvania Press.

CISCO (2018). The next-generation digital learning environment and a framework for change for education institutions. White Paper. https://www.cisco.com/c/dam/m/digital/elq-cmcglobal/OCA/Assets/Education/Framework_for_Change_White_Paper.pdf.

Clark, B. (1998). *Creating Entrepreneurial Universities: Organizational Pathways of Transformation*. Bingley: Emerald.

Collins, A. and Halverson, R. (2018). *Rethinking Education in the Age of Technology: The Digital Revolution and Schooling in America*. Teachers College Press.

Conrads, J., Rasmussen, M., Winters, N., Geniert, A. and Langer, L. (2017). *Digital Education Policies in Europe and Beyond*. JRC Science for policy report.

Deloitte (2017). *The Digital Workplace: Think, Share, Do: Transform your Employee Experience*. Canada: Deloitte.

Dennis, M.J. (2019). Recommendations for colleges and universities to avoid closing or merging. *Enrollment Management Report*, **23**(2), 1–3.

Dörner, R., Grimm, P. and Abawi, D.F. (2002). Synergies between interactive training simulations and digital storytelling: A component-based framework. *Computers & Graphics*, **26**(1), 45–55.

Douglas, D., Angel, H. and Bethany, W. (2012). Digital devices, distraction, and student performance: Does in-class cell phone use reduce learning? *Astronomy Education Review*, **11**(1), 0101081-0101084.

Eesley, C. and Wu, L. (2015). Entrepreneurial adaptation and social networks: Evidence from a randomized experiment on a MOOC platform. Available at SSRN, 2571777.

Entwistle, N. and Ramsden, P. (2015). *Understanding Student Learning* (Routledge Revivals). Routledge.

European Commission (2006). *Best Practices and Pedagogical Methods in Entrepreneurship Education in Europe. Socrates, Education and Culture*. Available at https://www.efmd.org/projects-test?download=10:13-qepe-best-practices.

European Union (2012). *Digital Literacy 2.0 – Train the Trainer and Qualify the User*. Brussels: European Union-Life Long Learning Program.

Gibb, A., Hannon, P., Price, A. and Robertson, I. (2013). A compendium of pedagogies for teaching entrepreneurship. IEEP, http://ieeponline.com/wp-content/uploads/2013/11/Wider-reading-draft-Ped-Note-compendium.pdf.

Giones, F. and Brem, A. (2017). Digital technology entrepreneurship: A definition and research agenda. *Technology Innovation Management Review*, **7**(5), 44–51.

Grand-Clement, S. (2017). *Digital Learning: Education and Skills in the Digital Age*. RAND Europe.

Guerrero, M. and Urbano, D. (2012). The development of an entrepreneurial university. *The Journal of Technology Transfer*, **37**(1), 43–74.

Guerrero, M. and Urbano, D. (2019). A research agenda for entrepreneurship and innovation: The role of entrepreneurial universities. In David B. Audretsch, Erik E. Lehmann and Albert N. Link (eds), *A Research Agenda for Entrepreneurship and Innovation*, pp. 107–133. Cheltenham, UK and Northampton, MA, USA: Edward Elgar Publishing.

Guerrero, M., Amorós, J.E. and Urbano, D. (2019). Do employees' generational cohorts influence corporate venturing? A multilevel analysis. *Small Business Economics*. DOI: 10.1007/s11187-019-00304-Z.

Guerrero, M., Cunningham, J.A. and Urbano, D. (2015). The economic impact of entrepreneurial universities' activities: An exploratory study of the United Kingdom. *Research Policy*, **44**(3), 748–764.

Guerrero, M., Heaton, S. and Urbano, D. (2020). Building universities' intrapreneurial capabilities in the digital era: The role and impacts of massive open online courses. *Technovation*. DOI: https://doi.org/10.1016/j.technovation.2020.102139.

Guerrero, M., Urbano, D., Fayolle, A., Klofsten, M. and Mian, S. (2016). Entrepreneurial universities: Emerging models in the new social and economic landscape. *Small Business Economics*, **47**(3), 551–563.

Guri-Rozenblit, S. (1993). Trends of diversification and expansion in Israeli higher education. *Higher Education*, **25**(4), 457–472.

Hollands, F.M. and Tirthali, D. (2015). *MOOCs in Higher Education. Institutional Goals and Paths Forward.* US: Palgrave Macmillan.

Kalar, B. and Antoncic, B. (2015). The entrepreneurial university, academic activities and technology and knowledge transfer in four European countries. *Technovation*, **36**, 1–11.

Kandri, S. (2020). How COVID-19 is driving a long-overdue revolution in education? Global Head of Education, IFC. https://www.weforum.org/agenda/2020/05/how-covid-19-is-sparking-a-revolution-in-higher-education/.

Karpati, A. (2011). *Digital Literacy in Education. Policy Brief.* Washington: UNESCO.

King, R.B., McInerney, D.M. and Nasser, R. (2017). Different goals for different folks: A cross-cultural study of achievement goals across nine cultures. *Social Psychology of Education*, **20**(3), 619–642.

Klofsten, M., Fayolle, A., Guerrero, M., Mian, S., Urbano, D. and Wright, M. (2019). The entrepreneurial university as driver for economic growth and social change – Key strategic challenges. *Technological Forecasting and Social Change*, **141**, 149–158.

Knox, J. (2014). Digital culture clash: 'Massive' education in the e-learning and digital cultures MOOC. *Distance Education*, **35**(2), 164–177

Liyanagunawardena, T.R., Adams, A.A. and Williams, S.A. (2013). MOOCs: A systematic study of the published literature 2008–2012. *The International Review of Research in Open and Distributed Learning*, **14**(3), 202–227.

Makarova, E.A. and Makarova, E.L. (2018). Blending pedagogy and digital technology to transform educational environment. *International Journal of Cognitive Research in Science, Engineering and Education*, **6**(2), 57.

Marinoni, G., van't Land, H. and Jense, T. (2020). *The Impact of COVID-19 on Higher Education Around the World.* Paris: International Associations of Universities.

Minola, T., Donina, D. and Meoli, M. (2016). Students climbing the entrepreneurial ladder: Does university internationalization pay off? *Small Business Economics*, **47**(3), 565–587.

Motiwalla, L.F. (2007). Mobile learning: A framework and evaluation. *Computers & Education*, **49**(3), 581–596.

Murray, O.T. and Olcese, N.R. (2011). Teaching and learning with iPads, ready or not? *TechTrends*, **55**(6), 42–48.

Nambisan, S. (2017). Digital entrepreneurship: Toward a digital technology perspective of entrepreneurship. *Entrepreneurship Theory and Practice*, **41**(6), 1029–1055.

Nambisan, S., Wright, M. and Feldman, M. (2019). The digital transformation of innovation and entrepreneurship: Progress, challenges and key themes. *Research Policy*, **48**(8), 103773.

Obschonka, M. and Audretsch, D.B. (2019). Artificial intelligence and big data in entrepreneurship: A new era has begun. *Small Business Economics*, 1–11.

O'Donoghue, J., Singh, G. and Dorward, L. (2001). Virtual education in universities: A technological imperative. *British Journal of Educational Technology*, **32**(5), 511–523.

OECD (2016). Skills for a digital world. Policy brief on the future of work. Paris: OECD. https://www.oecd.org/els/emp/Skills-for-a-Digital-World.pdf.

Ospina-Delgado, J. and Zorio-Grima, A. (2016). Innovation at universities: A fuzzy-set approach for MOOC-intensiveness. *Journal of Business Research*, **69**(4), 1325–1328.

Pacheco, D.F., Dean, T.J. and Payne, D.S. (2010). Escaping the green prison: Entrepreneurship and the creation of opportunities for sustainable development. *Journal of Business Venturing*, **25**(5), 464–480.

PWC (2018). The 2018 digital university. Staying relevant in the digital age. https://www.pwc.co.uk/assets/pdf/the-2018-digital-university-staying-relevant-in-the-digital-age.pdf.

QS (2020). Global opportunities in the new higher education paradigm. QS International Student Survey.

Rindfleisch, A., O'Hern, M. and Sachdev, V. (2017). The digital revolution, 3D printing, and innovation as data. *Journal of Product Innovation Management*, **34**(5), 681–690.

Rippa, P. and Secundo, G. (2019). Digital academic entrepreneurship: The potential of digital technologies on academic entrepreneurship. *Technological Forecasting and Social Change*, **146**, 900–911.

Scuotto, V. and Morellato, M. (2013). Entrepreneurial knowledge and digital competence: Keys for a success of student entrepreneurship. *Journal of the Knowledge Economy*, **4**(3), 293–303.

Sussan, F. and Acs, Z.J. (2017). The digital entrepreneurial ecosystem. *Small Business Economics*, **49**(1), 55–73.

Teece, D.J. (2018). Managing the university: Why 'organized anarchy' is unacceptable in the age of massive open online courses. *Strategic Organization*, **16**(1), 92–102.

The Conversation (2019). Universities must prepare for a technology-enabled future. https://theconversation.com/universities-must-prepare-for-a-technology-enabled-future-89354.

Tiven, M.B., Fuchs, E.R., Bazari, A. and MacQuarrie, A. (2018). *Evaluating Global Digital Education: Student Outcomes Framework*. New York, NY: Bloomberg Philanthropies and the Organisation for Economic Co-operation and Development.

Tomlinson, M. (2017). Introduction: Graduate employability in context: Charting a complex, contested and multi-faceted policy and research field. In *Graduate Employability in Context I*, pp. 1–40. Palgrave Macmillan UK.

UNESCO (2020a). COVID-19 crisis and curriculum: sustaining quality outcomes in the context of remote learning. UNESCO. https://unesdoc.unesco.org/ark:/48223/pf0000373273.

UNESCO (2020b). Distance learning strategies in response to COVID-19 school clo-sures. UNESCO. https://unesdoc.unesco.org/ark:/48223/pf0000373305.

Vieira, A.I., Oliveira, E., Silva, F., Oliveira, M., Gonçalves, R. and Au-Yong-Oliveira, M. (2019). The role of technologies: Creating a new labor market. In *World Conference on Information Systems and Technologies*, pp. 176–184. Springer, Cham.

Waller, M.A. and Fawcett, S.E. (2013). Data science, predictive analytics, and big data: A revolution that will transform supply chain design and management. *Journal of Business Logistics*, **34**(2), 77–84.

WEF (2018). The future of job reports. Switzerland: Centre for new economy and society. http://www3.weforum.org/docs/WEF_Future_of_Jobs_2018.pdf.

Wright, M., Clarysse, B., Mustar, P. and Lockett, A. (2007). *Academic Entrepreneurship in Europe*. Cheltenham, UK and Northampton, MA, USA: Edward Elgar Publishing.

Zysman, J. and Kenney, M. (2018). The next phase in the digital revolution: Abundant computing, platforms, growth, and employment. *Communications of the Association of Computing Machinery*, **61**(2), 54–63.

10 Sources of science and power: emerging organizational forms and professions in the entrepreneurial university

Jarrett B. Warshaw

Introduction

As entrepreneurial universities compete in science and for resources, they develop new organizational forms and professions for leading and managing them. A prominent change in academic organization entails creating an array of STEM-focused organizational units (SOUs), which consist of centers, institutes, schools, and departments, and engendering their crosscutting, orthogonal linkages in the administrative hierarchy (Warshaw, 2019; 2020). These linkages, according to advocates of such designs, may open the flow of knowledge-production and knowledge-exchange throughout segments of the campus and with industry, governmental agencies, non-profit entities, and other external partners (Crow and Dabars, 2015). The flexible arrangement, its supporters suggest, could expand the creative possibilities for science because it groups researchers and resources by programmatic areas rather than by departmental lines. In concert with these reforms are core shifts in the professional roles and boundaries of faculty and administrators. Administrative capacity and oversight tends to expand in entrepreneurial universities, reducing faculty, researchers suggest, to managed professionals (Gonzales et al., 2014; Rhoades, 2014). Meanwhile, some professors are "managerialized" as they become administrative leaders of SOUs. They suggest a potentially new profession forming in relation to this distinctive institutional context and the global knowledge economy.

SOUs offer campus stakeholders and external partners a variety of ways by which to organize – and anchor – the production of science in and through entrepreneurial universities. Many centers and institutes serve as organized research units (ORUs), which produce new knowledge in capital-intensive areas of science that other units, such as traditional academic departments, may not have the capacity or infrastructure to conduct (Gumport, 2016). Not all ORUs are bricks-and-mortar entities with steep start-up and operating costs. Some are virtual units, which exist via websites and utilize existing facilities on campus, while others are "paper" and/or "shadow" units (e.g., existing in letterheads and/or in signs or plaques posted by office doors). Their different forms and cost structures support flexible organizational designs and budgets. For these reasons, senior-level administrators, academic deans and chairs, teams of faculty, and individual investigators may each, through collaborative and semi-autonomous efforts, form and develop centers and institutes. In the USA, the federal government, states, philanthropic foundations, and donors establish centers and institutes as well. Recent estimates in US higher education suggest that the total number of ORUs has increased over time and that campuses may feature a dozen to hundreds of such units (Gumport, 2016).

Schools and departments, in relation to centers and institutes, comprise the core academic heartland (Clark, 1998). They serve as the primary contexts for hiring and tenure-and-promotion processes for faculty and for conducting the institutional mission of research, teaching, and service. Schools can be located within an overarching college or serve as stand-alone units comprised of departments and/or programs. Several US research universities have reorganized departments into interdisciplinary schools to support cost-efficiencies and to foster what advocates believe are more societally responsive and relevant approaches to teaching and research (Crow and Dabars, 2015). Departments are still considered the basic building blocks of academic organization for most institutions, as reflected in campus administrative hierarchies and also in academic budgets. Schools and departments are more focused on teaching than ORUs, though ORUs can and do offer classes, training opportunities and workshops, and certificates and degrees (Geiger and Sá, 2008). Yet schools and departments advance scientific research through their connections to centers and institutes on campus (via joint appointments and the flow of funding and intellectual property) and to industry (Mendoza, 2012).

SOUs and their network-based configurations suggest illustrative examples of prominent organizational changes taking place in entrepreneurial universities (Pinheiro and Stensaker, 2014). Such institutions feature strong administrative steering to tailor organizational designs to optimize campus-wide goals. But there are also decentralized, and less outwardly visible, forces of change emanating from the ground level among SOUs. For example, SOUs' leadership, management, and governance contain localized social processes and practices that shape entrepreneurial universities and pull them into the global knowledge economy. Governance refers to setting organizational purposes and goals and creating structures and processes to pursue them. Management focuses on daily work and operations, while leadership is the glue that synergizes governance and management and the unit as a whole (Bastedo, 2012). These three elements occur throughout multiple levels of colleges and universities. To foreground them in SOUs offers a unique vantage point for examining entrepreneurial universities, because it attributes evolving sources of science and power, in these settings and in the global knowledge economy, to units' strategic actions and alliances.

The organizational changes in entrepreneurial universities are connected to the shifting professional work and boundaries of administrators and faculty. Entrepreneurial universities have in part created – and leveraged – managerial professionals (Clark, 1998; McClure, 2016; Rhoades and Stensaker, 2017). These managerial professionals are administrators who hold advanced degrees and who, based on their specialized training, support their institutions across an array of offices and operational domains. They are associated with a reduction in the prominence of faculty, by way of performing selected academic work (e.g., instructional and curricular design), evaluating and assessing professors (e.g., quality control initiatives), and strengthening the overall administrative reach of executive-level leaders to whom they report (Gonzales et al., 2014; Rhoades, 2014). Such dynamics may exacerbate conflicts between administrators and professors and fragment the professoriate (Johnson, 2017). Yet there are numerous faculty who are becoming administrative leaders of SOUs, and we know relatively little about them and the extent to which they could be empowered as members of an emerging professional class of managerialized faculty. Through SOUs, might managerialization constitute a mechanism to corner a newer jurisdiction of work and resources in the knowledge economy. This mechanism may reify SOUs as key organizational sources of science and power.

Theories of academic capitalism and professionalization offer helpful accounts for why and how entrepreneurial universities are developing newer organizational forms and professions. The theory of academic capitalism accounts for organizational networks that are created and harnessed to compete for external funds (market-like initiatives) and to profit from intellectual property in the knowledge economy (market efforts) (Cantwell and Kauppinen, 2014; Slaughter and Rhoades, 2004). Theory of professionalization addresses the conditions that allow for new occupations to emerge and to monopolize niches in the labor market (Abbott, 1988). It suggests a means by which to analyze the connection of academic capitalism to professors and their professional motivations and outcomes. Professionalization is thus linked to contests for power and control of scientific production in entrepreneurial universities and the broader society (Brint, 1994; Foucault, 1994). These contests can effect change through overt conflicts and social movements; however, there are also subtle forms of collective action that, over time, redistribute access to resources and positions of influence (Fligstein and McAdam, 2012; Jacobs, 2014). Theory of professionalization may capture the form and range of academic capitalist processes, which move managerialized faculty, as a profession, toward the locus of scientific production.

This chapter aims to advance theory and future lines of research on the organizational forms and professions that entrepreneurial universities are developing. Specifically, its contribution lies in extending theories of academic capitalism and professionalization to mobilize new research on SOUs and on faculty who become administrative leaders of them. The chapter does not address research methods, which goes beyond its aim and scope, but may complement recent work indicating a variety of suitable designs and analytical techniques for developing an agenda on this topic (see, for example, Slaughter and Taylor, 2016). With these considerations in mind, the chapter is organized as follows: the first section discusses academic capitalism and professionalization as helpful theoretical perspectives for advancing research on organizational forms and professions in entrepreneurial universities. The second section attends to SOUs' leadership, management, and governance and poses lines of research within each of these elements. The third section focuses on the process and outcomes of managerializing faculty through SOUs; it identifies streams of research connected to the collapsing of boundaries between administrators and faculty and to the increasing fragmentation within the scientific profession. The final section offers concluding remarks about situating this chapter's research agenda in local, national, and global contexts.

Theoretical perspectives

The theories of academic capitalism and professionalization are helpful for motivating new lines of research on organizational forms and professions in entrepreneurial universities. In this section, each theory is discussed to frame the material in the chapter that follows.

Academic capitalism

The theory of academic capitalism explains why and how entrepreneurial universities engage the global knowledge economy (Cantwell and Kauppinen, 2014; Slaughter and Rhoades, 2004). Since the 1980s, universities – and their administrators and professors – have had unprecedented opportunities to pursue new competitive arenas for funding and to profit in the open marketplace. Policy changes in that era and thereafter in the USA, analogous to comparable movements in Australia, Europe, and Asia, have folded higher education into economic competitiveness agendas and campaigns. US policies, for instance, have granted ownership to universities and professors of intellectual property (IP) developed from federally funded research. The process to patent and license IP, in concert, has become streamlined. By loosening other elements of the legal, regulatory system, policymakers have widened the scope of what can be patented (such as basic algorithms and living organisms) and strengthened protections, through domestic and international initiatives, for patents and inventors. Such efforts leverage knowledge-as-raw-material to stimulate economic development, as reflected in start-up firms, technology transfer with industry, and regional clusters.

Broadly considered, academic capitalism calls attention to market-like and market behaviors and mechanisms that entwine entrepreneurial universities in the knowledge economy (Slaughter and Rhoades, 2004). Market-like initiatives encompass using public subsidies to offset the costs associated with competing for external sources of funding (and prestige). Market efforts entail seeking to profit from public aspects of institutions – intellectual property, trademarks, and copyrights – to generate revenues but that eschew public purposes and social goals (Rooksby, 2016). The theory, at heart, is one of networks. Entrepreneurial universities may develop new organizational forms and professions to amplify the exchange of knowledge across segments of campuses and with external partners (i.e., new circuits of knowledge). They create increasingly interdependent pockets of academic units within the university that also pull the enterprise as a whole into the knowledge economy (i.e., interstitial organizational emergence). Finally, entrepreneurial universities rely on administrators (i.e., managerial professionals) and some professors to shape and sustain these organizational networks and to re-norm the academy through market-driven mindsets and reward systems.

The theory of academic capitalism offers insight into the above-noted organizational networks that are forming. It also attends to the changing reward systems within the academic profession that stratify professors and disciplinary fields (Johnson, 2017; Rosinger et al., 2016). Moreover, researchers and analysts have extended the theory to account for disproportionate increases in administrators and managerial professionals and their influence on faculty work lives (Gonzales et al., 2014; McClure, 2016; Rhoades, 2014). This chapter suggests that academic capitalism can be reconnected to professionalization theories to deepen our understanding of core changes taking place in entrepreneurial universities and of the faculty who are "managerialized" as they lead and manage the newer organizational forms on their campuses.

Professionalization

Theory of professionalization offers a means by which to examine the conditions that shape the emergence of new occupational categories of specialists and experts in labor markets. Foucault (1994) studied the development of the intellectual class that resulted in the obedience of citizens through what he termed "disciplinary regimes". He observes how the aristocracy had historically relied on public corporal punishment, such as drawing and quartering, to instruct citizens about which behaviors were appropriate. But that regime shifted in the years thereafter, Foucault notes, to sanctioning and utilizing new groups of workers – neither bourgeois capitalists nor proletariat wage laborers – to discipline the society as a whole through less violent and more rationalized mechanisms. The new group of workers were intellectuals and professionals, who by way of advanced educational training and governmental certification, entered into positions of prominence and authority across an array of social institutions: hospitals, universities, prisons, and social welfare agencies. They helped to re-norm society by affirming and recalibrating powerful cognitive understandings of behavior considered normal and thus diminishing deviance. Foucault emphasizes the publicly stated altruistic motivations of semi-autonomous professionals to serve the greater good. Meanwhile, the motivations and status differentials of professionals shifts again in light of capitalism, in which economic gains rather than altruism confer status on select experts over their peers (Brint, 1994; Larson, 1979). These dynamics indicate the movement of knowledge and power in organizations and in society as a whole.

As re-situated with academic capitalism, theory of professionalization gives helpful analytical attention to one potentially newer profession of academics: faculty who become administrative leaders of emerging organizational forms in the entrepreneurial university. Professional status and jurisdictions (i.e., labor market niches) of occupational groups are fluid because of competition within and across the professions (Abbott, 1988; Jacobs, 2014). From an historical perspective, Abbott (p. 3) observes that new professions develop "when jurisdictions become vacant, which may happen because they are newly created or because an earlier tenant has left them altogether or lost its firm grip on them". This chapter posits that the organizational forms in entrepreneurial universities are, vis-à-vis academic capitalism, potentially opening an occupational space for a new profession to lead and manage the changes taking place. In turn, theories of academic capitalism and professionalization may anchor empirical work on how, by whom, and to what end these organizational forms and professions are developing.

Leadership, management, and governance of SOUs

The formation of SOUs, and the crosscutting, orthogonal linkages among them, suggests an illustrative example of newer organizational forms in entrepreneurial universities. This section calls attention to the leadership, management, and governance of SOUs; each of these elements contains decentralized social processes and practices shaping the changes taking place.

Leadership

The leadership of SOUs merits attention because it influences the viability of newer organizational forms and indicates a pathway to professionalization for administrative leaders. At the unit level, leadership entails legitimacy-building to enhance resources and opportunities for knowledge-production and knowledge-exchange. Leaders influence the sustainability of SOUs (and their networks) by setting the scope and nature of their collaborative and competitive strategies. Research on leadership in SOUs could examine several key aspects, such as the identification and selection of leaders, leadership styles/ approaches, and leadership departures and transitions.

For the identification and selection of SOU leadership, it remains unclear which faculty become SOU leaders and how and why they enter into these positions of formal bureaucratic authority and, in many cases, fiscal responsibility. Conventional wisdom suggests that a strong proportion of center and institute directors may be career academic administrators (Warshaw, 2020). They hold faculty appointments and have run a number of units over the years. Meanwhile, prior research suggests that the average academic administrator, such as a school director, department head, provost, or president, may be a less productive researcher while serving as an administrator, and she or he is likely to have been a less productive researcher before taking on an administrative role (Etzioni, 1964; see also Goodall, 2009). As such an observation suggests, star scientists, who are heavily grant-funded and produce disproportionate numbers of publications and patents, may be precluded from, or perhaps avoid, administrative leadership positions. Researchers could employ theory of academic capitalism to probe a potentially stratifying shift in which faculty gain unit-level leadership positions over others.

Star scientists in entrepreneurial universities preside over "quasi-firms" in their laboratories of graduate and undergraduate students, postdoctoral researchers, technicians, and other personnel (Etzkowitz, 2003). It could be that star scientists, in the era of academic capitalism, are receiving disproportionate opportunities to run – and leverage for their research agenda and teams – the newest, cutting-edge, and generously-resourced SOUs. Central administrators and deans could utilize new, endowed SOUs to retain star scientists and to recruit more of them from other campuses or from industry or federal laboratories. In this way, the theory of academic capitalism may cast light on emerging fault lines of stratification in which the less productive scholars, as compared to their more prominent peers, are left to run the SOUs of old. That stratification could be reflected, then, in widening asymmetries among SOUs (e.g., newer vs. older, innovative vs. traditional, well-resourced vs. resourced-constrained, etc.) and professors (star researchers vs. teaching-focused faculty, outside hirers vs. internal candidates, etc.). These asymmetries may thus limit the extent to which entrepreneurial universities can foster and harness alliances among segments of units and among the leaders of these units.

The leadership styles in SOUs will likely reflect an array of different approaches to legitimacy-building. While researchers and analysts can apply to research in this arena various theories of leadership (transformational, transactional, behavioral, etc.), they may do well to consider the social skills employed. A focus on social skills is especially important in studies of entrepreneurial universities, where organizational boundaries and reward systems are changing and being renegotiated. The social skills-based perspective moves analyses beyond prior leadership theories by attending to specific repertoires of practice that mobilize collective action.

Fligstein and McAdam (2012, p. 46) define social skills as "the ability to induce cooperation by appealing to and helping to create shared meanings and collective identities". Social skilled actors "read" the organizational context and external environment to seize openings for change and "link actors or groups with widely different preferences and help reorder those preferences" (p. 52). Examples of social skills include utilizing direct authority, aggregating interests, agenda-setting, using bricolage (taking whatever the system gives), brokering relationships, and leveraging rhetorical strategies. As applied to SOUs in entrepreneurial universities, there are knowledge gaps about which social skills are used; at what points in time some are emphasized over others; and how social skills effect unit-level outcomes.

The social skills used during SOUs' parturition, for example, could be different from those deployed in subsequent stages of their lifecycles. Some social skills may improve SOUs' technical efficiency and effectiveness, allowing them to secure additional or newer funding critical for long-term survival. Objective measures of SOU performance, such as grant activity, publications, patents, job placement of graduates, and the like, weigh in funding decisions and formal evaluations; however, the rapport between unit leaders and evaluators can mediate assessment ratings and results (Davis and Bryant, 2010). From a power-based perspective: certain types or sets of social skills could be used to manage "up" the administrative hierarchy to shape perceptions of unit-level legitimacy. The strategic use of social skills may explain why and how some SOUs can live on past their primes. SOUs vary in their levels and sources of funding and accountability, suggesting that specific practices may also differ based on these conditions that delimit units' opportunities and constraints.

Meanwhile, the concept of social skills is applicable to examining strategies and tactics by which SOU leaders engage in networks. The linkages of SOUs could engender a paradox of collaboration and competition, as entities balance their own resource-related needs and goals with those of the collective (Geiger and Sá, 2008). SOU leaders navigate network relationships for their respective units and for the broader enclave, and the navigation of these dynamics and interdependencies would likely entail a variety of social skills as featured in practice.

Relatedly, it may be helpful to consider the connection of social skills to the tenure of leaders themselves. SOUs may change leaders as they advance in their organizational lifecycles. The leader who is right or appropriate for an SOU can vary over time and based on internal developments (e.g., expansion and formalization of operations, policies, and procedures) and on emerging challenges that confront the entity. To the extent that social skill helps SOU leaders and their units mediate, or thrive, within conditions of change, further research is needed.

Management

SOU leaders have a number of options for managing daily work and operations. Bozeman and Youtie (2017) examined strategies for managing scientific teams and created a typology of them based on their modal characteristics, frequency of use, and effectiveness. They identified five strategies: Tyrannical Collaboration Management, Directive Collaboration Management,

Pseudo Consultative Collaboration Management, Assumptive Collaboration Management, and Consultative Collaboration Management. They conclude that Consultative Collaboration Management is not frequently practiced but may be the most effective. As compared to the other four, it entails open, inclusive, and frequent communication across team members, engenders trusting relationships, and fosters respect for different values and perspectives and sensitivity to power and status differentials. Might such an approach be appropriate for managing SOUs? Team-based science can constitute one aspect of SOUs' portfolio of work, funding streams, and operations. Teams can also form independently of organizational units on campus (Corley et al., 2006). In turn, SOUs could feature managerial strategies (and typologies) unique to them and that explain their organizational outcomes.

Entrepreneurial universities create new organizational networks on their campuses and with external partners for economic activities and entrepreneurship. As such, SOU leaders could vary in how much of their management is focused on external audiences (marketing and branding, developing relationships, and the like) and campus-based and within-unit stakeholders. There are different managerial strategies that may become salient at various points in time, such as ongoing recruitment-focused initiatives to attract and retain faculty, intervening periodically in team-centered efforts to facilitate productivity and pursuits of grants, and conducting annual evaluations and assessments to gauge performance and associated outcomes. A time-dynamic approach to examining managerial work and strategies may thus be appropriate.

Professional training and development for management is critical to consider. Many department chairs take on leadership roles due to felt needs to serve their units and colleagues, and they do not always receive pay increases or support for growing and developing as academic administrators (Gardner and Ward, 2018). Beyond their laboratories, center and institute directors may not have had much prior managerial experience. They could have very different levels of sensitivity to timelines and deadlines imposed by funding agencies and/or industry partners, formal reporting and accountability mechanisms, evaluating staff, and budgeting. Such considerations imply that SOU management may be ripe opportunities for professional growth and development and for opening new networks of collaboration and resources. But they also indicate that, without formal training or mentoring, SOU leaders might be constrained in their ability to help their organizations collaborate with other units and become sustainable.

Finally, the use of data in managerial decision-making suggests a promising line for research. The extent to which and how SOU leaders and their teams compile, analyze, interpret, and act on data can shape what they do and why. Academic capitalism suggests that there are many different types of markets of competition for individual units and their collaborative enclaves. To consider how, and by whom, these markets are defined, identified, and pursued is especially critical in studies of university segmentation and stratification (Rosinger et al., 2016).

Governance

Governance-related research calls attention to decision-making structures, processes, and practices (1) between SOUs and (2) within them. The study of governance between SOUs is distinctive in entrepreneurial universities, due to organizational designs that heighten inter-unit collaboration and competition. Such a perspective suggests that the configuration of interdependent SOUs could be adopted for external perceptions of legitimacy, conforming to external norms and shared understandings about what entrepreneurial universities should look like (Pinheiro and Stensaker, 2014). At the ground level, meanwhile, competition among SOUs may fuel semi-autonomous actions for resources and status and drive them apart. Some of the generously-resourced SOUs, run by star scientists, may secure select lines of communication with the highest levels of campus administrators, industry partners, policymakers, and program officers at funding agencies (Louvel, 2016). These delimited enclaves of governance could preclude wider and more productive collaborations and thus constrain scientific advancement.

Researchers and analysts could bring renewed attention to studying decision-making and choice processes within SOUs. Eckel and Morphew (2009) suggest that decision-making in units with close ties to revenue streams will take on corporatized, rational-bureaucratic forms of choice. The prospects of such dynamics occurring in entrepreneurial universities are strong because these institutions create new research- and revenue-focused units and expand their external peripheries in concert with emerging market opportunities. In such settings, these new units and configurations attract the attention and involvement of executive-level administrators and managerial professionals due to felt needs to enhance and diversify institutional revenues. Eckel and Morphew hypothesize that privatization – and institutional pursuits of revenues – dramatically increase the number of units (and collaborations among them) and thus choice opportunities throughout a campus as a whole. Their perspective suggests increasing complexity and fragmentation in decision-making that could potentially limit coherent, coordinated strategy for entrepreneurial universities.

Schools and departments could feature some top-down, corporatized decision-making on particular issues, yet largely focus on shared governance with less-linear, more unstructured, and lengthier choice processes that include a broad set of faculty. The type and form of governance in centers and institutes could potentially feature increasing degrees of centralization: decision-making concentrated among center and institute leaders and/or their supervisory boards of campus administrators and/or industry partners. Centers and institutes do not usually serve as the tenure homes for faculty, and they may have their own full-time research scientists, graduate and undergraduate research assistants, postdoctoral researchers, and administrative staff. Tenure-line and tenured faculty who are affiliated with centers and institutes could be precluded from unit-level decision-making, while the other personnel associated with these units could also lack formal governance roles and responsibilities. There could, of course, be SOUs that utilize information technology in innovative ways to facilitate quick, collaborative, and analytical decision-making in "real time" as choice opportunities unfold. Researchers and analysts may thus aim to link governance between and within SOUs to the relative effectiveness and longevity of these entities. We know so little about failure in entrepreneurial universities (Rhoades and Stensaker, 2017). For scholarly and practical reasons, then, it may prove useful to examine how governance structures and processes shape which SOUs and networks fold or survive over time.

The managerialization of professors

As the total number of SOUs and their networks has increased in more recent years, so, too, has the total number of faculty who lead and manage them (Gumport, 2016). The surge in "managerialized" faculty – and in their interactions as SOU leaders with each other and with administrators – suggests a critical mass is forming and may constitute a newer profession. Entrepreneurial universities, by way of academic capitalist activity, are especially susceptible to: (1) collapsing the professional roles and boundaries between administrators and faculty; and (2) fragmenting the scientific profession. This section situates in each of these two streams new lines of research on processes and outcomes associated with the managerialization of professors.

Fluid boundaries between administrators and faculty

The academic capitalism-focused literature on faculty and administrators often focuses on one group or the other (Gonzales et al., 2014; Rhoades, 2014).

Rarely are both discussed together, suggesting an opportunity to research equilibria between administrators and faculty and bureaucracy and science. For example, administrators and faculty (especially senior professors) are both critical to stewarding entrepreneurial universities (Clark, 1998; McClure, 2016). They may work together in campus-wide committees and in episodic or sustained collaborations that engage the global knowledge economy. SOU leaders are in unique positions relative to other faculty, for they represent their units and/or networks in academic capitalist activity with an array of administrators and administrative offices and external partners. Their daily work may span involvement as principal investigators, as managers of intellectual property, indirect cost recovery, and/or equity-stake agreements, and as arbiters of multi-institution and multi-sector partnerships. Yet knowledge gaps remain about the interactions (the synergies and conflicts) that transpire between administration and SOUs and about how these interactions blend, for SOU leaders in particular, administrative and academic work, careers, and identities.

The managerialization of faculty is reflected in professors becoming SOU leaders and in the collapsing professional roles and boundaries between them and administrators. When faculty become SOU leaders, they gain access to positions of formal and symbolic authority, to resources, and to direct lines of communication with administrators and external stakeholders. Rather than transitioning away from faculty and into academic administration (deans, provosts, or presidents), SOU leaders are the nexus bridging multiple organizational levels and stakeholder groups. Managerialization is rooted in emerging organizational forms and networks, which create new types of academic/administrative experts, but also in social processes entwining administrators and faculty in academic capitalist activity. The convergence of bureaucracy and science in entrepreneurial universities may thus managerialize more faculty and move them, as a critical mass of potentially new professionals, toward the locus of scientific production.

SOU leaders differ from managerial professionals (administrators with advanced degrees reporting to executive-level leaders) and from other scientists (Rhoades, 2014). Many SOU leaders gain selective access to positions of bureaucratic influence and power that others cannot attain because they are neither faculty nor prominent scientists (Foucault, 1994; Larson, 1979). They could shape the distribution of resources to their colleagues, to their teams and units, and in ways that advantage members of their network of peers. Yet SOU leaders may aim to expand the types and forms of academic work they do because they are transitioning into different stages of their careers as scientists. Managerialization, for them, becomes a way to elaborate or extend the scientific career rather than to chart a new profession. That elaboration or extension may entail seeking to lead the younger generation of scientists through SOUs and to build up new ventures and entities of scientific and societal relevance. Meanwhile, some SOU leaders could approach their managerialization as a competitive strategy to situate themselves – and their newer occupational group – favorably on campus and in the research economy (Abbott, 1988).

It would thus be helpful to know the extent to which SOU leaders perceive themselves, and are perceived by colleagues and peers, as administrative scientists occupying a new, unique occupational space in entrepreneurial universities and in the global knowledge economy. The professional motivations and goals of SOU leaders are also important to examine. It remains unclear why faculty become SOU administrative leaders and how these positions effect, over time, their academic work (norms, practices, and reward systems), productivity and resources (publications, patents, and grant funding), and careers (progression, advancement, and stature). Motivations and goals can vary by academic rank, career stage, salary and funding considerations, institutional setting, and other characteristics such as gender (on which this chapter elaborates next). A disaggregated view is thus warranted. Attention is also needed to studying group-level outcomes for managerialized faculty relative to principal investigators of laboratories and other segments of professors who are not SOU leaders. The cross-group comparative perspective may highlight any positive, marginal gains, vis-à-vis managerialization and net of other factors, which separates a newer professional class from others in science.

Fragmentation within the scientific profession

The changing political and economic contexts can prompt strains and fissures within academic science. Consider gender inequities. Women have typically been disadvantaged by academic capitalism, which is used to justify the concentration of resources and power to fields and disciplines with relatively high proportions of men (Metcalfe and Slaughter, 2008). Meanwhile, many US states fund "eminent scholars" to drive economic development through entrepreneurial universities (Warshaw and Hearn, 2014). The disproportionate flow of resources to eminent faculty could encourage entrepreneurship among these scholars and also their peers, but potentially widens the status-differentials within the scientific community. Professional norms and reward systems tend to change over time for faculty, resettling into a hierarchy that separates higher- and lower-status forms of academic work and careers (Johnson, 2017). Changes to long-established reward systems could be beneficial by broadening understandings of legitimacy, of what constitutes appropriate work and who is suitable to enter and become a member of professions. These changes may come with unintended consequences that increasingly splinter, and thus deprofessionalize, scientists.

The managerialization of faculty and its connection to fragmentation in the scientific profession warrants close attention. As faculty become administrative leaders, and as they advance their scientific work and careers through these positions, their emerging professional class may increase the hierarchical differentiation on campus and in academic science. Scholars could thus probe the extent to which – and how – managerialized faculty are a professional class, embodying and/or encouraging the collective redistribution of knowledge and power in entrepreneurial universities and the scientific profession. This chapter suggests ways in which such positions, when viewed through the theories of academic capitalism and professionalization, may be empowering and professionalizing. Indeed, becoming administrative leaders of SOUs could be pathways to institutional leadership (Goodall, 2009) and to positions of authority and influence in national research policy (Warshaw, 2019). But there could be resistance from other scientists and professional associations that precludes a newer profession from emerging. And external challenges may weaken or suppress a new profession.

To the extent that managerialized faculty are classified, from a legal perspective, as managers, the prospects for them and for other professors to unionize may diminish (Rhoades, 2014). A trade-off may ensue between managerialization and unionization as potentially competing forms of collective action. Religious and sociopolitical factors could each constrain the ascendance of a new science-related profession. Witness in the USA the persistent challenges to scientific evidence of evolution (a religious issue) and climate change (a political concern), as well as the refusal of some families and communities, despite the prevailing medical wisdom, to vaccinate children from life-threatening diseases (a social factor). The economic relevance of SOUs and their leaders, meanwhile, may buffer them from such external threats and strengthen their interdependencies as a collective and as a potentially newer profession.

As Weber (1958) observes, the era of industrialization elevates the value of specialists rather than generalists in the labor market. Higher education, he suggests, becomes more central in society than in previous eras when it trains experts and specialists for the industrial economy. In postindustrial contexts of academic capitalism, SOUs and their leaders could be indicative, and facilitative, of another shift in the image of the ideal educated self and profession. The sources of science and power – in entrepreneurial universities and the global knowledge economy – could increasingly flow through neither specialists nor generalists but the emerging class of administrative scientists and their organizational networks. To examine these dynamics may bring to light mechanisms for reconciling disequilibria between organizational forms and professions, bureaucracy and science, in entrepreneurial universities and the broader society.

Concluding remarks

The emerging organizational forms and professions in entrepreneurial universities offer opportunities to advance new theory-driven lines of research. This chapter focuses on SOUs and their configurations as illustrative examples of core organizational changes taking place, and it highlights a potentially new profession of managerialized faculty who become their administrative leaders. Such changes can and do often emanate from decentralized social processes and practices among SOUs. When these ground-level processes and practices are made explicit through theory and research, they could indicate unique insights into the redistribution of science and power in entrepreneurial universities and in the broader society.

In this chapter, theories of academic capitalism and professionalization address why and how entrepreneurial universities are forming organizational units and networks and creating an occupational space for a newer professional class to develop. They are suitable conceptual anchors for advancing research on the leadership, management, and governance of SOUs and on social skills and mechanisms for building legitimacy and cross-campus and cross-sector partnerships in the knowledge economy. Moreover, the theories may help scholars probe further the movement of SOUs and their administrative leaders toward the locus of scientific production.

While the material presented here primarily focuses on developments in the USA, it can be extrapolated to other national contexts. The USA has historically featured centers and institutes within postsecondary institutions as part of its national ecology of knowledge-production and knowledge-exchange. Meanwhile, in countries such as Japan, Germany, and the Netherlands, independent research institutes external to higher education have served key scientific and economic functions. These institutes are, in recent years, becoming entwined with and, in some cases, folded into entrepreneurial universities to enhance research capacity and anchor regional clusters for economic growth (Dill and Van Vught, 2010). Such changes reveal different pathways across national contexts toward comparable end-goals of entwining university structures and processes with broader economic imperatives. They also suggest more recent developments in which newer organizational forms and professions are likely to emerge.

To pursue this chapter's research agenda may thus require close attention to context. Rhoades and Stensaker (2017) note that prior research on entrepreneurial universities includes studies from different countries, yet largely perpetuates a common view of them as bounded organizations seeking self-determinism. They call for situating future research in local, national, and global contexts, where various ecosystems (e.g., public policies, multi-university and multi-sector partnerships, economic development councils, etc.) are entwined with campus-based structures and processes. The analytical challenge, then, is one of specification. By attributing change in organizational forms and professions, and in science and power, to localized, ground-level actions, might we eclipse broader influences and vice versa. An empirical-based determination about the locus of action – and of scientific production – can be difficult to make in the era of academic capitalist networks and globalization. Yet to make that determination is vital to advancing our understanding of who shapes entrepreneurial universities, how, and to what end.

References

Abbott, A. (1988). *The system of professions: An essay on the division of expert labor.* Chicago, IL: University of Chicago Press.

Bastedo, M. (Ed.). (2012). *The organization of higher education: Managing colleges for a new era.* Baltimore, MD: Johns Hopkins University Press.

Bozeman, B. and Youtie, J. (2017). *The strength in numbers: The new science of team science.* Princeton, NJ: Princeton University Press.

Brint, S. (1994). *In an age of experts: The changing role of professionals in politics and public life.* Princeton: Princeton University Press.

Cantwell, B. and Kauppinen, I. (Eds) (2014). *Academic capitalism in the age of globalization.* Baltimore, MD: Johns Hopkins University Press.

Clark, B.R. (1998). *Creating entrepreneurial universities: Organizational pathways of transformation.* New York: IAU Press.

Corley, E.A., Boardman, P.C. and Bozeman, B. (2006). Design and the management of multi-institutional research collaborations: Theoretical implications from two case studies. *Research Policy*, **35**(7), 975–993.

Crow, M.M. and Dabars, W.B. (2015). *Designing the new American university.* Baltimore, MD: Johns Hopkins University Press.

Davis, D.D. and Bryant, J.L. (2010). Leader-member exchange, trust, and performance in National Science Foundation industry/university cooperative research centers. *Journal of Technology Transfer*, **35**(5), 511–526.

Dill, D.D. and Van Vught, F.A. (Eds) (2010). *National innovation and the academic research enterprise: Public policy in global perspective.* Baltimore, MD: Johns Hopkins University Press.

Eckel, P.D. and Morphew, C.C. (2009). The organizational dynamics of privatization in public research universities. In C.C. Morphew and P.D. Eckel (Eds), *Privatizing the public university: Perspectives from across the academy* (pp. 88–108). Baltimore, MD: Johns Hopkins University Press.

Etzioni, A. (1964). *Modern organizations.* New Jersey: Prentice Hall.

Etzkowitz, H. (2003). Research groups as "quasi-firms": The invention of the entrepreneurial university. *Research Policy,* **32**, 109–121.

Fligstein, N. and McAdam, D. (2012). *A theory of fields.* New York: Oxford University Press.

Foucault, M. (1994). *Essential works of Foucault, 1954–1984: Volume three: Power.* New York: The New Press.

Gardner, S.K. and Ward, K. (2018). Investing in department chairs. *Change,* **50**(2), 58–62.

Geiger, R.L. and Sá, C.M. (2008). *Tapping the riches of science: Universities and the promise of economic growth.* Cambridge: Harvard University Press.

Gonzales, L.D., Martinez, E. and Ordu, C. (2014). Exploring faculty experiences in a striving university through the lens of academic capitalism. *Studies in Higher Education,* **39**(7), 1097–1115.

Goodall, A.H. (2009). *Socrates in the boardroom: Why universities should be led by top scholars.* Princeton, NJ: Princeton University Press.

Gumport, P.J. (2016). Graduate education and research: Interdependence and strain. In M.N. Bastedo, P.G. Altbach and P.J. Gumport (Eds), *American higher education in the twenty-first century: Social, political, and economic challenges* (4th ed.) (pp. 110–154). Baltimore, MD: Johns Hopkins University Press.

Jacobs, J.A. (2014). *In defense of disciplines: Interdisciplinarity and specialization in the research university.* Chicago, IL: University of Chicago Press.

Johnson, D.R. (2017). *A fractured profession: Commercialism and conflict in academic science.* Baltimore, MD: Johns Hopkins University Press.

Larson, M.S. (1979). *The rise of professionalism: A sociological analysis.* Los Angeles, CA: University of California Press.

Louvel, S. (2016). Going interdisciplinary in French and US universities: Organizational change and university policies. In E.P. Berman and C. Paradeise (Eds), *The university under pressure: Research in the sociology of organizations,* Vol. 46 (pp. 329–359). Bingley, UK: Emerald.

McClure, K.R. (2016). Building the innovative and entrepreneurial university: An institutional case study of administrative academic capitalism. *Journal of Higher Education,* **87**(4), 516–543.

Mendoza, P. (2012). The role of context in academic capitalism: The industry-friendly department case. *Journal of Higher Education,* **83**(1), 26–48.

Metcalfe, A.S. and Slaughter, S. (2008). The differential effects of academic capitalism on women in the academy. In J. Glazer-Raymo (Ed.), *Unfinished agendas: New and continuing gender challenges in higher education* (pp. 80–111). Baltimore, MD: Johns Hopkins University Press.

Pinheiro, R. and Stensaker, B. (2014). Designing the entrepreneurial university: The interpretation of a global idea. *Public Organization Review,* **14**(4), 497–516.

Rhoades, G. (2014). Extending academic capitalism by foregrounding academic labor. In B. Cantwell and I. Kauppinen (Eds), *Academic capitalism in the age of globalization* (pp. 113–134). Baltimore, MD: Johns Hopkins University Press.

Rhoades, G. and Stensaker, B. (2017). Bringing organisations and systems back together: Extending Clark's entrepreneurial university. *Higher Education Quarterly*, **71**(2), 129–140.

Rooksby, J.H. (2016). *The branding of the American mind: How universities capture, manage, and monetize intellectual property and why it matters*. Baltimore, MD: Johns Hopkins University Press.

Rosinger, K.O., Taylor, B.J., Coco, L. and Slaughter, S. (2016). Organizational segmentation and the prestige economy: Deprofessionalization in high- and low-resource departments. *Journal of Higher Education*, **87**(1), 27–54.

Slaughter, S. and Rhoades, G. (2004). *Academic capitalism and the new economy: Markets, state, and higher education*. Baltimore, MD: Johns Hopkins University Press.

Slaughter, S. and Taylor, B. (Eds) (2016). *Higher education, stratification, and workforce development: Competitive advantage in the US and Canada*. New York: Springer.

Warshaw, J.B. (2019). Leadership in US public research universities: Design-based strategies and academic organization. In J. Jameson (Ed.), *International perspectives on leadership in higher education: Critical thinking for global challenges* (pp. 69–90). New York: Routledge.

Warshaw, J.B. (2020). University as knowledge-based enterprise: Organizational design and technology transfer. In J. Rooksby (Ed.), *Research handbook on intellectual property and technology transfer* (pp. 92–130). Cheltenham, UK and Northampton, MA, USA: Edward Elgar Publishing.

Warshaw, J.B. and Hearn, J.C. (2014). Leveraging university research to serve economic development: An analysis of policy dynamics in and across three U.S. states. *Journal of Higher Education Policy and Management*, **36**(2), 196–211.

Weber, M. (1958). Bureaucracy. In H.H. Gerth and C.W. Mills (Eds), *From Max Weber: Essays in sociology* (pp. 196–244). New York: Oxford University Press.

11 Between academia and business: research agenda for acapreneurship

Andrew Creed, Jarna Heinonen and Ambika Zutshi

Introduction: why acapreneurship?

Since Clark's seminal book *Creating entrepreneurial universities* (1998a), we understand that the university stakeholders impose significant, conflicting demands for universities and academics, adding pressure to alter their character (Clark, 1998b). Furthermore, globalization and increasing demands of the knowledge-based economy have pushed universities to undergo significant transformations not only to their internal structure, but also to the nature of collaboration between universities and their external stakeholders. This has reconfigured the university sector's role in economic development (Sam and van der Sijde, 2014). The concepts of academic entrepreneurship and entrepreneurial university have helped to explain the phenomenon, related challenges and transformations from the perspective of the university. In their analysis of academic entrepreneurship literature, Mars and Rios-Aguilar (2010) revealed that implications of academic entrepreneurship on individuals (faculty members) need further study.

By chance, when studying a non-profit biomedical research institute and its commercialization in close collaboration with business, we familiarized ourselves with the institute's 'acapreneurial model' of working. We became intrigued with this model, which was explained as 'a hybrid culture that integrates, in a single facility, academic, entrepreneurial, clinical and population health elements' (Glaser, 2015; LIMR, 2018, p. 1). The model extends to individual researchers working in the institute. There are core principles incorporated into the acapreneurial model to strengthen the integration of researchers with biotechnology businesses' operations and start-ups. The principles include:

(1) researchers' goals include a proof-of-concept, patent and peer-reviewed publication rather than an academic grant-and-publish cycle only; (2) a hybrid management implying a middle pathway for a researcher between the independence of the tenured academic researcher and the top-down direction of the corporate researcher; and (3) a researcher intensively co-inventing with companies as advisors, board members and science officers, for example. The future of this acapreneurial model is envisaged to emphasize not only the development of core medical products but also population health and patient care solutions, implying a shift of focus from commercialization to social impact.

We bring these acapreneurial principles to the university context with an agenda to extend the discussion about academic entrepreneurship and entrepreneurial university. We focus on how universities ask academics to behave in more entrepreneurial ways in executing all university tasks (Leih and Teece, 2016; Wright and Phan, 2018; Miller et al., 2018) and to become more commercially and business oriented to bolster the financial sustainability of the universities as well as to contribute to the surrounding economy.

From the university perspective, a number of entrepreneurial academics have always operated at the boundaries of discovery research (Toole and Czarnitzki, 2009) and helped to spawn industries and applications that run to the heart of what ultimately become commercial interests (Laukkanen, 2003; Brennan et al., 2005). Universities attract extra funding, prestige, global ranking elevation, and higher tuitions when they promote the society-changing inventions that emanate into the commercial sector on the back of their research initiatives. It is natural that pressures will continue within universities for entrepreneurial academics to continue innovating for such benefits. Thus, the entrepreneurial activities in universities have developed in parallel with those emergent in commercial research sectors, such as biomedicine (Glaser, 2015; LIMR, 2018). Although entrepreneurship in universities is not to be understood as synonymous with commercialization, market-orientation or academic capitalism (see e.g. Clark, 2004; Mars and Rios-Aguilar, 2010; Taylor, 2012) the concurrent entrepreneurial developments invite us to consider a role and related expectations for an entrepreneurial academic working in between the academia and business. Next, we bring acapreneurship to the university context by building upon the literature of academic entrepreneurship and entrepreneurial university.

Academic entrepreneurship, entrepreneurial university and acapreneurship

University faculty members can engage in various entrepreneurial activities ranging from more traditional academic activities, such as publishing academic research and teaching graduates, to more entrepreneurial and commercially-oriented activities, such as patenting, licencing, and spin-off firm formation and start-ups. Commissioned contract research, consulting and professional training courses fall between these 'soft' academic and 'hard' entrepreneurial activities on the spectrum (Klofsten and Jones-Evans, 2000; Philpott et al., 2011). Particularly, the above commercialization activities of academics make up academic entrepreneurship. The wider academic community may not consider the softer activities like academic publishing to be entrepreneurial activities because they align better with the traditional academic culture (Klofsten and Jones-Evans, 2000). However, in the knowledge-based society, the production of scientific knowledge forms a basis for new job creation and economic growth (Etzkowitz, 2014).

The original rationale for academic entrepreneurship was that it enhances the commercialization of university research and serves as a source of revenue for the university. Academic entrepreneurship resembles entrepreneurship in the business context with some exceptions. Unlike traditional forms of entrepreneurship, academics involved in university entrepreneurial ventures of commercialization of science usually continue to work for the university and the ownership of intellectual property lies, at least in part, with the university (Siegel and Wright, 2015). Furthermore, academics engaged in entrepreneurship continue to apply scientific norms, standards and values, unlike conventional entrepreneurs, although adapted to the new situation (Siegel et al., 2003).

Academic entrepreneurship not only encompasses technology transfer and enterprise-formation, but it also extends the nature of teaching and research activities of universities (Etzkowitz, 2014). As to the teaching task, universities are expected to produce highly qualified entrepreneurial graduates who are prepared for life-long learning to secure their employability during their careers (Sam and van der Sijde, 2014). As to the research task, knowledge production increasingly transforms from 'Mode 1' to 'Mode 2', highlighting a transdisciplinary form of knowledge production instead of a disciplinary-based one.[1] This transformation implies that scientific and technological knowledge generates both from within and beyond the university boundaries, and scientists need to move closer to real world problems and collaborate with businesses

(Gibbons et al., 1994). Finally, the knowledge society drives a university to play an entrepreneurial role as its third task by collaborating with business and government for socio-economic development (Etzkowitz et al., 2000).

This second academic revolution[2] brought about the concept of an entrepreneurial university, which encompasses all three university tasks: research, teaching and a third task of socio-economic development (Etzkowitz et al., 2008). An entrepreneurial university is a university that undertakes entrepreneurial activities 'with the objective of improving regional and national economic performance as well as the university's financial advantage and that of its faculty' (Etzkowitz et al., 2000, p. 313).

When pursuing its entrepreneurial activities in the boundaries of academia and business, an entrepreneurial university challenges traditional university rituals and procedures around knowledge that pre-dates the global commercialism of today (Billis and Rochester, 2020). Although higher education and universities have also become a kind of global business where the fittest will survive and succeed (Bridgman, 2007), even policy makers do not consider universities as businesses (Lambert, 2003). However, universities are becoming more business-like and entrepreneurial in managing their affairs. Universities are casting off their ivory tower image by taking a more active role in economic development. For some entrepreneurial universities, an entrepreneurial academic may be narrowly defined in commercial terms, but one can be entrepreneurial in different ways, which affirms the role of the autonomous and critical academic (Bridgman, 2007).

Siegel and Wright (2015) argue that academic entrepreneurship literature has focused too narrowly on commercializing university research by academic faculty and university-business links and suggest extending academic entrepreneurship with emerging perspectives. These emerging perspectives relate to addressing the questions of why, what, who and how academic entrepreneurship takes place. The original rational for academic entrepreneurship, that is, commercialization of university research and provision of financial returns for the university, has extended to reflect the wider entrepreneurial university ecosystem, thus incorporating wider social and economic impacts on the ecosystem. Similarly, the forms of entrepreneurial activity widen from academic spin-offs, licensing and patents to cover also student and alumni start-ups, entrepreneurially equipped students and job creation. The key actors are not only faculty members, but also students; and their entrepreneurship societies, alumni, surrogate entrepreneurs and entrepreneurs in residence are engaged in academic entrepreneurship. Finally, the technology transfer offices and science parks are not the sole institutional means of supporting academic entrepreneurship, but more informal entrepreneurship garages, business plan competitions, collaborative networks, accelerators and incubators as well as employee mobility are flexibly exploited (Siegel and Wright, 2015).

The acapreneurial model taken from the non-profit research institute highlights the ways in which researchers integrate with businesses and start-ups. The principles resonate clearly with entrepreneurial university and academic entrepreneurship, particularly its new emerging perspectives (see Siegel and Wright, 2015). The goal of acapreneurship implies that academics target beyond the commercialized product or concept to make an impact on the surrounding ecosystem and wider society. Furthermore, the actors who are involved, the forms of acapreneurship and the modes of supporting acapreneurship expand the traditional understanding of academic entrepreneurship.

To summarize, we suggest that an academic applies acapreneurship when, on the one hand, moving from the traditional academic perspective to an entrepreneurial perspective (see Philpott et al., 2011) and, on the other hand, extending the activities from faculty members to include students and business stakeholders (see Siegel and Wright, 2015). Furthermore, acapreneurship can take place and produce different societal contributions in different types of universities with different focuses, as depicted in Figure 11.1. A teaching university is dedicated merely to capacity building of students. A research university engages with the creation of new knowledge in addition to teaching; whereas an entrepreneurial university encompasses teaching, research and the third task of socio-economic development. The university contributions respectively relate to business practice, innovation and impact on the ecosystem and society (Etzkowitz and Zhou, 2008).

Bringing acapreneurship to the university context makes the bridges between academia and business more visible. It also balances the three university tasks of academics and incorporates teaching of students into the third task informed by research. Furthermore, the emphasis shifts from practice and innovation towards the impacts upon the surrounding ecosystem and society. Next, we focus on the tensions that academics face when working as acapreneurs between academia and business.

Expectations and challenges in acapreneurship

Contemporary academic performance, irrespective of the discipline, level of employment (including contract, part or full time) or even country of employment, is evaluated on three criteria: research, teaching, and the third task, that is socio-economic development. Universities have transformed from

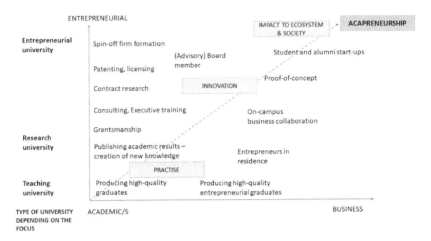

Figure 11.1 Acapreneurship integrating academic, entrepreneurial and business perspectives

traditional tasks of teaching and research to encompass also the third task of economic development (Sam and van der Sijde, 2014), although the primary focus depends on the university's strategic direction, and whether it attempts to fulfil its mission acting primarily as a teaching, research or entrepreneurial university. This common trend challenges academics in their respective universities because moving along the academic and business perspectives creates tensions for an acapreneur when attempting to achieve objectives, which are reviewable in formal performance appraisals. The expectations placed on an acapreneur, as well as related challenges derived from the literature on academic entrepreneurship and entrepreneurial university in the previous section, are summarised in the Table 11.1. The more the academic moves towards an entrepreneurial perspective, and the more acapreneurial s/he behaves, the more challenges s/he likely faces.

Academics are expected to conduct high-quality multidisciplinary research and publish in high-impact, peer-reviewed journals. Furthermore, academics must share preliminary findings of research projects during conferences, and seek and secure research grants for quality research. Collaborating across faculties, institutions and with individuals are some of the main research activities (Hansson and Mønsted, 2008). Reviewing papers of their peers for conferences and journals, along with providing informal feedback to colleagues, is a common contribution of academics. In addition, researchers need to collaborate with academic peers nationally, internationally and through

Table 11.1   Expectations and challenges in acapreneurship

	Expectation	Challenge
Research	• Attracting research funds to conduct quality research that makes it possible to further invest in quality research. • Shift from Mode 1 to Mode 2 knowledge production and to move closer to the real world problems.	• Funding policy may not align with multidisciplinary research interests/new ideas. • University organizational structures can stifle innovative endeavours across faculties and with businesses. • Working with business problems is time consuming and uncertain without any clear/secure payoffs. • Balancing between rigorous and relevant science.

	Expectation	Challenge
Teaching	• Producing research-based quality and relevant teaching/learning. • Producing high-quality entrepreneurial graduates to cope with a changing environment by applying principles of lifelong learning and entrepreneurship education.	• Subject matters and university organizational structures may hinder multi-disciplinary approach needed for relevance and employability. • Soft skills undervalued in comparison to academic knowledge. • Identification of changing future needs.
Third task	• Producing social and economic impact and outreach to the ecosystem through new innovations and intensive co-creation.	• Weak professional recognition of the third task including lack of incentives, and time-constraint due to heavy demands in research and teaching. • Fear of losing academic integrity over business needs. • Organizational structures might stifle the multi-disciplinary collaboration needed within and outside the university.

external networks (such as commercial, industrial, not-for-profit and govern-ment stakeholders) in order to increase the impact, quality and relevance of academic research.

Meeting the challenges is far from straightforward. According to the Mode 2 knowledge production, a multi-disciplinary approach is expected, but it may be hard to accomplish due to organizational and structural impediments of the university and/or research programmes of the financiers. Working with relevant business problems may not only be time-consuming but may also be insecure in terms of unexpected results. In addition, some disciplines are more suited to contributing to socio-economic development (Philpott et al., 2011). In order to meet the expectations posed to the research, academics may also need to consider the balance between scientific rigour and relevance of the research as new research ideas from business influence the academic research agenda (Etzkowitz, 2014).

In teaching, an academic is expected to execute high-quality, research-based and relevant teaching. This can extend to related learning opportunities for the students and increasingly to business executives and stakeholders. Outcomes are usually assessable through teaching evaluation scores (with benchmarks varying from one discipline and university to another), although the learning needs stem from the changing environment and students' future employ-ability. Designing fair and equitable assessment that evaluates theoretical aspects of the topics covered in the relevant course is also an academic role. Academics are also required to incorporate student feedback in their teaching style, content and assessment. Furthermore, combining research findings as part of teaching material, including updated, relevant information for the teaching program, helps academics because university teaching is expected to be research-based and relevant. Academics are also expected to integrate the principles and perspectives of life-long learning and entrepreneurship educa-tion into teaching of the curriculum (see e.g. Wright and Phan, 2018; Sam and van der Sijde, 2014). University structures with subject-related issues giving priority to the Mode 1 type of knowledge production and teaching thereof may also pose a challenge to research-based and relevant teaching expected from academics. It may also be hard for them to look beyond the current skills needs of the future employment (Sam and van der Sijde, 2014).

Another monitored aspect of academic performance is the third task, as in addition to research and teaching tasks, academics are expected to contribute to the social and economic development of the surrounding environment through new innovations and intensive co-creation (Etzkowitz et al., 2000). Depending on the level of the academic within the university hierarchy these roles can be specialized, for example senior academics are often required to engage with committees and community, internal and external to the university, and to be spokespeople for the university.

Although the importance of the third task has been highlighted in the universities, it seems that the task is not professionally recognized and incentives for active stakeholder engagement continue to be scarce (Philpott et al., 2011). Academic recruitment practices value journal publication, which may further work against the third task (Bridgman, 2007). In addition, university structures may pose an impediment to multidisciplinary collaboration needed to co-create new innovations with stakeholders. Execution of the third task may further be challenged by a fear of letting business overrule academic freedom and integrity, and thus the traditional mission of the university (Etzkowitz, 2014; Bridgman, 2007). The third task is often presented as subordinate to research and teaching tasks, implying that the third task is achievable only through fulfilment of research and teaching tasks (Sam and van der Sijde, 2014). In addition, there is a risk of losing one's reputation as a convincing researcher, especially among colleagues and the wider scientific community, when executing the third task.

Tensions when working between academia and business

Acapreneurship provides many opportunities for academics, but there are political and bureaucratic constraints to securing the new opportunities (Leih and Teece, 2016; Baruch and Rousseau, 2019). Balancing the various expectations related to the university tasks can create an environment of stress, low morale, backstabbing and the decline of academia as a lifelong career choice (Coates et al., 2009). The challenges acapreneurs face when attempting to meet the expectations create tensions, which need to be overcome for acapreneurship to flourish in the university setting. Based on the literature we have identified tensions in four related areas: goals and strategies, accountability and performance, management and incentives, and culture for collaboration.

One tension relates to university goals and strategies and the ways in which business perspectives are integrated into the university mission and tasks. For some, *commercial business* values pose a threat to *academic freedom and ethos* as they deviate from the traditional academic mission (Etzkowitz, 2014; Bridgman, 2007). A sense of vision and strategy is required, but is not always pragmatic, for academics, since collective targets are imposed by the university, which, sometimes, do not align with the individual's vision and values.

Another tension relates to what academics are expected to be accountable for, and how their performance is being measured. In terms of entrepreneurial activities, quality research and publications in the top-tier journals are *soft entrepreneurial activities* and outcomes, whereas, activities closer to business, such as patenting, licensing and start-ups, are considered as *hard entrepreneurial activities* (Philpott et al., 2011). Understandably, it is challenging as well as time-consuming to be a master of both, creating a tension for an acapreneur. How to balance these soft and hard entrepreneurial activities is definitely an individual challenge.

A tension, relating to university management and incentives, is informative of how a university values and supports academics to achieve the mission that that university has chosen in its strategy. Acapreneurial activities work best when allowed to emerge *bottom-up* from the individual initiatives. On the other hand, the university is putting *top-down* pressure on academics to behave entrepreneurially. However, the reality is that rigid university structures pose barriers from a number of directions to such entrepreneurial behaviour. Furthermore, traditional university reward structure is based on *publications* (soft activities) and does not reward (hard) *entrepreneurial activity* (Philpott et al., 2011). The multiplicity of university structure, policies and operations can serve to stifle some acapreneurial behaviours. For instance, before an individual or a team can apply for grants for innovative projects, they need to cross a number of hurdles internally to receive permission and fill forms at different levels. All these tasks need to pre-empt grant official deadlines due to the differently prioritized internal deadlines. When multiple institutions are involved on a project, the layers and demands of *bureaucracy* further compound to reduce the flexibility and responsiveness that an entrepreneur might normally be expected to express. This can mount pressure and, at times, frustration for an acapreneur who is trying to be *entrepreneurial* and responsive but held back systemically. Essentially, the university as a working environment may not necessarily offer the optimal support for acapreneurs to execute proactively all the three core tasks of the university. The irony is that universities are striving to be more dynamic, competing at the global level for survival and aiming to run more like businesses (Firmansyah et al., 2018). Academics are pushed to become multi-skilled acapreneurs to achieve their competing targets and priorities within research, teaching and the third task, while meeting with numerous barriers. Acapreneurs are, thus, facing *double tension* as the university on the one hand expects and requires acapreneurial activities, but on the other hand does not give enough room and encouragement for such ventures.

Finally, one tension relates to culture for collaboration in academia. Acapreneurship stems from multidisciplinary collaboration of faculty with external business and its stakeholders. It is about arranging internal collaboration within the university (coupling) and fostering external partnership (bridging) at the same time (Pinheiro and Stensaker, 2014). Different disciplines are more open than others to external outreach and collaboration with businesses. Collaboration is a powerful way to build and realize opportunities. Within universities there are power structures and informal hierarchies embedded in the organizational culture that influence the realization of the opportunities. University faculties and academics do not usually share a *unified drive* towards integrating the third task to research and teaching. Such goals and top-down visioning may actually create *academic disharmony* across faculties. (Philpott et al., 2011) and, thus, hinder multidisciplinary collaborative endeavours. In all, it seems that acapreneurs are lacking acapreneurial role models within the university with whom to associate (Philpott et al., 2011). Furthermore, concrete and applicable working practices to balance academia and business are only just emerging.

Research agenda for acapreneurship

The focus of this chapter was to bring acapreneurship to the university context by discussing and positioning it in the frame of academic entrepreneurship and entrepreneurial university. We suggest that an academic applies acapreneurship when moving from a traditional academic perspective to an entrepreneurial perspective (see Philpott et al., 2011) and extending the activities from faculty to include students and surrounding businesses (see Siegel and Wright, 2015) at the same time. This movement towards acapreneurship creates tensions for academic work and a doubt emerges whether universities' administrators fully understand what it means to expect academics to become acapreneurial. More awareness of the implications of this direction travelled by universities is required (Gutierrez and Worley, 2020).

Based on the existing literature on academic entrepreneurship and entrepreneurial universities, we identified expectations and challenges which an acapreneur faces (see Table 11.1) and revealed some related tensions. More research is needed to enlighten other potential conflicts around acapreneurship and how such tensions might be bridged. Acapreneurship implies close collaboration and co-creation between university researchers and businesses. What are the new forms of acapreneurship that engage both small and larger businesses to work with universities? What are the related implications for the teaching and curricula design? Furthermore, it is useful to gain better understanding of the impacts of acapreneurship in academia, businesses and wider society. New innovative research designs and measures are probably also needed to capture such impacts. The existing studies on academic entrepreneurship and entrepreneurial university approach university-business collaboration from the perspective of the university or researcher. It would be relevant for the future research agenda to approach acapreneurship also through the eyes of an entrepreneur and investigate the collaboration, motivation for it, practices and related outcomes from the business perspective in order to identify areas of mutual understanding and potential conflicts. What business practitioners, especially entrepreneurs, understand about the change in the academic role and its overlap with their own roles deserves further investigation. These broad themes ought to be included in the future research agenda of acapreneurship. The suggested research agenda for acapreneurship guides future directions making it easier to align acapreneurship throughout the university and business sectors for mutual benefit. Adding to identified broader themes, we suggest some more detailed research directions based on the revealed tensions. These include the following.

Goals and strategies

Tensions related to university goals and strategies are visible both at individual and university level. More research will unfold the ways in which commercial and academic priorities can align for best practice acapreneurship. It is equally important to understand parallels between university and individual priorities of acapreneurship.

Performance and accountability

Performance in entrepreneurial activities is typically measured by hard activities such as patenting and licencing, whereas softer activities such as academic publishing and contract research are less prominent as yardsticks of entrepreneurial performance (Philpott et al., 2011). Diverse universities with various faculties and strategies apply entrepreneurial activities differently. It would be useful to investigate the context-dependency of soft and hard entrepreneurial activities and the ways in which universities contribute to economic and social development. Perhaps, softer entrepreneurial activities will reveal a high contribution to economic and social development. More research on performance measures in teaching, research and the third task will prevent misalignments and capture the breadth of impacts. Furthermore, the funding structure of universities and financiers needs to be critically analysed to create schemes making it possible for acapreneurs to create multi-disciplinary and relevant research and teaching programmes including a co-creational component with businesses.

Management and incentives

Acapreneurs are facing the double tension of expectations for being entrepreneurial and limitations on the freedom to do so. Better knowledge and understanding is to be encouraged for the appropriate organizational arrangement supporting acapreneurship. Existing studies suggest that balancing is needed (see Pinheiro and Stensaker, 2014), but how it occurs in different contexts remains unresolved. For instance, we do not yet know how to balance between university bureaucracy and acapreneurial behaviour; and between a collegial, democratic bottom-up and centrally governed top-down approach with a strong steering core. In essence, the question is how to manage and lead acapreneurs and traditional academics in the same university. This further relates to incentives to reward acapreneurial behaviour, namely what performance appraisal systems are aligned to support acapreneurship at individual and university level. Logically, this leads us to suggest investigating the nature of an acapreneurial career and the factors affecting career advancement in different universities.

Culture for collaboration

Acapreneurship inherently involves intensive and goal-oriented co-creation between academia and business, which builds upon multi-disciplinary collaboration within academia. Academic freedom and Mode 1 knowledge production are dominant normative ethos in a traditional research university, whereas Mode 2 knowledge production and user-inspired basic research with a united drive towards the third task are more dominant in the acapreneurial model. Future research should investigate how to align academic freedom and strategic collaboration both within academia and with the stakeholders. Other research can explore the conditions and processes for how acapreneurs can capitalize on their business connections (networks) to help achieve their academic objectives. Furthermore, the role of students, entrepreneurs and business partners in generating innovative ideas and further co-creating them with the academia for the mutual and societal benefit will be of value in research findings.

The suggested research agenda incorporates multiple research approaches, depending on the concrete aim and research questions of the studies. A diverse range of methodologies may be required according to the research direction pursued. In-depth interviews with a cross-section of acapreneurs representing different levels and disciplines to identify the challenges and tensions faced within a certain discipline should be undertaken. Action research and other mixed method approaches will yield deep and rich insights for some psychological and sociological research directions for example.

These approaches, augmented with quantitative survey data and ongoing meta-analyses, will enable the wider literature of acapreneurship research to be continuously improved. Future research may involve surveys of acapreneurs to get a broader and more comprehensive picture of their perceptions of their roles, responsibilities and challenges, and their reasons for applying acapreneurship in academia. The practical policy and procedural changes affecting acapreneurship, as imposed by the university administrators to support university transformation, also need elucidation.

We hope that the research agenda for acapreneurship encourages researchers to address important bridges between academia and business. Following these new research directions will also provide managerial implications for university administrators and leaders, as well as policy implications for those making education and science policy decisions.

Acknowledgement

The second author would like to acknowledge the financial support provided by the NordForsk NCoE program 'NordAqua' (#82845).

Notes

1. Mode 1 form of knowledge production is a disciplinary-based knowledge production that is carried out within a disciplinary boundary with regard to cognitive and social norms governing academic sciences, implying the absence of practicality in nature. Mode 2 is a transdisciplinary form of knowledge production that is carried out within a context of application and needs considerations of the interests of stakeholders (Gibbons et al., 1994).
2. The first academic revolution refers to a transition from teaching institutions to research universities. The second academic revolution implies bringing the third task, a socio-economic development, to universities (Etzkowitz et al., 2008).

References

Baruch, Y. and Rousseau, D. (2019), 'Integrating psychological contracts and ecosystems in career studies and management', *Academy of Management Annals*, **13** (1), 84–111.

Billis, D. and Rochester, C. (2020), *Handbook on hybrid organisations*. Cheltenham, UK and Northampton, MA, USA: Edward Elgar Publishing.

Brennan, M., Wall, A. and McGowan, P. (2005), 'Academic entrepreneurship: Assessing preferences in nascent entrepreneurs', *Journal of Small Business and Enterprise Development*, **12** (3), 307–322.

Bridgman, T. (2007), 'Freedom and autonomy in the university enterprise', *Journal of Organizational Change Management*, **20** (4), 478–490.

Clark, B. (1998a), *Creating entrepreneurial universities: Organizational pathways of transformation*. Oxford: IAU Press/Pergamon.

Clark, B. (1998b), 'The entrepreneurial university: Demand and response', *Tertiary Education and Management*, **4** (1), 5–16.

Clark, B. (2004), 'Delineating the character of the entrepreneurial university', *Higher Education Policy*, **17** (4), 355–370.

Coates, H., Dobson, I., Edwards, D., Friedman, T., Goedegebuure, L. and Meek, L. (2009), *The attractiveness of the Australian academic profession: A comparative analysis*. Melbourne: ACER.

Etzkowitz, H. (2014), 'The entrepreneurial wave. From ivory tower to global economic engine', *Industry and Higher Education*, **28** (4), 223–232.

Etzkowitz, H. and Zhou, C. (2008), 'Introduction to special issue: Building the entrepreneurial university: A global perspective', *Science and Public Policy*, **35** (9), 627–635.

Etzkowitz, H., Webster, A., Gebhardt, C. and Cantisano Terra, B.R. (2000), 'The future of the university and the university of the future: Evolution of ivory tower to entrepreneurial paradigm', *Research Policy*, **29** (2), 313–330.

Etzkowitz, H., Ranga, M., Benner, M., Guaranys, L., Maculan, A. and Kneller, R. (2008), 'Pathways to the entrepreneurial university: Towards a global convergence', *Science and Public Policy*, **35** (9), 681–695.

Firmansyah, D., van der Sijde, P. and van den Besselaar, P. (2018), 'Academics coping with business logic: A study at Indonesian universities', *Journal of Engineering and Technology Management*, **49** (2018), 91–108.

Gibbons, M., Limoges, C., Nowotny, H., Schwatrzman, S., Scott, P., Trow, M. and Agassi, J. (1994), *The new production of knowledge: The dynamics of science and research in contemporary societies*. London: SAGE Publications Ltd.

Glaser, V. (2015), 'Interview with Mel Reichman, PhD', *Assay and Drug Development Technologies*, **13** (1), 11–15.

Gutierrez, K. and Worley, J. (2020), 'Pondering an ideal worker in academia and consideration of a "new" normal of faculty work-life'. In: las Heras Maestro, M., Chinchilla Albiol, N., and Grau Grau, M. (eds), *The new ideal worker. Contributions to management science*. Cham, Switzerland: Springer.

Hansson, F. and Mønsted, M. (2008), 'Research leadership as entrepreneurial organizing for research', *Higher Education*, **55** (6), 651–670.

Klofsten, M. and Jones-Evans, D. (2000), 'Comparing academic entrepreneurship in Europe: The case of Sweden and Ireland', *Small Business Economics*, **14** (4), 299–309.

Lambert, R. (2003), *Lambert review of business-university collaboration*. London: HM Treasury.

Laukkanen, M. (2003), 'Exploring academic entrepreneurship: Drivers and tensions of university-based business', *Journal of Small Business and Enterprise Development*, **10** (4), 372–382.

Leih, S. and Teece, M. (2016), 'Campus leadership and the entrepreneurial university: A dynamic capabilities perspective', *Academy of Management Perspectives*, **30** (2), 182–210.

LIMR (2018), 'Organizational model of biomedical research: A mix of academic and entrepreneurial cultures means that knowledge and invention are equally weighted for maximum return on investment', *Catalyst*, Spring/Summer. Lankenau Institute for Medical Research (LIMR), https://www.mainlinehealth.org/-/media/files/pdf/basic-content/research/limr/catalyst/catalyst-2018-spring-summer.pdf?la=en.

Mars, M. and Rios-Aguilar, C. (2010), 'Academic entrepreneurship (re)defined: Significance and implications for the scholarship of higher education', *Higher Education*, **59** (4), 441–460.

Miller, K., Alexander, A., Cunningham, J. and Albats, E. (2018), 'Entrepreneurial academics and academic entrepreneurs: A systematic literature review', *International Journal of Technology Management*, **77** (1–3), 9–37.

Philpott, K., Dooley, L., O'Reilly, C. and Lupton, G. (2011), 'The entrepreneurial university: Examining the underlying academic tensions', *Technovation*, **31** (4), 161–170.

Pinheiro, R. and Stensaker, B. (2014), 'Designing the entrepreneurial university: The interpretation of a global idea', *Public Organization Review*, **14** (4), 497–516.

Sam, C. and van der Sijde, P. (2014), 'Understanding the concept of the entrepreneurial university from the perspective of higher education models', *Higher Education*, **68** (6), 891–908.

Siegel, D. and Wright, M. (2015), 'Academic entrepreneurship: Time for a rethink?', *British Journal of Management*, **26** (4), 582–595.

Siegel, D., Waldman, D. and Link, A. (2003), 'Assessing the impact of organizational practices on the productivity of university technology transfer offices: An exploratory study', *Research Policy*, **32** (1), 27–48.

Taylor, M. (2012), 'The entrepreneurial university in the twenty-first century', *London Review of Education*, **10** (3), 289–305.

Toole, A. and Czarnitzki, D. (2009), 'Exploring the relationship between scientist human capital and firm performance: The case of biomedical academic entrepreneurs in the SBIR program', *Management Science*, **55** (1), 101–114.

Wright, M. and Phan, P. (2018), 'From the editors: The commercialization of science: From determinants to impact', *Academy of Management Perspectives*, **32** (1), 1–3.

12 Relationship development patterns of university-based start-ups

Lise Aaboen, Anna Dubois and Leena Aarikka-Stenroos

Introduction

Entrepreneurial universities are centres of learning that create and disseminate new knowledge, organise multidisciplinary and boundary-spanning activities and facilitate novel partnership arrangements with support from state and private-sector partners (Klofsten et al., 2019). Previous research addresses how scientific knowledge is transferred to the market (Boehm and Hogan, 2013; Debackere and Veugelers, 2005; Gilsing et al., 2011), how start-ups may have a catalysing effect on domestic industries, and how start-ups may take on active roles in disseminating new technologies (Autio, 1994). Taken together, previous studies of entrepreneurial universities show how various actors from industry, universities and other fields shape start-ups' business; however, they focus less on start-ups' performance after they leave the university and the incubator (Soetanto and van Geenhuizen, 2019). Moreover, previous studies do not capture how the early relationships formed by start-ups influence their business ideas or how business emerges. In light of the assumption that the context of start-ups plays a vital role in their development, it is necessary to develop an understanding of the interaction between start-ups and relevant actors in university and industry context(s).

In this chapter, we focus on how start-ups become embedded in the university and industry context(s), and we suggest a research agenda for a more systemic approach to studying university and industry actors in the context of start-up development in entrepreneurial universities. The story of a firm should not end at the achievement of business; an entrepreneurial university should have a role in the ongoing development of start-ups originating both from universities and industry. Therefore, we focus on how start-ups develop over time through interactions with relevant university and industry actors. We use examples of transport-related start-ups in Western Sweden to explore how start-ups become embedded in these two contexts by identifying and analysing their relationship development patterns.

Key actors and embeddedness in the university and industry context(s)

Key actors

Universities are organisations that gather a critical mass of educated individuals, such as students and researchers, in one place to generate new ideas. Some of these ideas can be diffused by start-ups (Westhead and Storey, 1995). Schools of entrepreneurship, which provide master's programmes related to action-based entrepreneurship education (Fogelberg and Lundqvist, 2013; Rasmussen and Sørheim, 2006), and incubators, which accelerate the development of start-ups (Grimaldi and Grandi, 2005; Mian, 1997), are two types of university-based actors that support start-ups. Incubators can prepare start-ups for potential obstacles by complementing and developing the entrepreneurial abilities of the founders, providing advice regarding financing and giving structure and credibility to firms. Often, an incubator provides a shared location for firms, business coaching and courses (cf. Aaboen, 2009; Bergek and Norrman, 2008; Hackett and Dilts, 2004; Phan et al., 2005). In addition, there are other supporting organisations connected to the university that provide soft funding, business support and legal advice. However, the role of technology transfer offices tends to be less important in Swedish universities compared with universities in other countries. This is because Sweden is one of the few countries in Europe that maintains the 'teacher's exemption' model, meaning that university-employed inventors own their inventions and have the ability to commercialise them (Fogelberg and Lundqvist, 2013; Jacobsson et al., 2013) and allocate ownership rights (Bourelos et al., 2012).

Industry or market-related actors, such as local and global firms in the value chain, industry experts and industry associations, are critical players that can facilitate knowledge development and market formation (Bergek et al., 2008; Clarysse et al., 2014) and thereby act as relevant actors for the start-up. Early interactions with potential customers and other stakeholders tend to facilitate the development of knowledge about customer preferences (e.g. Aarikka-Stenroos and Lehtimäki, 2014), as these actors articulate demand.

Furthermore, first customers play a critical role, as they teach the start-up how to interact with customers (cf. Aaboen et al., 2011). Subsequently, they can become reference customers, which facilitate further sales and funding, increase the start-up's credibility in the market and showcase the initial customers' commitment to the start-up (see, e.g., Ruokolainen and Aarikka-Stenroos, 2016; Partanen et al., 2014).

Another relevant actor group is funders, such as venture capitalists (Wright et al., 2006; Shane and Cable, 2002) and angel funders (Shane, 2004; Erikson and Sørheim, 2005), who are able to contribute more financing in later stages of development than soft funders. Governmental actors and regulators, who shape markets by determining the standards and preferences of a whole society or market, are also relevant. Governmental actors are particularly important as providers of soft financing to fill the gap between private funding and private equity financing (Mustar et al., 2006).

Embeddedness

Previous research (e.g. Ciabuschi et al., 2012; Ingemansson and Waluszewski, 2009; Perna et al., 2015) pointed out that in order for a start-up to develop, it needs to be embedded in specific development, producing and using settings. Perna et al. (2015) argue that embeddedness is achieved by interfacing the new solution with other products that are already in use, produced, supplied, marketed and sold. Moreover, Jack and Anderson (2002: 484), who focus on the social relationships of the entrepreneur, maintain that embeddedness 'is about joining the structure'. Thus, the embeddedness of start-ups in the university and industry contexts is highly relevant for start-up development.

The concept of embeddedness was introduced by Granovetter (1985: 481) to highlight the importance of considering how 'economic action is embedded in structures of social relations'. According to Uzzi (1997: 36–37), structural embeddedness creates 'economic opportunities that are difficult to replicate via markets, contracts, or vertical integration'. However, the positive effects of embeddedness are only valid until a certain threshold, and then embeddedness starts to become a liability since it makes the firm vulnerable to exogenous shocks and unable to access information outside the network. The strength of 'weak ties' (Granovetter, 1973: 1360) is a key notion that highlights the importance of ties between networks in which relationships are strong(er). Weak ties facilitate the 'diffusion of influence and information, mobility opportunities and community organisation'. Hence, in addition to strong relationships, firms need access to so-called 'acquaintances' through weak ties in order to gain access to more 'distant' actors.

Studies of start-ups that are grounded in the industrial network approach emphasise the emergence of adjustments to, and interdependencies with, other organisations during firm development, the formation of business relationships that enable start-ups to become embedded in industrial networks and, most importantly, the interaction processes that take place between the start-up and its network of various counterparts (Aaboen et al., 2013; Ciabuschi et al., 2012; La Rocca et al., 2013). In addition to building direct relationships with various actors, it is vital for start-ups to consider the connectedness between relationships. When investigating start-ups' relationships, it is important to consider the network effects produced by the interconnectedness among relationships (see, e.g., Ritter 2000). For example, third-party connections are important when considering the mediation of contacts and potential development of connections between relationships (Aarikka-Stenroos, 2011).

A key issue for start-ups is how their early relationship formation helps to embed them in the industry and university contexts. The entrepreneurial university must also consider how to support the formation of relationships that result in embeddedness and have a positive effect on the start-ups' business development. There are latent networks of relationships (based on business exchanges as well as social interactions) in the university and industry contexts of firms, and while these relationships and networks always 'exist', they are also always specific to the actors involved. Whether or not they can be accessed or utilised by a particular (new) actor depends on the situation and on the initial relationships developed by the start-up within the network.

The conceptual framework for this study, which explains start-ups' efforts to interact and form relationships with actors in the industry and university contexts, is illustrated in Figure 12.1. Together, the industry and university contexts (Baraldi and Perna, 2014; Baraldi and Ingemansson Havenvid, 2016; Fini et al., 2011) form the context for business development (Clarysse et al., 2011; Isenberg, 2010). The underlying assumption is that start-ups need to build and develop relationships with industry and university actors in order to access resources to develop their technology and offerings.

The features (i.e. relationships among actors) in the two contexts are important since indirect links to other actors are enabled by forming (direct) relationships with 'the right' actors in the two context(s). Vital features include the actors and their relationships as well as how relationships are connected within and across contexts. Hence, the entrepreneurial university needs to consider its ability to support its start-ups' embeddedness processes by developing these contexts as well as start-ups' opportunities to access them.

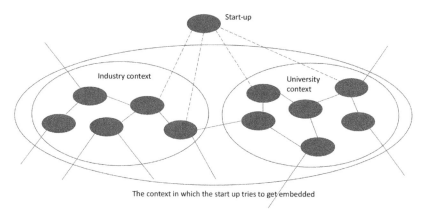

Figure 12.1   The conceptual framework: a start-up trying to become embedded in the industry and university context(s), which together form the context for business development

Method

This case study's starting point is the automotive and transport cluster in Western Sweden, which was established as both an academic context and an industry context. To capture as much information as possible about how start-ups become embedded in the university and industry context(s), we relied on both secondary data concerning the case and primary data about the relationship development patterns of the start-ups.

Identification of transport-related start-ups

After consulting with the university's investment company and the School of Entrepreneurship, 14 transportation-related start-ups were identified, all of which were contacted to confirm that they were actually related to *both* the transport industry and the university. During the selection process, it was discovered that three of the firms no longer existed, two of the firms had changed their names (which means that they were listed twice under different names in the original list) and one firm's business did not relate to transport. Additionally, a representative of one firm wrote an e-mail explaining that the firm did not want to participate in the study since start-ups need to prioritise their time and resources. In total, nine start-up firms were included in further analysis (see Table 12.1).

Table 12.1   Background information about the start-ups

Start-up	Business focus within the transportation industry	Firm age (years at the time of case selection)	Number of employees at the time of case selection	Approximate net turnover at the time of case selection (SEK)
1	Booking system, online services, certification and business intelligence for a specific form of transport.	9	~70	46 000 000
2	Storing and distribution for Internet shopping and marketing material. Both physical and software facilities.	4	4	0
3	Prolonging the life of forklift batteries.	2	1	490 000
4	Advanced measurement instrument.	1	2	84 000
5	Electric moped.	2	2	0
6	Lightweight materials for the automotive industry.	8	32	25 000 000
7	Applications involving hardware, software and communication methods for bus operators.	12	18	18 000 000
8	Optimisation software for waste logistics.	1	3	Not a public company
9	Applications involving hardware, software and communication methods for heavy trucks.	10	~50	53 000 000

Data collection

The main method used to gather data was theme interviewing (see Flick, 2009). The interviewees were CEOs, heads of sales or heads of development. They were selected by the firms as the persons who are most knowledgeable about the firm and its relationships. All our interviewees were part of the start-up's founding team except for interviewee 1, who was the first additional employee to join the team. In some of the start-ups, the CEO was the only employee, and in three of the firms, there were only two or three employees. In these start-ups, all employees participated in the interviews.

During the interviews, the development of the start-up firms was discussed, placing particular focus on (1) the relationships that firms build with customers, the university and other actors, such as investors (i.e. both industry and university relationships); (2) start-ups' business development processes and the role of industry or university relationships in these processes; and (3) start-ups' perceived needs in terms of relationship formation and goals and business development plans for the next five years, including potential collaborations with the university or other actors. A mind map of the relationships of firms was created by the interviewer in order to keep track of the data and enable follow-ups. The map was shown to the interviewee(s) during the interviews in order to avoid misunderstandings and trigger memories about other relationships. The majority of the interviews lasted between one and two hours. The interviews were recorded and transcribed. Secondary data were obtained from various sources, including previous studies of actors within the university's innovation infrastructure and companies in Western Sweden. Based on the data, the industrial relationships of the university's transport researchers were compared with the stated needs of the start-ups.

Data analysis

Data from the transcripts and secondary data were structured both start-up by start-up and in tables summarising a certain part of the data for all cases simultaneously. We first conducted an in-depth exploration of a single case to determine how the start-up processes occurred in each sub-case and to identify the roles of different actors from the industry or university during this process. Then, to capture patterns across processes, we performed cross-case analysis and compared the start-ups with regard to their development processes, the involved actors and the developed industry- and university-based relationships.

The case of transport-related start-ups in Western Sweden

The key industry and university actors in the transport cluster of Western Sweden

Western Sweden has a long history of automotive development and vehicle production (see, e.g., Brown, 2000; Engström et al., 2004; Fredriksson and Gadde, 2005). The port of Gothenburg is the largest port in Scandinavia (see, e.g., Woxenius and Bergqvist, 2011). Also, in this region, many companies of all sizes manufacture vehicle components or provide services related to transport (see, e.g., Brown, 2000; Johannisson and Lindholm Dahlstrand, 2009). The majority of smaller technology-based firms in the region originate from local universities and large companies, and relationships with previous employers and universities are important (Lindholm Dahlstrand, 1999). The importance of transport-related companies in the region is reflected in the activities and investments made by the university. Since 2010, transport has been one of eight 'areas of advance' at the university, representing a substantial share of the research and education activities at the university. Currently, research within the transport area of advance is conducted together with researchers at another university in the region. In total, around 200 senior researchers and 350 PhD students (about 15 per cent of whom were associated with the other university) are involved in this research. Moreover, the teaching activities in which transport-related researchers are involved cover more than half of the 40 master's programmes at the university.

A historical account of the development of the infrastructure for innovation and entrepreneurship at the university was presented by Jacob et al. (2003). In 2015, a new organisational set-up was introduced in order to boost venture creation by making the system of involved actors more coherent and visible. Among the set of actors involved in the innovation infrastructure, the two entities that were most often mentioned by our interviewees were the School of Entrepreneurship and the incubator. The School of Entrepreneurship was founded in 1997 with the purpose of developing high-tech entrepreneurs and high-tech ventures through technology transfer (Fogelberg and Lundqvist, 2013; Rasmussen and Sørheim, 2006). A key feature of the programme is that teams of students are paired with an inventor who already has an idea instead of coming up with an idea themselves. The projects are financed with up to SEK 100 000 raised from local public seed funds (Åstebro et al., 2012). The incubator was founded in 1999 by a five-million-euro donation from a business angel (see Fogelberg and Lundqvist, 2013). Rasmussen et al. (2006) and Clarysse and Bruneel (2007) both describe how the incubator operated prior to the new organisational setup in 2015, and they emphasise the strong connection to business angels, the seed money fund and the five per cent equity share that the start-ups give to the incubator.

The innovation system of the university included various actors, such as a venture capital firm founded in 1994 due to the investment of a university initiative and a seed-financing company in high-potential technology-based firms, mainly those from the university (Rasmussen et al., 2006). In addition, there were the university's institute for commercial R&D (Fogelberg and Lundqvist, 2013), the university's technology licensing organisation, and the university's advanced management programs (Jacob et al., 2003). The university's science park serves as an 'office hotel' for start-ups and new ventures originating from existing companies that wish to co-locate with the research resources at the university. The interviewees mentioned that ALMI is a source of soft financing and counselling. ALMI is a policy actor owned by the government and regional development actors. In addition, the interviewees also frequently identified Venture Cup (a business plan competition) and the Connect Foundation as part of the university's innovation infrastructure. In Venture Cup, the teams present and develop ideas in several steps. The Connect Foundation, which is sponsored by regional universities, innovation actors and companies, is a non-profit organisation focusing on increasing employment in many regions and nations around the world. During the Connect 'springboard', the entrepreneurial team is able to improve their business plan, identify important contacts and improve their ability to present their ideas.

The business development processes of nine transport-related start-ups

In this section, we present and analyse the business development processes of nine identified transport-related start-ups, placing particular focus on their relationships with industry- and university-based actors. Based on the individual start-up case analyses and cross-case comparisons, we identify relationship development patterns, which are summarised in Table 12.2. However, it should be noted that the firms were in different stages of development. Consequently, some have become more embedded than others in the industrial and/or university context, which may affect the results of this study. Next, we provide brief descriptions of the nine start-ups, presenting their processes from development of a business idea to development of the business.

Start-up 1

The first start-up aims to provide information-system-based services via a two-sided platform that can be scaled up. Currently, it is growing. In the first phase of development (i.e. early development of the business idea), an employee at a large transport-related company generated the original idea and shared it with a childhood friend, who was a student at the School of Entrepreneurship. A team was formed at the School of Entrepreneurship to create a start-up, and the idea was soon transformed into a rather different idea related to the same industry. The School of Entrepreneurship provided the necessary office space, coaching and business education, even though it did not initially believe that the business idea was good. Other relationships with university-related actors were either weak or non-existent. During the next phase (i.e. realisation of

Table 12.2 Identified patterns among the nine start-ups

Pattern	Start-ups	Explanation
Industry–University–Industry	1	Even though the initial idea was generated by a person employed in the transport industry, it was developed further within the School of Entrepreneurship. Few relationships were formed with actors connected with the university, but the relationships with customers are diverse. These interactions influence the development of firms and products. We therefore view the start-up as embedded in the industry from the time it reaches its first group of customers.
	3	In this case, the sister companies contributed knowledge of the product and the organisation of the company. However, since the product targeted the Scandinavian market and the sister companies were located in other parts of the world, the sister companies were not able to mediate contact to the local market. The potential legitimacy of being located in the incubator was not enough to solve this problem. Therefore, the firm has been struggling to form relationships in its intended market.
	7	The technological idea was generated by the transport industry, but the firm's many relationships within the university enabled the founders to re-formulate the technology to become a business idea for a different industry and find several investors. This initial business idea enabled the firm to become embedded enough in the industry to be able to find customers for consultancy services. Then, again, the start-up re-formulated its business idea through an interaction with a customer and continues to sell this product to additional customers. The story of this firm emphasises that customer interaction is more important than financial and technical resources.
	9	Bringing basic technology to the School of Entrepreneurship contributed to the identification of a business idea that was suited to different industries. The business idea fitted the needs of the industry well enough for the first customer to start interacting with the firm. Together, the first customer and the firm modify the business idea. Thus, the product enables the firm to become embedded within its industry niche.

Pattern	Start-ups	Explanation
Industry–University–Industry/University	2	The embeddedness of the business idea in the idea generator's network seems to have been partly maintained, complemented by the social relationships of the founder and the relationships of the founder and actors connected to business development at the university. However, the start-up's relationships have tended to contribute additional business ideas rather than ways to achieve sufficient business within the areas that the firm is exploring.
University	4	Even though the firm is partly located outside the campus area and has external investors and suppliers, it has always remained embedded in the university context and has utilised relationships with university actors both for production and for identifying customers. The product is completely developed in a laboratory setting. So far, it seems to have been difficult to build enough industrial relationships to realise the perceived industrial potential and application of the product.
Industry–University	5	The business idea came from the industry and was accompanied by a network of suppliers. The firm became very embedded in the university as a student project while the founders were part of the School of Entrepreneurship; students performed most of the roles within the firm. The firm did not become embedded enough in the industry to form customer relationships and develop its business.
	8	The business idea came from industry but soon became very embedded in the university as a student project and part of the School of Entrepreneurship. Students performed most roles within the firm and the product development process. The firm was not able to become embedded in industry by forming enough customer relationships.
University–Industry	6	Initially, the firm interacted only within the university sphere. Because the firm sought new relationships with industry through trade fairs, these relationships were not mediated by university actors. Starting with the first customer relationship, the firm became increasingly more embedded in industry by letting one customer relationship lead to the next. In this way, the firm was able to utilise current relationships and relevant knowledge when building new relationships.

the initial business plan, facing markets and establishing relationships with its first customers), two unrelated foreign transport companies became the first customers. Further international relationships were developed without any Swedish market/industry connections. The product was developed through intensive interaction with these customers. The founders approached the first customers without any external support and later managed to use both existing and potential customers as reference customers. A fast-growing customer base was important for obtaining feedback regarding the use of the product, since the product would become more valuable with more users. When the start-up reached the third phase, relationships with European transport authorities were developed. Products were continuously developed based on customers' needs, which entailed expansion of the customer network. Students from the university were involved and engaged in master's projects. European transport authorities were important for improving the quality of their services, and interaction with customers was still important for developing new products and services. The start-up displayed organic development except for a few acquisitions of firms that offered complementary services.

Start-up 2

The second start-up developed storing and distribution services for Internet shopping (both physical and software facilities). In the early phase, a spin-off idea came from a non-transport-related company, which did not regard the idea as related to its core activities and gave it to the School of Entrepreneurship to be developed into a start-up. The idea generator became the first customer since he had another start-up, an Internet shop, that was in need of distribution services. The start-up was able to gain diverse customers (generally Swedish) in distribution networks. However, early establishment of relationships with some small customers has not been enough to enable the firm to reduce its dependence on support from actors at the university for soft financing. To further develop its business, the start-up formed connections with ALMI to gain additional funding. The start-up moved to another part of Sweden and is well-connected to the local community through social ties. The start-up is still developing its business idea by trying out new services and spinning out firms when the scope of services becomes too large.

Start-up 3

The third start-up's business idea is to prolong the life of forklift batteries, and it is still trying to achieve this goal. The start-up started at the incubator and is based on the same idea as its sister companies in other countries. Because the founder comes from a family that is active in this industry in other countries, the founder has social contacts that provide expertise regarding both the product and the industry. These contacts were more highly valued than the coaching associated with the incubator. The start-up is still in its initial phase, as it has no specific local or regional connections except for some potential customers (i.e. logistics companies) in Sweden. It developed its business idea

through interactions with its social contacts at the international sister companies and other local actors in the sister companies' network, and it has tried
to initiate customer contacts. However, these customer relationships usually
ended after the first trial delivery. The start-up has moved out of the incubator
and has no connection with the university. It uses a modified business model
to keep the start-up in business while still seeking customers for the initial
business idea.

Start-up 4

The fourth start-up is still trying to develop a business to produce advanced
measurement instruments (hardware and software). The idea was generated
by a research group at the university and elaborated upon as part of a project at
the School of Entrepreneurship. There were several areas of application for the
product, including the automotive industry. During the year of start-up development in the School of Entrepreneurship, the firm participated in a competition for start-ups and achieved good results. This made it easier for the firm to
attract venture capital and soft financing from Innovation Bridge, VINNOVA
and ALMI (about 50 per cent loans and 50 per cent venture capital). However,
the firm admits that the financing comes with a price: 'We approached them
with a plan and they expect us to follow that plan in order for them to want
to invest more money later'. The research group and a collaboration partner
in another country became the first two customers. The key component was
produced using the university's equipment. The start-up continued to network
through the university's researchers to gain additional customers. It has two
small suppliers for the mechanical product and the software. After a few
years with an office in an office hotel, the firm moved to a science park connected to the university, thereby increasing its potential embeddedness among
university-related actors.

Start-up 5

The fifth start-up tried to make a business with small electrical vehicles
but eventually gave up. The idea was generated by an external innovator
over a long time period and later developed as a project at the School of
Entrepreneurship. Then, the product was developed in collaboration with
researchers/teachers and students at the university. Seed funding was obtained
from Innovationsbron and VGR. Since the idea had already been developed by
the external innovator, suppliers were already involved and willing to supply
parts to the start-up. Additionally, the suppliers were already knowledgeable
about the product and the small electrical vehicle industry. The product was

similar to a delivery tricycle but included new technology. Students at the university were extensively involved in product and production management as part of their projects and master's theses. The start-up was able to draw upon the university's networks of senior managers within the automotive industry to provide credibility to the project. It initiated contact with potential customers in need of, for example, short-distance transportation and gathered them for focus groups. At the time of the interview, the start-up was looking for a production partner. The start-up had a list of 30 potential production partners and narrowed the list to four candidates. The CEO elaborated: 'Since we will more or less marry the production partner, due to shared certificates, for instance, it is important to find a company that feels good'. However, currently, there is low activity in the firm and the founder has been recruited by a multinational company that develops electrical vehicles.

Start-up 6

The sixth start-up focuses on lightweight materials for the automotive industry. It is growing. The idea was generated by a researcher at the university. The firm started at the School of Entrepreneurship, and the university's investment company invested in it. It further developed for a few years at the incubator and participated in Connect. The first customers came from the foreign automotive industry. The firm participated in trade fairs, which connected it to a car manufacturer that wanted to evaluate the application of the developed material for future generations of cars and therefore requested a trial order. This led the start-up to construct a pilot production machine. A large investment from a private venture capitalist enabled the firm to move to another location, which is still in the region but close to other actors that are exploring similar production techniques; and offices and larger production equipment with the potential for expansion were set up. The firm's first paying customer was BMW. Through interactions with this customer, the firm realised that it wanted customers with faster product development processes than the ordinary automotive industry. Therefore, it started to initiate relationships with customers within the Formula 1 industry. The CEO explained that this is an industry in which the actors always try to make improvements: 'if everything is according to plan and they fix all the details and lower the weight, it [components made from our material] will be included in the next race'. Furthermore, the product development process was perceived as faster and less complex than the ordinary automotive industry: 'You have one year, then you have to meet them [the customer], because that is when they are testing new materials. You have to know when that is. And if you get it then you have made it, then production starts about six months later'. The firm's positive experience with the

Formula 1 industry encouraged it to include firms within other sports sectors, such as those that produce indoor hockey sticks, golf handles and surfboards, in their customer portfolio. The university's investment companies are minority owners. Students from the university and other universities in the region have been involved in projects.

Start-up 7

The seventh start-up is focused on applications of hardware, software and communication methods for bus operators. In the early business development phase, two inventors working at a global information and communications technology company with a local presence generated initial ideas for a product. The idea was developed further in a master's project at the university. The start-up collaborated extensively with university researchers in several research areas. It found investors easily but eventually realised that the margins were too small for the initial product idea. Therefore, it started to provide consultancy services regarding the technology underlying the product. When generating business, a new product was developed while providing consultancy services to a customer within the local transport network, who became the first paying customer. The product was based on the same technology as the previous one but was targeted at a different type of vehicle and a different industry segment with better margins. The new product has enabled the firm to expand through sales, mostly among Swedish customers. The product is adjusted to each new customer and therefore requires close customer interaction. The firm has been involved in EU projects and various social organisations related to its business and has taken part in Connect. However, the main focus has been market development.

Start-up 8

The eighth start-up focused on optimisation software for waste logistics but eventually gave up. The initial business idea was generated by an employee at a local firm specialising in transport based on identified needs. A project was initiated at the School of Entrepreneurship, and seed funding was gained from Innovationsbron. Potential local customers were involved in the pilot project to test the hardware, which was financed by the potential customers. Parts of the product development process were carried out by master's students from the university. Other parts of the development were carried out by a specialised supplier who was accessed through the School of Entrepreneurship's contacts. Although the firm was a small customer of this supplier, the supplier was interested in supporting the firm since the relationship enabled the supplier to learn more about the technology that the firm used. The founding team has now found employment elsewhere, even though the start-up still officially exists.

Start-up 9

The ninth start-up focuses on hardware, software and communication methods for heavy trucks and long-haul transporters. The business idea was generated by an inventor employed at a global information and communications technology company with a local presence and was developed as part of a project at the School of Entrepreneurship. The university's investment company was involved as a partial owner. The start-up moved to the incubator and obtained seed funding from VINNOVA, Teknikbron and VGR. The first customer was a road carrier, and the firm developed the product in interaction with this customer. During the development process, the road carrier realised that it could save 10 per cent on fuel consumption (SEK 100 000 per vehicle per year) by never driving faster than 83 km/h. The customer decided to install a monitoring product in all their vehicles and implement a policy to never drive faster than 83 km/h. The customer then started to boast that it was 'Sweden's most overtaken road carrier' in its marketing after implementing the policy and product. The start-up expanded both by finding new customers and by developing additional services for new and existing customers and then moved out of the incubator. The firm broke even after six years and started to expand its product portfolio within its narrow niche three years later. Subsequently, it expanded internationally. Almost all employees recruited during the expansion period were from the university of origin, and many had started their careers as master's students. The firm has continued to grow in this way. Today, the firm is present in a handful of countries.

Conclusions

The role and contribution of entrepreneurial universities to new venture formation is not limited to research commercialisation and academic spin-off activities; but through these cases, we demonstrate the multi-faceted links and the way in which the university can contribute to these start-ups during various development phases. In contrast to the rather linear perspective on entrepreneurial pathways in the literature on research commercialisation and spin-offs (Klofsten et al., 2019), each individual start-up described in this chapter underwent a unique and interactive journey in the 'patterned landscape'. Within the incubator literature, the 'nested' view of incubation (Mian et al., 2016) treats incubation as a multi-faceted, complex and context-dependent phenomenon rather than the activities of a stand-alone organisation (Baraldi and Ingemansson Havenvid, 2016). This view implies that more actors are active in the incubation process than the incubator itself. Therefore, according to Roig-Tierno et al. (2015), in order to develop and succeed, start-up firms need to combine help from different network structures. In other words, there are some parts of the entrepreneurial university literature that attempt to view development paths as less linear and more directed by the start-ups and their embeddedness in different contexts. The 'patterned landscape' described in this chapter includes both the industry and university contexts. From a university point of view, there is a challenge to design the context in light of the general need for support that characterises start-ups' development. While business ideas often come from industry, interactions with industry and university actors complement each other in fulfilling certain important functions for the development processes of start-ups, such as developing the product and business plan, securing financing and getting in contact with the first paying customers. By capturing and comparing start-ups' development processes, we contribute to the understanding of the starting-up process as a context-dependent and idiosyncratic process. However, identifying and supporting general patterns in the unique journeys of these firms remains a challenge that should be investigated further.

Based on our study of all the university-based start-ups at the focal university at a certain point in time, we know that around 200 senior researchers are engaged in transport research at the university. Interestingly, only two of the start-ups originated from research; the rest are based on product ideas originating from industry, in contrast to the traditional models of knowledge or technology transfer (Debackere and Veugelers, 2005; Gilsing et al., 2011). Despite this foundation in industry, several start-ups had to start from scratch when identifying and developing relationships with industrial customers. The customers that were identified were often distant or marginal actors in the industry rather than initial industrial contacts. Furthermore, university actors are involved in a very limited way in the start-ups' development, especially when it comes to getting in contact with the first paying customers. We therefore agree with Soetanto and van Geenhuizen (2019) that future research on entrepreneurial universities should focus on how to support start-ups post-incubation. However, as shown by this study, both the entrepreneurial university and the surrounding industry are active participants in the landscape in which start-ups develop. Hence, the importance of ties across the two contexts, which embed start-ups in both contexts, requires further scrutiny.

Future research agenda

We argue that the development and success of university-based start-ups must be understood in terms of how they are embedded in their context(s). This has several important implications for further studies. In this section, we elaborate on these implications and suggest three research questions for future studies.

First, how do university-based start-ups become embedded in (business) networks? To answer this question, further description and analysis of cases in which university-based start-ups developed relationships in their network contexts are needed. In this chapter, we provided brief descriptions of nine such cases in order to illustrate a few aspects of the variety of their relationship development patterns. However, much more detail is needed to capture the interactions of start-up companies and, thus, to understand the roles of the different involved actors and the interplay among them. One key feature of the networks in which companies try to become integrated is how the relationships among actors are connected and how these connections can be utilised by start-ups. Although every case is unique, there may be possibilities to learn more about the variety of needs and paths of these companies and to contradict the often-simplified assumptions about how universities spin off new companies.

Second, what roles do universities play in the networking and embedding of start-ups in their network context(s)? It is important to better understand universities' various roles in start-ups' development-related needs in the network context, which contains numerous internal actors and university functions. Also, the various time-related and sequential aspects of these roles require further description and analysis. Understanding the roles that universities play in the networking and embedding of start-ups will have strong implications for entrepreneurial university metrics. It is not sufficient to count only spin-offs, since universities' contribution to start-ups' networking and embedding is much wider and more complex than this.

Third, how can collaborative platforms be designed and developed to enable start-ups to gain access to partners with whom they can interact in fruitful ways? In recent years, public funding agencies have put a lot of effort and investment into programmes aiming to facilitate collaboration among various actors (industrial actors, academic actors, public authorities, etc.) to deal with 'big challenges' such as transformation of the transport system. However, little is known about how the various types of actors benefit from the collaboration that takes place on these platforms or in the networks that are formed as a result. It thus is important to further investigate how start-ups make use of these programmes to become embedded and gain access to various kinds of resources.

References

Aaboen, L. (2009). Explaining incubators using firm analogy. *Technovation*, **29** (10), 657–670.

Aaboen, L., Dubois, A. and Lind, F. (2011). Start-ups starting up – Firms looking for a network. *IMP Journal*, **5** (1), 42–58.

Aaboen, L., Dubois, A. and Lind, F. (2013). Strategizing as networking for new ventures. *Industrial Marketing Management*, **42** (7), 1033–1041.

Aarikka-Stenroos, L. (2011). Reference communication and third actors in the initiation of relationship. Dissertation. Turku School of Business, University of Turku, Series A-6.

Aarikka-Stenroos, L. and Lehtimäki, T. (2014). Commercializing a radical innovation: Probing the way to the market. *Industrial Marketing Management*, **43** (8), 1372–1384.

Åstebro, T., Bazzazian, N. and Braguinsky, S. (2012). Startups by recent graduates and their faculty: Implications for university entrepreneurship policy. *Research Policy*, **41**, 663–677.

Autio, E. (1994). New, technology-based firms as agents of R&D and innovation: An empirical study. *Technovation*, **14** (4), 259–273.

Baraldi, E. and Ingemansson Havenvid, M. (2016). Identifying new dimensions of business incubation: A multi-level analysis of Karolinska Institute's incubation system. *Technovation*, **50–51**, 53–68.

Baraldi, E. and Perna, A. (2014). When do start-ups stop being start-ups? A business network perspective on four cases of university spin-offs. Presented at IMP Conference, Bordeaux.

Bergek, A. and Norrman, C. (2008). Incubator best practice: A framework. *Technovation*, **28** (1–2), 20–28.

Bergek, A., Jacobsson, S., Carlsson, B., Lindmark, S. and Rickne, A. (2008). Analyzing the functional dynamics of technological innovation systems: A scheme of analysis. *Research Policy*, **37** (3), 407–429.

Boehm, D. N. and Hogan, T. (2013). Science-to-business collaborations: A science-to-business marketing perspective on scientific knowledge commercialization. *Industrial Marketing Management*, **41** (4), 564–579.

Bourelos, E., Magnusson, M. and McKelvey, M. (2012). Investigating the complexity facing academic entrepreneurs in science and engineering: The complementarities of research performance, networks and support structures in commercialization. *Cambridge Journal of Economics*, **36**, 751–780.

Brown, R. (2000). Clusters, supply chains and local embeddedness in fyrstad. *European Urban and Regional Studies*, **7** (4), 291–305.

Ciabuschi, F., Perna, A. and Snehota, I. (2012). Assembling resources in the formation of a new business. *Journal of Business Research*, **65** (2), 220–229.

Clarysse, B. and Bruneel, J. (2007). Nurturing and growing innovative start-ups: The role of policy as integrator. *R&D Management*, 37 (2), 139–149.
Clarysse, B., Bruneel, J. and Wright, M. (2011). Explaining growth paths of young technology-based firms: Structuring resource portfolios in different competitive environments. *Strategic Entrepreneurship Journal*, 5 (2), 137–157.
Clarysse, B., Wright, M., Bruneel, J. and Mahajan, A. (2014). Creating value in ecosystems: Crossing the chasm between knowledge and business ecosystems. *Research Policy*, 43 (7), 1164–1176.
Debackere, K. and Veugelers, R. (2005). The role of academic technology transfer organizations in improving industry science links. *Research Policy*, 34 (3), 321–342.
Engström, T., Blomquist, B. and Holmström, O. (2004). Reconstructing the history of the main Volvo Tuve plant. *International Journal of Operations & Production Management*, 24 (8), 820–839.
Erikson, T. and Sørheim, R. (2005). 'Technology angels' and other informal investors. *Technovation*, 25, 489–496.
Fini, R., Grimaldi, R., Santoni, S. and Sobrero, M. (2011). Complements or substitutes? The role of universities and local context in supporting the creation of academic spin-offs. *Research Policy*, 40 (8), 1113–1127.
Flick, U. (2009). *An introduction to qualitative research*. Sage.
Fogelberg, H. and Lundqvist, M. A. (2013). Integration of academic and entrepreneurial roles: The case of nanotechnology research at Chalmers University of Technology. *Science and Public Policy*, 40, 127–139.
Fredriksson, P. and Gadde, L-E. (2005). Flexibility and rigidity in customization and build-to-order production. *Industrial Marketing Management*, 34 (7), 695–705.
Gilsing, V., Bekkers, R., Bodas Freitas, I. M. and van der Steen, M. (2011). Differences in technology transfer between science-based and development-based industries: Transfer mechanisms and barriers. *Technovation*, 31 (12), 638–647.
Granovetter, M. (1973). The strength of weak ties. *American Journal of Sociology*, 78 (6), 1360–1380.
Granovetter, M. (1985). Economic action and social structure: The problem of embeddedness. *American Journal of Sociology*, 91 (3), 481–510.
Grimaldi, R. and Grandi, A. (2005). Business incubators and new venture creation: An assessment of incubating models. *Technovation*, 25 (2), 111–121.
Hackett, S. M. and Dilts, D. M. (2004). A systematic review of business incubation research. *Journal of Technology Transfer*, 29 (1), 55–82.
Ingemansson, M. and Waluszewski, A. (2009). Success in science and burden in business. On the difficult relationship between science as a developing setting and business as a producer-user setting. *The IMP Journal*, 3 (2), 20–56.
Isenberg, D. J. (2010). How to start an entrepreneurial revolution. *Harvard Business Review*, 88 (6), 40–50.
Jack, S. L. and Anderson, A. R. (2002). The effects of embeddedness on the entrepreneurial process. *Journal of Business Venturing*, 17, 467–487.
Jacob, M., Lundqvist, M. and Hellsmark, H. (2003). Entrepreneurial transformations in the Swedish University system: The case of Chalmers University of Technology. *Research Policy*, 32, 1555–1568.
Jacobsson, S., Lindholm-Dahlstrand, Å. and Elg, L. (2013). Is the commercialization of European academic R&D weak? A critical assessment of a dominant belief and associated policy responses. *Research Policy*, 42 (4), 874–885.

Johannisson, B. and Lindholm Dahlstrand, Å. (2009). Bridging the functional and territorial rationales – Proposing an integrating framework for regional dynamics. *European Planning Studies*, **17** (8), 1117–1133.

Klofsten, M., Fayolle, A., Guerrero, M., Mian, S., Urbano, D. and Wright, M. (2019). The entrepreneurial university as driver for economic growth and social change – Key strategic challenges. *Technological Forecasting & Social Change*, **141**, 149–158.

La Rocca, A., Ford, D. and Snehota, I. (2013). Initial relationship development in new business ventures. *Industrial Marketing Management*, **42** (7), 1025–1032.

Lindholm Dahlstrand, Å. (1999). Technology-based SMEs in the Göteborg region: Their origin and interaction with universities and large firms. *Regional Studies*, **33** (4), 379–389.

Mian, S. A. (1997). Assessing and managing the university technology business incubator: An integrative framework. *Journal of Business Venturing*, **12** (4), 251–285.

Mian, S., Lamine, W. and Fayolle, A. (2016). Technology business incubation: An overview of the state of knowledge. *Technovation*, **50–51**, 1–12.

Mustar, P., Renault, M., Colombo, M. G., Piva, E., Fontes, M., Lockett, A., Wright, M., Clarysse, B. and Moray, N. (2006). Conceptualising the heterogeneity of research-based spin-offs: A multi-dimensional taxonomy. *Research Policy*, **35** (2), 289–308.

Partanen, J., Chetty, S. K. and Rajala, A. (2014). Innovation types and network relationships. *Entrepreneurship Theory and Practice*, **38** (5), 1027–1055.

Perna, A., Baraldi, E. and Waluszewski, A. (2015). Is the value created necessarily associated with money? On the connections between an innovation process and its monetary dimension: The case of Solibro's thin-film solar cells. *Industrial Marketing Management*, **46**, 108–121.

Phan, P. H., Siegel, D. S. and Wright, M. (2005). Science parks and incubators: Observations, synthesis and future research. *Journal of Business Venturing*, **20** (2), 165–182.

Rasmussen, E. and Sørheim, R. (2006). Action-based entrepreneurship education. *Technovation*, **26** (2), 185–194.

Rasmussen, E., Moen, Ø. and Gulbrandsen, M. (2006). Initiatives to promote commercialization of university knowledge. *Technovation*, **26** (4), 518–533.

Ritter, T. (2000). A framework for analyzing interconnectedness of relationships. *Industrial Marketing Management*, **29** (4), 317–326.

Roig-Tierno, N., Alcázar, J. and Ribeiro-Navarrete, S. (2015). Use of infrastructures to support innovative entrepreneurship and business growth. *Journal of Business Research*, **68** (11), 2290–2294.

Ruokolainen, J. and Aarikka-Stenroos, L. (2016). Rhetoric in customer referencing: Fortifying sales arguments in two start-up companies. *Industrial Marketing Management*, **54**, 188–202.

Shane, S. A. (2004). *Academic Entrepreneurship*. Cheltenham, UK and Northampon, MA, USA: Edward Elgar Publishing.

Shane, S. A. and Cable, D. (2002). Network ties, reputation, and the financing of new ventures. *Management Science*, **48**, 154–170.

Soetanto, D. and van Geenhuizen, M. (2019). Life after incubation: The impact of entrepreneurial universities on the long-term performance of their spin-offs. *Technological Forecasting and Social Change*, **141**, 263–276.

Uzzi, B. (1997). Social structure and competition in interfim networks: The paradox of embeddedness. *Administrative Science Quarterly*, **42** (1), 35–67.

Westhead, P. and Storey, D. J. (1995). Links between higher education institutions and high technology firms. *Omega*, **23** (4), 345–360.

Woxenius, J. and Bergqvist, R. (2011). Comparing maritime containers and semi-trailers in the context of hinterland transport by rail. *Journal of Transport Geography*, **19**, 680–688.

Wright, M., Lockett, A., Clarysse, B. and Binks, M. (2006). University spin-out companies and venture capital. *Research Policy*, **35**, 481–501.

13 Research spin-offs and their role within the entrepreneurial university in the digital age: a framework for future research from Italian case studies[1]

*Elisa Salvador, Raffaella Manzini, Andrea Urbinati,
Gloria Puliga and Valentina Lazzarotti*

Introduction

The interest around research spin-offs (RSOs)[2] has increased continuously over the last 15 years, while their number is rising all over Europe (De Cleyn, Festel, 2016). Consequently, several academic debates about the effective success, convincing strategy, and real performance of this particular kind of start-up company are open and arouse tricky questions. Furthermore, universities are more and more involved in their so-called "third mission" (Treibich, et al., 2013; Goldstein, Glaser, 2012) and RSOs are considered to be one of the main strategic options for the external transmission and valorisation of scientific knowledge activities carried out in universities.

Following the Internet revolution, we are witnessing the rise of high-growth firms, gazelles, "unicorns" and other kinds of companies that go beyond the traditional (old) vision of doing business (Visintin, Pittino, 2016). Open innovation, lean start-up and design thinking are currently some of the strategies emerging for doing business. Embeddedness in a business ecosystem, whether it be physical or digital, is also considered to be a useful complement or alternative to traditional industrial partnerships (Benghozi, Salvador, 2014). RSOs depict this new way of doing business. The link with the university of origin (usually referred to as the parent institute), which may or not have an active involvement, influences the company creation, development and growth. This occurs not only because the RSO is founded by at least one member of the university staff, but also because it transfers the results of knowledge developed inside the university to the market. Knowledge spillovers are usually linked to originality, differentiation, uniqueness and creativity, as well as to the creation of high-quality jobs. RSOs are also expected not to escape from the consequences of the information and communication technologies (ICTs) revolution, as is the case in the overall world of business. New business models (Benghozi, et al., 2017) and value chains structures appear in all the business sectors, laying the foundation for a new business landscape.

In this context, the potential impact of digital technologies on academic entrepreneurship is actually an under-researched field of analysis and there is an emerging need to map and categorize the new forms of academic entrepreneurship linked to the influence of digital technologies (Rippa, Secundo, 2019). The creation of RSOs enhanced by digital technologies is one of the main representative examples of these new forms of entrepreneurship. Despite the growing relevance for companies of ICTs (Urbinati, et al., 2018), the role and influence of the university's entrepreneurial strategy for RSOs that deal specifically in the digital sectors and provide digital products/services through the exploitation of new digital technologies (hereafter called Digital RSOs) still remains unexplored.

Accordingly, the aim of this contribution is to bridge the gap in the intersection between Digital RSOs and the entrepreneurial university, by answering the following research question: How do Digital RSOs work within the entrepreneurial university and what are the critical factors characterising them? And, consequently, is there a need for further research specifically dedicated to the role played by the entrepreneurial university regarding RSOs in the digital age?

Providing an answer to this question is pivotal because digital tools are more and more pervading every aspect of activities at business, society and education levels, and, consequently, this analysis would make it possible for us to suggest a focus for the future research agenda of the entrepreneurial university in the digital age. In order to answer this research question, we leverage on a multiple case study analysis of four Digital RSOs from the Polytechnic of Milan (Italy) and on a set of interviews with experts on the subject. The results coming from the investigation show that the peculiarities of Digital RSOs ask the entrepreneurial university to enrich its role, with a new set of competences and services. Thus, we outline a new focus for existing research on the entrepreneurial university.

Research spin-offs and the entrepreneurial mission of universities in the digital age: a brief overview

RSOs are considered a peculiar kind of start-up company with the particularity of coming from a traditionally non-commercial context, that is, the research world (Siegel, Wright, 2015). As with every company, RSOs also have a business purpose when dealing with the market, even if, at the same time, they come from the university world. RSOs are the commercialisation of scientific knowledge that has been developed in universities or research centres. This means that the business mission of a company (i.e., generating profits) could be in contrast with the traditional mission of universities to produce scientific knowledge as a public good (Callon, Bowker, 1994). The issue of ad hoc university regulations (Salvador, 2009) has formally solved this potential conflict.

The key role that RSOs have in technology transfer processes has been widely recognised. RSOs have often been described in the literature as pivotal drivers of the valorisation, technological development, and economic growth of university research results (Shane, 2004; Wright, et al., 2004). RSOs were initially seen through optimistic eyes with regards to their growth potential (Heirman, Clarysse 2004), with the expectation that they would contribute to local economic growth by providing high-quality business opportunities.

The scientific literature has focused on several aspects related to the creation, growth and development of RSOs (Benghozi, Salvador, 2014; van Geenhuizen, Soetanto, 2009; Wright, et al., 2007). Several typologies, theories, perspectives and taxonomies have been proposed (Rasmussen, Wright, 2015; Bathelt, et al., 2010; Mustar, et al., 2006). From among the main topics of analysis and elements of open debate about Italian RSOs, it is possible to mention some specifically, i.e., the more or less effective role and brand effect (Salvador, 2011) played by technology transfer offices (TTOs) and/or by science parks and incubators, the relationship with the university of origin (Salvador, Benghozi, 2015), as well as location issues (Lejpras, Stephan, 2011), and the potential influence on company success and performance of regional and innovation policies, which are among the sharpest in the European Union (Iammarino, et al., 2009).

Gaps in business management capabilities and in finance possibilities (Wright, et al., 2007; Shane, 2004) usually characterise RSOs because of the influence from the university's non-commercial culture (Clarysse, et al., 2011; Wright, et al., 2004, 2007). RSOs take on an attitude of low level risk (Chiesa, Piccaluga, 2000) as well as one of autonomy and independence (O'Shea, et al., 2005). It has been said that "academics and businesspeople effectively speak different languages" (Mustar, Wright, 2010: 52). The presence of a TTO inside the university is one of the factors that could influence the generation of RSOs in an academic institution, smoothing down any non-commercial attitude (Algieri, et al., 2013). TTOs' mission should be to foster the valorisation of the research outcomes, through facilitating the creation of RSOs with dedicated assistance and providing an intermediary role between the university and the other actors of the innovation system in the business and government world, meaning the third mission of the university (Algieri, et al., 2013; Muscio, 2010).

Digital RSOs are well represented in the universe of Italian RSOs: 26 per cent deal in services for innovation and 22 per cent in ICTs, thus representing the widest sectors (Netval, 2018). The link between digital and RSOs deserves, therefore, deeper attention. Generally speaking, the diffusion of powerful digital technologies is transforming entrepreneurship in significant ways through the emergence of new initiatives that cross traditional boundaries and tighten networks and communities, giving rise to unexpected forms of ecosystems and evolutive kinds of ventures (Nambisan, et al., 2019). According to Sussan and Acs (2017: 71), digital entrepreneurship is related to "entrepreneurial activities that optimize the utilization and reconfiguration of digital infrastructure in the form of new systems, new platforms, and new networks". In this context, "entrepreneurial university" and "academic entrepreneurship" have become prevalent research topics. Academic entrepreneurship has evolved over the years and is also subject to the influence of digital technologies that reshape the overall markets and societies, as well as open up new connections to consumers (Nambisan, et al., 2017). Universities are nowadays facing the challenge of adapting to unpredictable environments on a global level. Rippa and Secundo (2019) have recently coined the concept "digital academic entrepreneurship", addressing the potential impact of new digital technologies[3] on academic entrepreneurship, a topic that is still under-investigated. This new competitive landscape demands adaptability, flexibility, leadership skills, and an adhocracy attitude (Klofsten, et al., 2019; Waterman, 1990). To this aim, RSOs can represent a pivotal opportunity, especially Digital RSOs, as they come from and are strictly linked to the Internet and ICTs, which are profoundly revolutionising every business. These companies are mostly supported in novel ways by new digital technologies in their products/services supply and they represent one of the main strategic options for the digital academic entrepreneurship strategy (Rippa, Secundo, 2019).

As highlighted by Sussan and Acs (2017), entrepreneurship in the digital age is not fully understood; we are witnessing a reversal of several aspects that undermine the traditional entrepreneurship process. For example, in the past, customers were looked for after the creation of a company. In the digital age, a young start-up can have millions of customers throughout the world from its birth. Notwithstanding the global impact of digital technologies, the creation of digital companies remains local, highlighting the need to explore regional clusters at the country level (Sussan, Acs, 2017).

Research framework and methodology

The above section highlighted that there is a need for further studies in the field of entrepreneurial university and Digital RSOs. Consequently, we conducted an empirical study to find out what (if any) the distinctive characteristics of Digital RSOs are, and how their relations with the parent institute actually work. Then, by looking at the results of our empirical study in the light of the current literature, we bring into evidence some suggestions for a future research agenda, one aimed at investigating the role of the entrepreneurial university towards Digital RSOs. We thus focused on selected case studies from a prestigious Italian higher education institution, the Polytechnic of Milan. Italian RSOs are particularly appropriate as an empirical setting for the scope of our analysis. Indeed, since the early 1990s (Chiesa, Piccaluga, 2000) Italy has been one of the European countries to experience a steady growth of RSOs (Ramaciotti, Rizzo, 2015). Several TTOs have been set up and are expected to play a key role in assisting the establishment of RSOs (Muscio, 2010). Various contributions about Italian RSOs have already been published.[4]

In order to answer the research question, our study relies on a multiple case study analysis of four Italian RSOs (Yin, 2003) and on a set of interviews with experts (Bogner, Menz, 2009). Multiple case studies are particularly suitable to explore phenomena in a comprehensive way and consolidate the suitability of the proposed, theoretical and conceptual setting (Siggelkow, 2007). Multiple case studies, in particular, are suited to answer the "how" questions, as in our case, and to investigate phenomena in their whole complexity and to obtain initial insights adopting a qualitative approach in the interpretive tradition (Walsham, 1995; Klein, Myers, 1999). In addition, thanks to real-time data collection, case studies avoid the weaknesses inherent in retrospective reconstruction and the associated errors tied to reinterpretation (Alblas, Wortmann, 2014). In line with Heirmann and Clarysse (2004), in order to limit the possible noise related to environmental factors, our study focuses on a single region, Lombardy.[5] We also focused on RSOs from a single university, the Polytechnic of Milan,[6] similarly to other previous studies (Neves, Franco, 2018), in order to include cases that experienced the same type of support and working conditions. In particular, we identified all the RSOs of the Polytechnic of Milan, looking at the list of RSOs incubated by PoliHub, the Innovation District & Startup Accelerator of the Polytechnic of Milan.[7] Therefore, the selection of the case studies has followed theoretical and convenience sampling criteria (Voss, et al., 2002), and was especially driven by the idiosyncratic characteristics of the four RSOs, i.e., proximity to the university of origin, influence on universities' entrepreneurial strategy and novelty of digital products or services provided. The number of RSOs involved in this research is enough for case study analysis, especially in exploratory research (Gioia, et al., 2013).

The semi-structured and open questions asked during the interviews were suggested by the existing literature on RSOs. The interview questions were submitted to the selected case studies from April to May 2018 and used as the main framework during face-to-face interviews. The focus of the interviews was in particular on the key features of RSOs: financial and human resources, products and/or services, competitive strategies, market characteristics, industrial relationships and links with the parent institute, and the managerial issues characterising RSOs. We mostly focused on the case studies' innovation strategies and their relationships with universities and scientific parks-incubators. All the interviews were recorded and transcribed later, enabling the inclusion of additional notes, comments, and ideas. The data from the interviews were coded using an iterative process that attempted to capture all of the useful information (Guest, et al., 2013). Information from the primary sources was triangulated with secondary sources, such as company reports and websites, in order to avoid post-hoc rationalisations and to enrich or modify the theoretical setting. Several follow-ups and phone calls to the involved co-founders followed between October and December 2018 in order to complete the collection of data.

Additionally, we organised interviews with experts, a research method widely used in social research (Flick, 2006), which can provide researchers with an "efficient and concentrated method of gathering data" (Bogner, et al., 2009: 2) especially in exploratory research. In particular, we interviewed experts who work in TTOs, incubators and observatories and who closely interact with RSOs. Therefore, we relied on interviews with so called "systematisation experts", i.e., experts characterised by "knowledge of action and experience, which has been derived from practice, is reflexively accessible, and can be spontaneously communicated" (Bogner, Menz, 2009: 47). Experts can go beyond the focal vision of the specific entrepreneur (i.e., each co-founder of each analysed RSO) and can capture a set of additional insights for the future research agenda of the entrepreneurial university.

The interviews with experts were conducted between January and February 2019 with two academics involved in digital entrepreneurship activities, and one expert of TTOs and science and technology parks. For the interviews, we decided to adopt an "interaction model" (Bogner, Menz, 2009), which does not have a rigid structure so that the interview becomes a sort of discussion in which there are pre-defined questions, but also allows for interviewers to ask numerous counter-questions. The questions followed the same topics as the interviews undertaken with Digital RSOs founders, and we added a specific question about potential interesting avenues for future research of the entre-preneurial university.

The empirical study: the case studies and the interviews with experts

Spin-off A is a crowd-testing platform that offers digital services quality-testing solutions that enable the release of apps and websites that are more effective, usable, and free of bugs on mobile devices. Spin-off A aims to lower software development costs and increase quality assurance. Spin-off B is a fraud detection product that supports the analysis and investigation of online banking fraud techniques. Spin-off B models user behavior and its evolution, and implements a white-box strategy for identifying fraudulent behaviors. Spin-off B was developed in cooperation with one of the largest national Italian banks. The project was also born as a partnership between a well-known Italian security firm and a company of experts in delivering high-quality software. Spin-off C conducts efficiency improvement activities of computer numerical control (CNC) machineries. This improvement involves the optimisation of machining programs, which are the set of operations required to perform a process. The innovation consists of a method for separating the geometric, techno-logical and management information contained in a machining program in order to set-up a base of reusable knowledge related to mechanical processing. Spin-off D is a unique reality of its kind, composed of engineers specialised in developing and applying innovative mathematical and numerical models. Spin-off D is a spin-off of a peculiar Polytechnic of Milan's Laboratory (also known as "PoM-Lab") with a business model based on the ability to effectively transfer technology and know-how from the world of research to the world of industry. It manages around 30 projects per year.

Table 13.1 summarises some general information about these RSOs, including the date of foundation, founders' information, age ranges of the founder(s),

236 A RESEARCH AGENDA FOR THE ENTREPRENEURIAL UNIVERSITY

Table 13.1   Research spin-offs' (RSOs) general information

	Spin-off A	Spin-off B	Spin-off C	Spin-off D
Date of foundation	2016	2016	2015	2010
Founders' information	3 founders: 1 assistant professor and 2 businessmen	2 founders: 1 researcher and 1 full professor	3 founders: 1 full professor, 1 researcher and 1 manager	4 founders: 1 entrepreneur and 3 full professors
Range ages of the founder(s)	35–44	25–34	25–34	45–54
Qualification of main partners	2 partners: 1 business angel and 1 digital company	2 partners: 1 cyber-security company and 1 software house	1 partner: the client is the technological partner	1 partner: 1 financial advice company
Stage of development	Growth stage	Start-up stage	Start-up stage	Later stage
Number of employees	6 employees	10 employees	0 ("job on call") employees	30 employees
Turnover	Over 800,000 €	Over 100,000 €	Over 100,000 €	Over 1.5 million €

qualification of main partners, stage of development, number of employees, and turnover.

We believe that the RSOs in Table 13.1 adequately fit the theoretical setting and, therefore, are suitable to respond to the research question, as they are: (i) heterogeneous from the point of view of the stages of development to explain the differences on how they organise their innovation strategy; and (ii) homogeneous from the point of view of the founders (i.e., at least one professor) to highlight the similarities (and differences) about the relationships with universities and science parks-incubators.

With regards to the additional interviews, the three experts were selected with the idea of choosing "people who possess special knowledge of a social phenomenon which the interviewer is interested in" (Gläser, Laudel, 2009). According to this criterion, we interviewed a professional working closely with RSOs and start-ups who also deals in the digital sectors and is based in the specific Lombardy region area, and two academics involved in the management of the Digital Innovation Observatories of the Polytechnic of Milan. Both of the latter deal with RSOs with the aim of investigating their main evolutionary trajectories in specific contexts. In the light of the characteristics described above, we believe that the three experts involved have "knowledge of action and experience derived from practice" (Bogner, Menz, 2009), which proved useful to the aim of our analysis.

Results

Innovation strategy and relationships with universities and science parks-incubators

Spin-off A innovates by providing an innovative economic model. Its innovation activities and outcomes are also possible thanks to the technological competences of the internal human resources. The idea of founding Spin-off A was mainly derived from a research fellow from the Polytechnic of Milan and from competences in the mobile sector, the sector being studied in its research grant, such as app developing and testing. The period of work at the Polytechnic of Milan allowed Spin-off A to create a user base of 8,000 contacts, which the company uses as "testers" of their solutions, before proposing them to the clients. In this context, PoliHub acts as a catalyst for new contacts or clients, and it provides the physical location or training opportunities.

Spin-off B is registered in the list of innovative start-ups according to the Italian Law 221/2012 and applied for the Start-cup Lombardia in the fintech area. In the same way as the previous company, Spin-off B is also incubated by PoliHub, which allows the company to benefit from a network of consulting companies that provides system integration services. Spin-off B is derived from a doctoral project undertaken by one of the founders, and the company continues to tap into the university's know-how and scientific competences.

Spin-off C is an innovative start-up and based its innovation strategy on improving the core components of its business model, i.e., the technology and the reliability of the software solution, already mentioned above. In particular, the innovation strategy of Spin-off C leverages on the patenting of software solution methodologies and on industrial secrets of related software solution applications. Spin-off C exploits the synergies between PoliHub, the Polytechnic of Milan and all the companies affiliated with these two institutions. In particular, PoliHub places a series of activities and services for start-ups at the service of all the incubated companies (including Spin-off C), such as mentoring, co-working, advertising, training programs and acceleration programs, which are difficult to find in other places.

The innovation activity of Spin-off D is prominent. In recent years, Spin-off D has generated two other realities, two innovative start-ups that also consolidate the innovative spirit and the diversification of the business model on business to consumer (B2C) markets. In the 2018–2020 three-year "Innovation Plan", Spin-off D plans to create another company and to consolidate itself as a group operating both in the B2B and B2C markets, with a consolidated turnover of more than five million euro. Spin-off D continues to co-operate with PoM-Lab with mutual collaboration agreements, aimed at exchanging knowledge, expertise and concrete actions, both on the industrial and on the research fronts. Moreover, all training courses, events and workshops organised by PoM-Lab are attended by Spin-off D employees in order to maintain the right level of updating in the areas of simulation and mathematical modelling. Spin-off D co-operates with PoliHub to exploit synergies that act as access to the network of other companies and physical location.

Managerial issues

The interviews with the four case studies have offered the opportunity to ponder some managerial issues that especially characterise Digital RSOs and that affect their future development, as well as the future research agenda (see p. 240 below) of the entrepreneurial university. Most of the time, and generally at the beginning, a Digital RSO is required to join and to be able to work with one or more large stakeholder companies. Once the customers are reached, the challenge is to establish a long-term relationship with them, because they usually do not consider sustainable relationships with small suppliers (i.e., Digital RSOs) that have no history (co-founders of Spin-offs A and C).

Talent management is also a difficult task: a Digital RSO has to find talent willing to take risks with it. During the first phases of an RSO lifecycle, it can be difficult to attract talent, as RSOs are not yet able to count on an adequate brand, organisational structure and incentive systems (such as remuneration policies). In addition, during the growing phases, it is important to "hire" people who are gradually included in the company, but who were not part of the original core (co-founder of Spin-off D). Finally, the success of an RSO is more due to the quality of the entrepreneur than to the idea, and consequently its leadership and soft skills influence the entry and growth of new people (co-founders of Spin-offs A and B).

Then, in the management of the growth phase, Digital RSOs have to anticipate the growth time and start thinking about how to reorganise the company as soon as they are on the market. When they exceed, for example, four or five employees, the entrepreneurs also have to give the right weight to staff functions and internal services (i.e., it is not just creative people, developers or engineers that remain important for the company in the growth phase). Thus, entrepreneurs have to delegate as soon as possible by avoiding the strong centralisation of decisions, which is typical of the initial phases of RSOs (co-founder of Spin-off D).

Digital entrepreneurs are often very market-oriented and not inclined to follow the obligations that are not tied to the business, such as norms and regulations (co-founder of Spin-off A). Nonetheless, sometimes the external contextual factors and the market in which the idea is proposed influence the acceptance of the business. Most of the time, environmental conditions define to what degree the business is necessary, how disruptive it is and how much it is perceived as an added value in the specific market and according to the specific external contextual factors (co-founders of Spin-offs B and C).

The ability of an RSO to scale-up into the market also depends on the network effects or innovation ecosystems that a specific area allows for reaching (in Italy, for example, Milan remains a "happy island" (cf. below) but in other geographical areas this aspect is much more complex) (co-founder of Spin-off B). In any case, an RSO must not be too tied to the idea of product or service from which it was started, but must constantly be available to adapt to market changes. Indeed, entrepreneurs have to remember that not only can large companies be challenged by new start-ups, but that the start-ups themselves have continually to be able to diversify to maintain their competitiveness (co-founder of Spin-off D).

Findings from the involvement of experts were very useful to capture additional insights that may suggest future research topics for entrepreneurship scholars and innovation management insiders. Experts highlighted a set of idiosyncratic elements that make the ventures dealing in the digital field different from the traditional ones, both in terms of entrepreneurial activity and from the perspective of innovation processes and outcomes. Experts underlined that the most evident characteristic of new ventures dealing in the digital field is that they are easier to create, but most of the time they are addressed to specific (niche) needs of the markets, and this way they are difficult to replicate (or be scaled-up) on a large scale (i.e., the ability of the firm to grow fast without being hampered by the restraint of existing structure and resources, compared to traditional ventures). This characteristic has two main consequences: the first is that the lifecycle of these ventures is shorter than traditional non-digital based companies, and whether, on the one hand, this means faster growth, or, on the other, it requires a continuous renewal of organisational capabilities, processes, management practices and skills, as well as a constant recruitment of talents. The second consequence is that the time spent to prepare the content of a venture's business plan is much less than what is required for a traditional company's business plan. This aspect is particularly important to highlight, as it also influences the evaluation logic and criteria for financial loans. In the seed phase, RSOs founders raise money easily. However, they often do not invest this capital with a long-term perspective and they run out of money even before the commercialisation of the product or service takes place. Lastly, according to the experts interviewed, another characteristic of Digital RSOs is that the business model of ventures dealing in the digital field is highly imitable, and this negatively affects the appropriability of the value generated and the sustainability of their competitive advantage compared to that of their counterparts. This happens because the business models of Digital RSOs are similar and the content of novelty is low.

Discussion and conclusions: why should we study the role the entrepreneurial university plays regarding RSOs in the digital age?

The present study has brought into evidence how some selected Digital RSOs actually work within the entrepreneurial university, and especially what the main critical factors are that characterise Digital RSOs. The findings make it possible to advance suggestions at a general level for rethinking academic entrepreneurship in the digital age (Siegel, Wright, 2015) and consequently advance the need to develop new avenues and approaches for future research (cf. p. 242 below).

From a theoretical perspective, the case studies analysed seem to operate – and this is true at least for those that are in their initial stages of diffusion – in markets that are still hard to define and where even competition is difficult to identify ex ante (cf. Figure 13.1). This is something different from traditional RSOs, which can find in the assistance provided by their parent institute (i.e., mostly through TTOs) one of the factors that allows them to start operating in a structured way against direct competitors in the business market, even from the early phases (Algieri, et al., 2013). On the other hand, they do not find the geographical location to be one of the main sources of cost of competitive advantage, as their business model is based on digital technologies and can

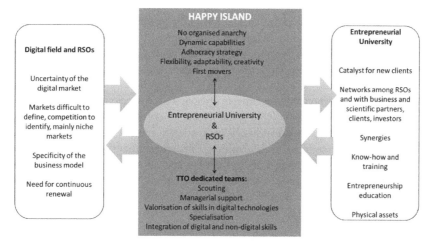

Figure 13.1   Research framework for entrepreneurial university and RSOs

be performed without the need to be physically close to their clients or other stakeholders (Sternberg, 2014; Lejpras, Stephan, 2011). The deep level of tacit and codified knowledge that is the foundation of any RSO should really make the difference. Thinking about the entrepreneurial university research agenda, this means that specific attention should first be devoted to the new form of assistance provided by universities, mostly the role that TTOs are expected to play in this uncertain and rapidly changing environment. Universities should go beyond the main pillar of providing general assistance: the digital world calls for a faster and more open-oriented strategy that considers the rapid and continuous changes appearing on the market. Therefore, a new direction should focus on testing and then investigating the efficacy of a complementary tool (Rosenberg, 1963) inside TTOs themselves: in our opinion, TTOs should be completed by a dedicated team composed of project managers with skills in digital technologies who are able to assist in the best way possible RSOs working in this field. In addition, in the case of the Digital RSOs investigated, it seems that their universities of origin still co-operate for the RSOs' innovation activities. In addition, all the analysed RSOs have strong relationships with the science park-incubator. However, none of the interviewed co-founders cite the TTO as one of the actors that influenced their creation. This confirms our suggestion of improving competences of TTOs (or other units dedicated to support Digital RSOs) in the ICTs field, and this is perfectly in line with the recent universities' objective of "third mission" development (Cesaroni, Piccaluga, 2015; Siegel, Wright, 2015). In other words, the increasing role played by TTOs (Algieri, et al., 2013), incubators, scientific and technological parks should not be underestimated (Salvador, 2011), but needs to be more oriented towards being more specialised and not only focused on generalist assistance. Our suggestion is further corroborated by Sanchez-Barrioluengo and Benneworth (2019), who highlighted very recently that TTOs do not have a strong added value for delivering entrepreneurial activities.

Second, as highlighted by the experts interviewed, the role of digital technologies or digitalisation in affecting the nature of entrepreneurial activity, and their long-term impact on industry competition, market developments, and society at large are yet to be determined. This means that this could be a new focus for the university research agenda: the goal should be to advance useful suggestions for universities having to anticipate this challenge and be prepared for its positive and/or negative consequences with a suitable strategy and a choice of "specialization" (cf. Figure 13.1).

Third, our investigation revealed that existing research does not properly deepen (a) how companies manage the recruitment of talents (either in terms of architecture of human resources or of the organisation of intellectual capital) and (b) the organisational and strategic variables (such as the incentive systems or the governance structure) that are necessary for scaling up and rapid growth (Simsek, et al., 2018; Lee, 2014; Baum, Bird, 2010; Zahra, et al., 2006). Accordingly, in our opinion, the future research agenda should focus on building a dedicated team inside the TTOs with the necessary skills in this direction: a databank could be built thanks to the activities of "talent scouting" and an ad hoc research project scheduled in the agenda could test its impact after a certain number of years.

Future research agenda: what are the suggestions for further studying the role the entrepreneurial university plays regarding RSOs in the digital age?

Highlighting possible avenues of future research is not enough to actually understand how to walk these new roads. From this perspective, the evidence emerging from our empirical study brings to light that there is the need to adopt a multidisciplinary approach, where research from different fields of study can be exploited jointly. For instance, many new opportunities for the research agenda of the entrepreneurial university exist in the intersection between digital technologies fields of study and entrepreneurship studies that dissolve boundaries and change the dynamics of traditional entrepreneurship, as well as innovation processes and outcomes (Kuester, et al., 2018;

Obschonka, Fisch, 2018; Nambisan, 2017; Nambisan, et al., 2017). According to Teece (2018), universities are like big businesses, sharing the same characteristics and problems but also benefiting from some peculiarities, like autonomy. Accordingly, this requires being in tune with the current competitive environment, thus overcoming "organised anarchy" and adopting strategic management decisions as well as dynamic capabilities (Teece, 2018). This suggests the opportunity to also include the strategic perspective, studying whether and how the entrepreneurial universities may adopt an adhocracy strategy (Waterman, 1990) showing flexibility, creativity and adaptability on the one hand (cf. Figure 13.1), but also a fine capacity for specialisation and anticipating and predicting future changes in order to play the role of first movers as frequently as possible (Benghozi, Salvador, 2015): this potential evolution would be perfectly coherent with the needs emerging from the world of Digital RSOs.

Furthermore, the literature on technology intelligence (Kerr, et al., 2006) may be fruitful to study because of the need – highlighted by the experts interviewed – to develop (or to access) skills in technological fields other than the digital field in order to capture opportunities for enlarging their business perspective to some more traditional and stable markets, and not only to temporary, small, "bubble" niche markets. Furthermore, like all RSOs, Digital RSOs need to have easy access to managerial know-how in order to support the growth and consolidation of their company. Thus, a sort of "happy island" for RSOs can be envisaged and outlined as shown in Figure 13.1, which could be the object of a multidisciplinary research, aimed at studying how universities can play the role of "facilitators" in enabling an evolution towards a new heterogeneous university model (Siegel, Wright, 2015; Martin, 2012), which, in our opinion, should be able to reconcile the winning factors of the digital world (i.e., dynamic capabilities, adhocracy, flexibility, creativity, etc.) with the new expected digital skills of TTOs teams. In this way, they can gain a mutual advantage, taking into account the specificities of the digital market for RSOs and the role envisaged for the new entrepreneurial university mission scheduled in Figure 13.1. TTOs should therefore play a role of intermediaries for making possible the creation of what we call a "happy island", meaning an original university ecosystem (Hayter, 2016; Benghozi, Salvador, 2014; Moore, 1996) merging the (third) mission of the entrepreneurial university with its RSOs in the new digital environment.

This does not mean denying the traditional university mission of teaching and research. On the contrary, future research could help in defending and strengthening it through fostering and valorising a complementary activity of targeted entrepreneurship that is not easily imitable and able to bring benefits to students (i.e., courses provided by Digital RSO founders), as well as to the brand name and persistent success of the university itself facing the disruption caused by the digital economy. The adoption of such a strategy would be winning in the long period: knowledge held by Digital RSOs could be valorised by the universities themselves through involving RSO staff in teaching entrepreneurship in the digital age. A background of very specific and deep competencies in this field could lead the university to develop unique capacities and core pedagogical attitudes of differentiation compared to its competitors. A multidisciplinary approach in research is always a big challenge, but we really believe that in this field it is potentially very powerful.

Some methodological considerations are required for defining how to study the role the entrepreneurial university plays regarding RSOs in the digital age. Case studies are probably the most interesting research method for this specific topic, given the need to merge different perspectives of study and to adopt a holistic view on the "happy island" described above. However, case studies obviously have several limitations in terms of generalisability. Hence, future research should aim at building a dedicated databank of Digital RSOs, through the identification of selected variables, for longitudinal quantitative analyses about the performance and growth of these companies. Comparisons between traditional RSOs and Digital RSOs could also be undertaken for understanding whether or not "digital" really has an influence on an RSO's mission. Universities need to understand whether their policy strategy has to be focused more on Digital RSOs than on traditional ones. Moreover, an approach focused on the theory of effectuation (Sarasvathy, 2009) could help in understanding the success of Digital RSOs and the role of their founders: a dedicated management and entrepreneurial theory about Digital RSOs could be suggested in the academic literature.

Last but not least, as highlighted by Salvador, et al. (2019), RSOs should be considered to be "creative" firms. Creativity is a pivotal source for innovation, and a new approach toward studying Digital RSOs and their contribution for the entrepreneurial university could be focused on creativity tools and techniques arising from these peculiar companies. A comparison between the business structure and strategy of companies from cultural and creative industries and Digital RSOs could inspire improvements for successful advancement and business transformation. Starting from these assumptions, a new (creative) approach could really make the difference in the globalised digital market. All these aspects need urgent deeper study, thus calling for future research directions in this way.

Acknowledgement

The authors thank all the interviewees for the time they devoted to this research project. They also thank Fabrizio Conicella, President of APSTI (Italian Association of Science and Technology Parks) for his useful suggestions.

Notes

1. A preliminary but significantly different version of this chapter was presented at the R&D Management Conference 2018 "R&Designing Innovation: Transformational Challenges for Organizations and Society", which was held on 30 June to 4 July 2018, in Milan, Italy, under the title "Research Spin-offs and the Digital Revolution: some evidence from Italian case-studies".
2. In this chapter we adopt the definition of RSOs provided by Benghozi and Salvador (2014, p. 51): "Firms established by current or former university/research centre members (e.g., professors, researchers, technical and administrative staff and Ph.D. candidates) for the purpose of exploiting research results, regardless of whether the firm holds a university share or patent".
3. "Such as social media, mobile, analytics, 3D printing, cloud and cyber-solutions, digital and cloud platforms, MOOCs, Fab Labs": Rippa and Secundo (2019: 907).
4. For example, among others, Salvador, et al., 2019; Salvador, Benghozi, 2015; Mariotti, Salvador, 2015; Benghozi, Salvador, 2014; Carree, et al., 2014; Algieri, et al., 2013; Colombo, Piva, 2012; Iacobucci, et al., 2011; Muscio, 2010; Grandi, Grimaldi, 2003; Chiesa, Piccaluga, 2000.
5. Lombardy provides for more than 22 per cent of the Italian GDP.
6. Polytechnic of Milan is the first Italian university in the Times Higher Education ranking and in the QS Graduate Employability ranking.
7. PoliHub is the third university startup incubator worldwide, with more than 1,200 ideas collected in 2017, eight major acquisitions, 113 start-ups incubated in 2017, more than 4,000 m^2 of incubation space and about 30 million of cumulative start-up turnover in 2017.

References

Alblas, A.A. and Wortmann, J.C. (2014). Function-technology platforms improve efficiency in high-tech equipment manufacturing: A case study in complex products and systems (CoPS). *International Journal of Operations and Production Management*, **34**(4), 447–476.

Algieri, B., Aquino, A. and Succurro, M. (2013). Technology transfer offices and academic spin-off creation: The case of Italy. *The Journal of Technology Transfer*, **38**(4), 382–400.

Bathelt, H., Kogler, D.F. and Munro, A.K. (2010). A knowledge-based typology of university spin-offs in the context of regional economic development. *Technovation*, 30(9), 519–532.

Baum, J.R. and Bird, B.J. (2010). The successful intelligence of high-growth entrepreneurs: links to new venture growth. *Organization Science*, 21, 397–412.

Benghozi, P.-J. and Salvador, E. (2014). Are traditional industrial partnerships so strategic for research spin-off development? Some evidence from the Italian case. *Entrepreneurship and Regional Development: An International Journal*, 26(1–2), 47–79.

Benghozi, P.-J. and Salvador, E. (2015). Technological competition: A path towards commoditization or differentiation? Some evidence from a comparison of e-book readers. *Systèmes d'Information et Management (SIM)*, 20(3), 97–135.

Benghozi, P.-J., Rayna, T., Salvador, E. and Striukova, L. (2017). Editorial, in Special Issue on: Leveraging Technological Change: The Role of Business Models and Ecosystems. *International Journal of Technology Management*, 75(1/2/3/4), 1–5.

Bogner, A. and Menz, W. (2009). The theory-generating expert interview: Epistemological interest, forms of knowledge, interaction. In Bogner, A., Littig, B. and Menz, W. (Eds), *Interviewing Experts* (pp. 43–80). London: Palgrave Macmillan.

Bogner, A., Littig, B. and Menz, W. (Eds). (2009). *Interviewing Experts*. London: Palgrave Macmillan.

Callon, M. and Bowker, G. (1994). Is science a public good? Fifth Mullins Lecture, Virginia Polytechnic Institute, 23 March 1993, *Science, Technology and Human Values*, 19(4), 395–424.

Carree, M., Della Malva, A. and Santarelli, E. (2014). The contribution of universities to growth: Empirical evidence for Italy. *The Journal of Technology Transfer*, 39(3), 393–414.

Cesaroni, F. and Piccaluga, A. (2015). The activities of university knowledge transfer offices: Towards the third mission in Italy. *The Journal of Technology Transfer*, 41, 753.

Chiesa, V. and Piccaluga, A. (2000). Exploitation and diffusion of public research: The general framework and the case of academic spin-off companies. *R&D Management*, 30(4), 329–340.

Clarysse, B., Tartari, V. and Salter, A. (2011). The impact of entrepreneurial capacity, experience and organizational support on academic entrepreneurship. *Research Policy*, 40, 1084–1093.

Colombo, M.G. and Piva, E. (2012). Firms' genetic characteristics and competence-enlarging strategies: A comparison between academic and non-academic high-tech start-ups. *Research Policy*, 41(1), 79–92.

De Cleyn, S.H. and Festel, G. (2016). *Academic Spin-offs and Technology Transfer in Europe. Best Practices and Breakthrough Models*. Cheltenham, UK and Northampton, MA, USA: Edward Elgar Publishing.

Flick, U. (2006). *Introduction to Qualitative Research*, 3rd edn. London: Sage Publications.

Gioia, D.A., Corley, K.G. and Hamilton, A.L. (2013). Seeking qualitative rigor in inductive research: Notes on the Gioia methodology. *Organizational Research Methods*, 16(1), 15–31.

Gläser, J. and Laudel, G. (2009). On interviewing "good" and "bad" experts. In Bogner, A., Littig, B. and Menz, W. (Eds), *Interviewing Experts* (pp. 117–137). London: Palgrave Macmillan.

Goldstein, H.A. and Glaser, K. (2012). Research universities as actors in the governance of local and regional development. *Journal of Technology Transfer*, **37**(2), 158–174.

Grandi, A. and Grimaldi, R. (2003). Exploring the networking characteristics of New Venture Founding Team. A study of Italian academic spin-off. *Small Business Economics*, **21**(4), 329–341.

Guest, G., Namey, E.E. and Mitchell, M.L. (2013). *Collecting Qualitative Data: A Field Manual for Applied Research.* California: Sage Publications.

Hayter, C.S. (2016). A trajectory of early-stage spinoff success: The role of knowledge intermediaries within an entrepreneurial university ecosystem. *Small Business Economics*, **47**, 633–656.

Heirman, A. and Clarysse, B. (2004). *The Initial Resources and Market Strategy to Create High Growth Firms.* Working Paper Steunpunt OOI 2004; October.

Iacobucci, D., Iacopini, A., Micozzi, A. and Orsini, S. (2011). Fostering entrepreneurship in academic spin-offs. *International Journal of Entrepreneurship and Small Business*, **12**(4), 513–533.

Iammarino, S., Sanna-Randaccio, F. and Savona, M. (2009). The perception of obstacles to innovation. Foreign multinationals and domestic firms in Italy. *Revue d'Economie Industrielle*, **125**, 75–104.

Kerr, C.I., Mortara, L., Phaal, R. and Probert, D.R. (2006). A conceptual model for technology intelligence. *International Journal of Technology Intelligence and Planning*, **2**(1), 73–93.

Klein, H.K. and Myers, M.D. (1999). A set of principles for conducting and evaluating interpretive field studies in information systems. *MIS Quarterly*, **23**(1), 67–94.

Klofsten, M., Fayolle, A., Guerrero, M., Mian, S., Urbano, D. and Wright, M. (2019). The entrepreneurial university as driver for economic growth and social change – Key strategic challenges. *Technological Forecasting and Social Change*, **141**, 149–158.

Kuester, S., Konya-Baumbach, E. and Schuhmacher, M.C. (2018). Get the show on the road: Go-to-market strategies for e-innovations of start-ups. *Journal of Business Research*, **83**, 65–81.

Lee, N. (2014). What holds back high-growth firms? Evidence from UK SMEs. *Small Business Economics*, **43**, 183–95.

Lejpras, A. and Stephan, A. (2011). Locational conditions, cooperation, and innovativeness: Evidence from research and company spin-offs. *Annals of Regional Science*, **46**(3), 543–575.

Mariotti, I. and. Salvador, E. (2015). On-park and off-park research spin-offs: some insights from an empirical investigation on Italy. *International Journal of Entrepreneurship and Innovation Management*, Special Issue on Inspired by Silicon Valley: a Cheap Copy or a Masterpiece?, **19**(5/6), 405–422.

Martin, B. (2012). Are universities and university research under threat? Towards an evolutionary model of university speciation. *Cambridge Journal of Economics*, **36**(3), 543–565.

Moore, J.F. (1996). *The Death of Competition: Leadership and Strategy in the Age of Business Ecosystems.* New York: Harper Business.

Muscio, A. (2010). What drives the university use of technology transfer offices? Evidence from Italy. *Journal of Technology Transfer*, **35**(2), 181–202.

Mustar, P. and Wright, M. (2010). Convergence or path dependency in policies to foster the creation of university spin-off firms? A comparison of France and the United Kingdom. *Journal of Technology Transfer*, **35**(1), 42–65.

Mustar, P., Renault, M., Colombo, M., Piva, E., Fontes, M., Lockett, A., Wright, M., Clarysse, B. and Moray, N. (2006). Conceptualising the heterogeneity of research-based spin-offs: A multi-dimensional taxonomy. *Research Policy*, **35**(2), 289–308.

Nambisan, S. (2017). Digital entrepreneurship: Toward a digital technology perspective of entrepreneurship. *Entrepreneurship Theory and Practice*, **41**(6), 1029–1055.

Nambisan, S., Wright, M. and Feldman, M. (2019). The digital transformation of innovation and entrepreneurship: Progress, challenges and key themes. *Research Policy*, **48**, 1–9.

Nambisan, S., Lyytinen, K., Majchrzak, A. and Song, M. (2017). Digital innovation management: Reinventing innovation management research in a digital world. *Mis Quarterly*, **41**(1): 223–238.

Neves, M. and Franco, M. (2018). Academic spin-off creation: Barriers and how to overcome them. *R&D Management*, **48**(5), 505–518.

Netval (2018). *La rete del trasferimento tecnologico si rafforza con la clinical innovation.* XIV Report Netval, edited by Ramaciotti, L., Daniele, C., Pavia, Netval, pp. 1–343.

O'Shea, R.P., Allen, T.J., Chevalier, A. and Roche, F. (2005). Entrepreneurial orientation, technology transfer and spinoff performance of U.S. universities. *Research Policy*, **34**(7), 994–1009.

Obschonka, M. and Fisch, C. (2018). Entrepreneurial personalities in political leadership. *Small Business Economics*, **50**(4), 851–869.

Ramaciotti, L. and Rizzo, U. (2015). The determinants of academic spin-off creation by Italian universities. *R&D Management*, **45**(5), 501–514.

Rasmussen, E. and Wright, M. (2015). How can universities facilitate academic spin-offs? An entrepreneurial competency perspective. *Journal of Technology Transfer*, **40**(5), 782–799.

Rippa, P. and Secundo, G. (2019). Digital academic entrepreneurship: The potential of digital technologies on academic entrepreneurship. *Technological Forecasting and Social Change*, **146**, 900–911.

Rosenberg, N. (1963). Technological change in the machine tool industry, 1840–1910. *The Journal of Economic History*, **23**(4): 414–443.

Salvador, E. (2009). Evolution of Italian universities' rules for spin-offs: The usefulness of formal regulations. *Industry and Higher Education*, **23**(6), 445–462.

Salvador, E. (2011). Are science parks and incubators good "brand names" for spin-offs? The case-study of Turin. *Journal of Technology Transfer*, **36**(2), 203–232.

Salvador, E. and Benghozi, P.-J. (2015). Research spin-off firms: Does the university involvement really matter? *Management International*, **19**(2), 22–39.

Salvador, E., Marullo, C. and. Piccaluga, A. (2019). Determinants of growth in research spin-offs: A resource-based perspective. *Recherches en Sciences de Gestion – Management Sciences – Ciencias de Gestión*, n. 133, pp. 53–78.

Sanchez-Barrioluengo, M. and Benneworth, P. (2019). Is the entrepreneurial university also regionally engaged? Analysing the influence of university's structural configuration on third mission performance. *Technological Forecasting and Social Change*, **141**, 206–218.

Sarasvathy, S.D. (2009). *Effectuation: Elements of Entrepreneurial Expertise.* Cheltenham, UK and Northampton, MA, USA: Edward Elgar Publishing.

Shane, S. (2004). *Academic Entrepreneurship. University Spinoffs and Wealth Creation.* Cheltenham, UK and Northampton, MA, USA: Edward Elgar Publishing.

Siegel, D.S. and Wright, M. (2015). Academic entrepreneurship: Time for a rethink? *British Journal of Management*, **26**, 582–595.

Siggelkow, N. (2007). Persuasion with case studies. *Academy of Management Journal*, **50**(1), 20–24.

Simsek, Z., Heavey, C. and Fox, B.C. (2018). Interfaces of strategic leaders: A conceptual framework, review, and research agenda. *Journal of Management*, **44**, 280–324.

Sternberg, R. (2014). Success factors of university-spin-offs: Regional government support programs versus regional environment. *Technovation*, **34**(3), 137–148.

Sussan, F. and Acs, Z.J. (2017). The digital entrepreneurial ecosystem. *Small Business Economics*, **49**, 55–73.

Teece, D.J. (2018). Managing the university: Why "organized anarchy" is unacceptable in the age of massive open online courses. *Strategic Organization*, **16**(1), 92–102.

Treibich, T., Konrad, K. and Truffer, B. (2013). A dynamic view on interactions between academic spin-offs and their parent organizations. *Technovation*, **33**(12), 450–462.

Urbinati, A., Chiaroni, D., Chiesa, V. and Frattini, F. (2018). The role of digital technologies in open innovation processes: An exploratory multiple case study analysis. *R&D Management*, **50**(1), 136–160.

van Geenhuizen, M. and Soetanto, D.P. (2009). Academic spin-offs at different ages: A case study in search of key obstacles to growth. *Technovation*, **29**(10), 671–681.

Visintin, F. and Pittino, D. (Eds) (2016). *Fast Growing Firms in a Slow Growth Economy. Institutional Conditions for Innovation*. Cheltenham, UK and Northampton, MA, USA: Edward Elgar Publishing.

Voss, C., Tsikriktsis, N. and Frohlich, M. (2002). Case research in operations management. *International Journal of Operations and Production Management*, **22**(2), 195–219.

Walsham, G. (1995). Interpretive case studies in IS research: Nature and method. *European Journal of Information Systems*, **4**(2), 74–81.

Waterman, R. (1990). *Adhocracy: The Power to Change*. Knoxville, TN: Whittle Direct Books.

Wright, M., Vohora, A. and Lockett, A. (2004). The formation of high-tech university spinouts: The role of joint ventures and venture capital investors. *Journal of Technology Transfer*, **29**(3–4), 287–310.

Wright, M., Clarysse, B., Mustar, P. and Lockett, A. (2007). *Academic Entrepreneurship in Europe*. Cheltenham, UK and Northampton, MA, USA: Edward Elgar Publishing.

Yin, R. (2003). *Case Study Research: Design and Methods* (2nd edn). California: Sage Publications.

Zahra, S.A., Sapienza, H.J. and Davidsson, P. (2006). Entrepreneurship and dynamic capabilities: A review, model and research agenda. *Journal of Management Studies*, **43**, 917–955.

Index

Printed and bound by CPI Group (UK) Ltd, Croydon, CR0 4YY